HISTORY OF THE 40TH DIVISION

HISTORY OF THE 40TH DIVISION

BY

LIEUT.-COL. F. E. WHITTON, C.M.G., p.s.c.

Late The Prince of Wales's Leinster Regiment and General Staff.

Author of
"The Marne Campaign," "A History of Poland," "Moltke,"
"The Decisive Battles of Modern Times," "The
History of The Leinster Regiment."

ALDERSHOT
GALE & POLDEN, LTD., WELLINGTON WORKS,
ALSO AT LONDON AND PORTSMOUTH

CONTENTS

LIST OF MAPS

___

PHOTOGRAPH

AUTHOR'S NOTE.

THE following errata have come to notice while this volume was in the press :—The " year headings " on pp. 7, 17, and 45 should read " 1915," " 1916," " 1916 " respectively, and not as now shown. On p. 124, line 14, *for* " 25th " *read* " 24th." The author expresses his apologies to the O.C. 229th Field Company, R.E., for the variation in the spelling of his name, which was not detected until too late.

Of the five maps illustrating this History, four were specially drawn for it. The exception is the map facing p. 200, which, in order to reduce expense, was reproduced photographically from a map supplied by H.M. Stationery Department. On the original the rivers and streams are shown by minute lines of faint blue. It was not realized until too late that these had eluded the camera. The paragraph which follows will, however, be sufficient to supplement the description of the Sensée Valley on p. 189.

The " bridge over the Sensée River " referred to is just west of the road junction west of Mory. Thence the valley trends generally west of north to about half a mile south of the " t " in Hamelincour*t*. Here it swings north-east. St. Léger is in the valley. The river continues north-east, leaving Croisilles on the left, Fontaine lez Croisilles on the right, and Chérisy and Vis en Artois on the left.

THE 40th DIVISION

CHAPTER I.

THE FORMATION OF THE DIVISION.

THE 40th Division was formed in September, 1915, and a comparison of its distinguishing numeral with the date at which it was raised will afford a good indication of the class of war in which it was soon to be engaged. The great European catastrophe had broken out in the early days of August, 1914. At that time the British effort—so far as an expeditionary force was concerned—was limited to a cavalry division, six divisions of all arms, and some lines of communication troops. But in little more than a year the number of divisions had reached forty; a second main theatre of war had come into being in the Near East; and so far from the war having been " over by Christmas " (*i.e.*, of 1914), as had for some time been the popular delusion, more than three years of terrible struggle had yet to be endured. Short, therefore, though the period had been since the Old Contemptibles had marched to the fray with their swan-song of " Tipperary," it had been long enough completely to alter the character of the war.

A brief retrospect of the war-year which preceded the formation of the 40th Division will be necessary if the conditions which faced that unit when it first entered the lists are to be correctly understood. The pages which immediately follow will undoubtedly seem dull, but to omit them would be to ask the reader to begin a serial with but a vague knowledge of what had occurred before the hero comes into the tale.

So far as the British contingent of the Allied Armies in France is concerned, no lengthy recapitulation of 1914 is here required; for so long as a memory of England endures, our children's children, and those later to succeed them, will speak of the pressure back from the frontier at Mons; the stubbornly-contested retreat; to be followed by the stand made by the Franco-British Armies between Paris and Verdun. The victory of the Marne checked the onrush of the invaders; it saved Paris; and it completely wrecked the grandiose plan of the German Supreme Command, who had gambled on a smashing victory over France within six weeks, after which Russia would be dealt with in turn. Following up their success, the victorious Allies were checked upon the Aisne, and there followed at once an attempt by each side to outflank the other towards the north. The attempt was continued until the right and left flanks of Germans and Allies respectively rested on the sea. For some six weeks, from October 11th, the Germans made frantic efforts to burst through at Ypres. But the effort was in vain, and the end of 1914 found the Belgians, British and French dug in along a line which extended from the North Sea to the frontier of Switzerland.

The purely military chronicle of the *annus mirabilis* of 1914 will be ever available from contemporary chronicles, but it will not be so easy to recapture the atmosphere which prevailed at its close; but it is essential to endeavour to produce it, for the history of the 40th Division would be incomplete without some revelation of the conditions, particularly so far as they affected recruiting, which prevailed at the moment of its birth. Briefly, the prevailing sentiment at the close of 1914 was one of inane optimism. The old Regular Army had been practically destroyed, but—outside the ranks of the remaining professional soldiers—a sure and early triumph was everywhere expected. There was a most amazing credulity in accepting as gospel idiotic calculations made by " well-known strategists " in the Press. It was "proved" by these experts in the most convincing manner that Germany was at the end of her tether; that her supply of men was running out; that her ranks were filled by old, fat men in spectacles or by very emaciated boys; that she was already robbing the cradle and the grave; that she had no money; that her people at home were starving; that the soldiers at the front hated fighting and had to be flogged into battle by their officers; that the German officers were nothing like so good as had been thought —that they cowered behind in dug-outs while the fighting was going on and spent the rest of the time getting extremely drunk. And much more pleasant information of this kind. This blatant twaddle formed the funeral march at the obsequies of the Old Army.

When the year 1915 opened the war had entered upon a new phase. War of movement had now become impossible, for owing to the construction of a continuous barrier from the North Sea to the Swiss frontier mobile operations now perforce gave way to trench warfare. For this class of fighting the Germans were considerably better equipped than the British; and, moreover, the ebb and flow of attack and defence had left the Germans in Flanders almost everywhere in possession of the higher and drier ground, while in the lower strips water was found at a few feet and in some cases a few inches below the surface. In this latter terrain the construction of adequate trenches was a physical impossibility, and, in such makeshift protection as could be got to stand, the conditions were terrible. Lying in sodden, or sometimes waterlogged trenches, exposed to the fire of a vastly superior artillery, and opposite an enemy possessed of weapons not at our disposal, the British infantry was called upon to endure as severe a test of constancy as occurred throughout the whole war.

It was not long before the advent of trench warfare convinced many that to carry serried lines of defence bristling with barbed wire and obstacles must prove a

costly and bloody business. These brains sought
eagerly for a way round the barrier which would lead to
a speedier and less expensive victory, and so began the
controversy between Easterners and Westerners which
endured while the war lasted. It was proposed to
transfer the bulk of the British Army to the Balkans
and to fight one's way into Central Europe by a back
door. Such an enterprise, although there were many
and obvious objections to it, was one in which the
command of the sea enjoyed by the Allies, and secured
for them by the British Navy, might have been
exploited to its full extent; and an operation derided
by the ignorant as a " side show " would possibly have
merited the description in history of a maritime
strategic counterstroke of the highest value. It is not,
however, here intended to argue the vast question of
such operations in general nor this one in particular.
All that need now be said is that the Balkan project
was condemned, but that an immediate result of the
controversy was, since Turkey had come into the war
against the Allies, the inception of the Dardanelles
adventure, with Constantinople as the objective.

The French generalissimo, General Joffre, was, however, an out-and-out Westerner. He laid stress on the
fact that the Germans were in occupation of a large
slice of France, that near Noyon they were barely fifty
miles from Paris, and that on the Somme they were
but twenty miles from Amiens, the point of junction
between the French and British Armies. He maintained that the security of the Western Front must be
a paramount consideration in Allied strategy, and that
to secure the position in the West it was necessary to
drive the enemy farther back. His method to ensure
this end was to attack on the Western Front at the
earliest possible moment and with the maximum of
force. With these views Sir John French, the British
commander-in-chief, was in general agreement. His
first proposal aimed at a combined naval and military
attempt against the Belgian coast, but when this was

found to be impossible of fulfilment he set himself wholeheartedly to co-operate with General Joffre's plans. Wishing to give his troops a wider experience of an attack against entrenchments, and being desirous of ascertaining the effect of a super-bombardment by artillery, Sir John French delivered an attack on Neuve Chapelle with his First Army on March 10th. Though Neuve Chapelle was not a complete success the result of the bombardment was impressive and was held to promise great things when there should be more guns and more ammunition.

Preparations for further battles, therefore, went forward. One was to be an attack by the French on Vimy Ridge. The Germans, however, were determined not to await attack tamely but to interfere with the Allied preparations. It so happened that in order to secure troops for the Vimy attempt, General Joffre had weakened the northern part of the Ypres salient of French troops. Against this portion of the front the Germans, confident of the efficacy of a weapon hitherto unknown—that of poison gas—made the vigorous attack or series of attacks now known as the Second Battle of Ypres. Although the Germans made but a slight advance in that sector, they at any rate achieved part of their purpose in weakening the forces and exhausting the meagre supply of ammunition which the Allies were accumulating for their great offensive of 1915. That offensive began on May 9th with an attack by the British First Army on either side of Fromelles which extended southwards to Festubert and petered out from lack of shells on May 25th. On the right of the British the French under General Joffre were at the same time making slow but costly progress up the Vimy Ridge, doggedly continuing the attempt even after the British offensive at Festubert had died away. This battle, which had opened simultaneously with the British effort at Fromelles, continued till July 13th. The French fought magnificently and twice gained the crest, only, however, to be driven off each time. General Joffre then decided to ring down the curtain and to stage a new piece.

The general situation seemed to call for an energetic offensive by the Allies on the Western Front, for the Russian Armies had been worsted and were in retreat, thus enabling the Germans to transfer forces from east to west; and although against this was the fact that Italy had come in on the side of the Allies, no active assistance could be looked for from her for the moment. The key of the whole question on the Western Front was the fact that the New Armies of England were now coming to hand. Two divisions had arrived in France by the end of May, and six more by the end of July, so that with this augmentation, plus divisions formed by units from overseas stations, from India, as well as Territorial divisions and the Canadians, the four divisions and the cavalry division which had fought at Mons had, in less than a year, swollen to twenty-eight divisions and five divisions of cavalry.

Put briefly, General Joffre's plan aimed at a double French offensive, one wing being supported by a British attack. The northern French offensive was to be a repetition of the attempts to gain Vimy Ridge, and this was to be in conjunction with a British effort against Loos on the left; while the southern French offensive was to take place in Champagne. This great forward movement began in the autumn. The French efforts to gain the Vimy Ridge failed almost completely, while the British movement against Loos, after some initial success on our part, terminated in a stalemate of mutual exhaustion. As for the French push in Champagne, after a beginning which led to high hopes, the battle ended in November without much material gain after the successes of the first four days.

The year 1915 was thus to end with the problem of breaking the German front still unsolved.

It was in these days of disappointment and hopes

unfulfilled that the 40th Division was born. Its life
began in a period of reaction when the storm of military enthusiasm which had followed immediately on
the outbreak of war had definitely spent itself, and in
a period when the discovery had been made that the
withdrawal from their trades, and the recruitment of
all fit men who offered themselves for enlistment, was
not conducive to the successful prosecution of the war.
Already, in July 1915, a National Registration Act
had been passed and the Local Government Board had
been allotted the task of supplying the particulars of
all males between eighteen and forty-one. From these,
registers were compiled in various recruiting areas,
and—to anticipate slightly—in October the " Derby
Scheme " or " Group System " was initiated by Lord
Derby on his appointment as Director General of
Recruiting. Under this system men were to be enlisted
for one day and immediately passed into the reserve,
with liability to be called to the colours when required.
Between October 25th and the middle of December
1915, 2,000,000 men were attested under this scheme,
of whom half were married men. As it was now clear
that the single men were not responding to the call for
voluntary recruits, the nation had no resource but to
introduce compulsory service. This received the Royal
assent in January, 1916.

Meanwhile, however, the 40th Division, which had
begun to assemble at Aldershot in the previous
September, had been feeling severely the inevitable
reaction of the enthusiasm of 1914. The War Office
had to do the best it could, and by lowering
the height required for an infantry soldier steps were
taken to form a " Bantam " division. In quality
these short and stocky soldiers were excellent, but
the quantity was insufficient, and the difficulty had
to be met by the enlistment of men who not only did
not reach the regulation height but whose general
physique was obviously unequal to the strain of military service. All honour to such men for coming

forward in their country's emergency. But it would have been folly to send them overseas; consequently, as will be seen, the 40th Division was faced with the necessity of a drastic weeding-out before it could take the field.

By the time the 40th Division was constituted the strictly territorial basis for larger new formations was a thing of the past, and the 40th Division was composed of a blend of English, Welsh and Scottish units, the infantry being known as the 119th, 120th and 121st Brigades. The state of transition between voluntary enlistment, which was drying up, and universal liability for service, which had not yet been definitely adopted, reacted naturally on the new division. Several of the units were under strength, but more contained a large proportion of unfit men; and the divisional and brigade commanders soon realized that a drastic weeding-out would be necessary before the Division could proceed overseas. This weeding-out began almost at once, and was continued throughout the winter of 1915/1916 and into the early spring of the latter year, as it became more and more evident that many of the men were unfit to undergo even the training to which they were submitted at home. How drastic this weeding-out process ultimately became may be shown by quoting the case of one battalion, which joined the Division at Aldershot over 1,000 strong, and later was reduced by medical rejections to little over two hundred.

Apart from the handicap to training which this constant change of personnel entailed, the wastage was not being made good from ordinary sources of supply, although the divisional commander had sent one of his staff officers to Lancashire, Edinburgh and Glasgow early in December in order to try to accelerate the flow of recruits to his weakest battalions. Accordingly, in the spring of 1916, he decided that he had no option but to represent to the authorities that his Division in its then state was unfit to go overseas, and that unless other, and stronger, measures were taken to supply it with the full complement of fit men, its departure must be indefinitely postponed. He coupled with this report a definite recommendation that he should be given four new battalions from some division which would, in the ordinary course, have been going overseas at a later date than himself, and undertook that, if this were done, his Division could soon be made fit for service. He based this request on the idea that, from the officers and men of the four battalions of each of the 120th and 121st Infantry Brigades, two good battalions could be formed, and that he could allot two new battalions intact, if he were given them, to each of these brigades, so as to complete them to establishment. The 119th Infantry Brigade, in which the wastage from medical causes had been much less, could, he considered, be brought up to strength, and rendered fit for service, in the ordinary way. This recommendation was approved by the War Office, who decided to send him the four battalions (*viz.*, the 13th East Surrey Regiment, 14th Argyll and Sutherland Highlanders, and 20th and 21st Middlesex Regiment) from another source.

The promise of these fresh units raised the spirits of all ranks of the 40th Division, from the divisional commander downwards, and no time was lost in carrying the necessary reorganization into effect. So anxious was the divisional commander to accelerate matters that he sent at once for the commanders of the 120th and 121st Brigades, informed them that they would each be given two new battalions, and gave them verbal instructions to proceed immediately with the necessary amalgamation of the battalions in their brigades, so as to convert their existing four battalions into two; and to report to him when this had been done. He explained that the best of the officers, non-commissioned officers and men should, of course, be selected, but that he would leave them a perfectly free hand in carrying this out; that the composition of the two re-formed battalions in non-commissioned officers and men and nominal rolls of the surplus (if any) were to be sent to the officers i/c records concerned, and that the composition of these battalions in officers, and a list of surplus officers, were to be sent to divisional headquarters for submission to the War Office.

These verbal instructions were not even confirmed in writing; but the commanders and staffs of brigades and battalions carried them out so ably, loyally and expeditiously, that the reorganization was carried out without a hitch, and was completed within three days. This reorganization was soon followed by the arrival of the new battalions which had been allotted by the War Office, and preparations were pushed on in all departments for the early departure of the Division overseas. Training became more intensive; deficiencies of personnel in other units were made good; equipment was completed. The cavalry squadron, machine gun companies, and other units (which were needed to complete) arrived, and the Division was then enabled to embark for France by the end of May, 1916.

The work done at Aldershot by the 40th Division was similar to that proceeding all over Great Britain— the building up, with the maximum of speed and from raw material, an army fit to encounter a trained nation-in-arms. But, instead of producing time-tables and programmes of work, it is thought that a better idea will be conveyed by some personal narratives, typical of many sent in for the composition of this History. And accordingly there are now given excerpts from the stories respectively of an " A " and " Q " staff officer, a regimental officer, and an officer of one of what are sometimes rather pedantically termed the "ancillary services."

The staff officer writes: " I duly reported at Aldershot on September 7th, 1915, and was told that the Division had not yet arrived, but that it would commence to do so in a few days time, and that the headquarters would be located in the officers' mess of Corunna Barracks, in the Stanhope Lines. Thither I repaired, and found complete solitude and emptiness. There was obviously nothing to be done for the moment, so I hurried back to London to collect a supply of stationery and works of military reference, with a view to starting an office. Fortified with these, I returned once more to Aldershot, and opened the office of the headquarters of the Division. I was not to be left long in my solitude. Soon other staff officers reported for duty, and before long the various formations commenced to arrive.

" Major-General H. G. Ruggles-Brise, who was acting temporarily as B.G., G.S. at Aldershot, was appointed to command the Division, with Lieutenant-Colonel H. A. Walker as his G.S.O.1; Major F. D. Finlay as G.S.O.2; Captain G. de C. Glover as G.S.O.3; Lieutenant-Colonel C. F. Moores as A.A. and Q.M.G.; Captain A. H. Bathurst as D.A.A. and Q.M.G.; and Captain A. R. Gordon as D.A.Q.M.G.

" There seems little to record during the months of October and November, 1915. Early in December I was sent to Lancashire and Scotland on a recruiting expedition, but although I received many promises of help, the results were disappointing. In December the Division moved to Blackdown, and we remained there until we went overseas. We were a very happy family, and we liked Blackdown (except for the mud, and, later, the dust—both of which were prodigious); but the weakness of our battalions, and our unreadiness on this account to go overseas, somewhat damped our spirits, until the solution of this difficulty (described above) was found.

" In March, 1916, we heard that we might be sent to Ireland, in consequence of the outbreak of the rebellion in Dublin; but, fortunately, we escaped this unpleasant duty. In the early months of the year various staff and regimental officers went on a ' Cook's tour ' to France, to see something of the work of a division in the line.

"The months of March and April, 1916, were chiefly taken up, in the ' A ' and ' Q ' office, with the plans, and execution, of the reorganization of the Division. Early in May the Division was inspected by His Majesty the King, who expressed himself most eulogistically regarding the turn-out and bearing of the men. Orders, long expected, to proceed overseas had arrived, and on May 28th, 1916, an advanced party, consisting of the D.A.A. and Q.M.G., the staff captains of brigades, the senior supply officer and the D.A.D.O.S. left Blackdown in motors for Folkestone. We arrived at Boulogne the same night (where we learnt that the Division was to join the I Corps of the First Army), and we left the following morning for Lillers, in order to arrange for billets, supplies, etc., for the whole Division in the neighbourhood of that place. The Division followed three days later.

" Every officer at divisional headquarters while the 40th Division was at Aldershot will agree that we owed a special debt of gratitude to Captain Stuart Grant, one of the divisional commander's A.D.C's. Captain Grant was a born mess president, and by his enterprise and natural ability he gave us a mess, both in England and France, which would have done credit to the most piping times of peace. We should have been almost ashamed of its comparative luxury, were it not that we felt that the difference between a well-run mess, such as ours, and a badly-run one was a difference of management and not of cost, and that we hoped that the superior comfort which he gave us might possibly conduce to our military efficiency. Unfortunately for us, Captain Grant's administrative ability came under the notice of I Corps headquarters soon after our arrival in France, and he was wafted away as their camp commandant.

" Next, I know that the ' A ' and ' Q ' staff will agree in expressing appreciation and gratitude for the services of our chief clerk (Q.M.S. Ward). A man of delicate physique, but with a high sense of duty, he performed his arduous duties, both in England and France, with great ability and unfailing good temper.

"Lastly, no account of the headquarters of the 40th Division, during its preparation at home and for the first few months after it went overseas, would be complete without mention of Major (now Lieutenant-Colonel) Finlay, our G.S.O.2. While many of us took our work, and the war generally, rather seriously, Major Finlay, with his imperturbability and cynical humour, provided a welcome relief and kept us amused. As a Staff College man, and Regular soldier of many years' standing, he was naturally a most useful and efficient member of the staff; but it is no disparagement to him to say that we shall remember him still more for his eye-glass and his quizzical manner."

A sidelight is thrown on regimental soldiering of those Aldershot days by the following narrative: "From forming part of the 118th Brigade of the 39th Division, we were soon transferred to the 40th Division, forming—with the 14th Highland Light Infantry, the 14th Argyll and Sutherland Highlanders, and the 11th King's Own Royal Lancaster Regiment—the 120th Brigade. Uniforms were issued, as well as rifles and equipment; companies were organized, non-commissioned officers appointed; and, all things considered, the battalion began to bear a marked resemblance to real soldiers. It was about this time—I forget whether it was just before or just after we had been transferred to the 40th Division—that a noteworthy incident took place. It was on the first occasion that we had been inspected by a general. The officers polished up their 'Infantry Drill'; the non-commissioned officers busied themselves sorting out the men who were most proficient in forming fours, in order that on the parade itself they should be found in the front ranks of the companies; buttons were polished vigorously; equipments fitted; and the battalion bugler betook himself to the fastness of the hills to add the 'General Salute' to his somewhat shaky repertoire which at present was comprised of ' Réveillé,' ' Cookhouse,' ' Last Post,' and a very confused idea of ' Orderly-Room.'

" The day arrived, the battalion paraded fully twenty minutes too soon, and the general was fully twenty minutes late. It was, of course, at this moment that the general approached along the one road upon which we had not posted a look-out, and instantly there was dire confusion. The colonel hurriedly gave the command, ' 'Shun! Slope—Arms!' followed by a short pause, during which the Great One himself left the road and approached us, then by ' General Salute, Present—Arms!' A long-drawn-out rustle of unaccustomed hands juggling with rifles, and out of the tail of my eye I saw Regimental Sergeant-Major Birch rushing stealthily towards the bugler, who was apparently over-awed by the situation, saw him whisper hoarsely in the manner of all sergeant-majors, saw that worthy bugler waver, gather together his scattered faculties, raise the bugle falteringly to his lips, and then the cloud seemed to pass from his mind and with a magnificent flourish he blared forth, and bugled as he had never bugled before—the ' Last Post.'

" The face of the general for a few moments was a study. But, thank heavens, he saw the humour of the situation, and what seemed to us at the time to be a tragedy passed by as one of the many such humorous little incidents that marked the progress of a battalion where we were all learners, but enthusiastic ones at that. And in such a manner the autumn months rolled by, while we delved into the mysteries of company drill, musketry, and such like; all the while getting to know one another and to like one another the better for the knowing.

" The officers came to know their non-commissioned officers and men. Those talks to the various members of our platoon during the halts on route marches or during the last visit to the huts just before ' Lights Out'; the usual ' Good-night, sir ' as we left the hut gradually became something more personal than the

mere recognition of our departure. We learned, as
time went on, who the men were who were going to be
short of kit at the kit inspection, and what their
excuses would be. We learned that behind the gruff
and forbidding exterior of grizzled old Corporal ' X '
was one of the best and kindest of natures. We learned
that because Private Blinks had been a dustman in
private life he was none the worse for that. Nor did
the interest in our men extend merely to the psychology
of their characters. At foot inspection, after a route
march, the corn on Tompkins's little toe was a matter
of the greatest concern to us. Sergeant Bone's little
girl of three, who came one day to visit daddy in
camp, became a personal acquaintance with whom we
enjoyed a most intimate friendship.

" On their side the men learned that their officers were
not the stuck-up prigs they had first supposed. They
learned to know that the officers used a certain amount
of discrimination in the manner in which they
'jumped on' them when they were at fault. They
most of them learned that straight dealings met with
straight treatment, and that the violent and powerful
string of language meted out by the sergeant-major on
occasions, or the seemingly drastic punishment of
'C.B.' for a dirty button on parade by the company
commander, was not the mark of a permanent feud or
expression of personal dislike but merely a step towards
efficiency and a deterrent to slackness. And out of
such knowledge gained of one another grew that fine
bond of friendship which was the foundation of that
fine quality which made life with the 40th Division a
more than ordinarily pleasant experience, and which
gave us those memories which we all prize so highly,
namely, *esprit de corps*.

" Three months had passed, and by this time the
effects of the healthy life and training showed itself in
the faces and in the very bearing of the men. In the
early days at camp the route marches we had taken, at
the most only about six miles, had resulted in numerous

casualties, and the battalion arrived back in camp with numbers sadly depleted by men who had fallen out. Now twelve or fifteen miles could be undertaken carrying a full pack, rifles and equipment, and return to camp without casualties, looking remarkably fresh as they marched in to the energetic efforts of the band playing the regimental march. Heads held high, arms swinging, and a new pride in their bearing—it was no longer merely a joke.

"Situated in one of the most beautiful parts of beautiful Surrey, life in camp must have been a wonderful experience to these Londoners, who had seldom seen anything of the country outside Wandsworth except on bank holidays when, perhaps, they took their families to some overcrowded heath or common a little way out of London. To live in this beautiful country, rising early in the morning, breathing clean, fresh air and the scent of the pine woods which surrounded the camp; spending the days in healthy outdoor exercises and feeling a fitness they would never have felt in the ordinary course of their lives—this was indeed a heaven-sent experience for them. When parades were finished for the day they wandered off in twos and threes to the surrounding villages, where some would consume vast quantities of beer and return to camp in a hilarious mood, whilst others would go off in search of the female society which the exigencies of camp life denied them.

"Christmas 1915 passed. As many as possible were allowed to go on leave, while the remainder celebrated the occasion in as royal a manner as the circumstances permitted. In the evening on Christmas Day a small deputation of the officers, led by the senior subaltern, visited the men's huts and canteens and the sergeants' mess, where they shared for a while the joys of Yuletide with the men. I think that in the canteen the practical demonstration that an 'orficer' could drink his 'pot o' beer' with the best of them did much to endear them to the men.

" By the New Year the battalion was taking the form
of a fighting unit—signalling and pioneer sections
were formed; men were trained in bombing and in the
use of Lewis guns; a full transport existed; and every
man had a rifle, and, what is more, was getting to know
how to use it.   We were now more or less proficient in
the usual routine of squad, platoon and company drill,
and more time was being devoted to musketry and field
training.

" As I have said, the battalion transport was now
complete, and as the full complement of officers'
chargers was available many of the officers had seized
the opportunity of learning to ride, and the spectacle
of an officer taking two cushions into mess to sit on was
no uncommon sight, whilst the number of those who
preferred to remain standing in the ante-room before or
after mess was really remarkable.   Sundays we usually
selected as the day for riding parties.   I remember one
such day when L—— (Captain C. E. L——), who was
a keen learner, and I, went for a ride over Thursley
Common.   L—— was riding a rather fractious pony he
called Ginger (partly on account of its colour and partly
on account of its nature).   It was a lovely day, and we
were both eager to get to the open country, where we
could stretch our horses' limbs.

" Just after leaving camp L—— dismounted to adjust
his stirrup lengths, and I went on to the common
thinking he would catch me up, as he knew the path
I would take.   Arriving on the common I took my
horse for a good stretch gallop for about a mile and
then slowed up to a canter.   The air was keen, the sun
was shining, and I was enjoying myself so thoroughly
that the passing of time and the absence of L—— did
not occur to me for half an hour, as I alternately
cantered, trotted and galloped over the springy turf of
Thursley Common.

" Then I came back to earth.   Where was L——?
He must have been thrown and probably hurt.   I put
heels to my horse and galloped back the way I had
come and the way L—— should have come, scanning

c

the country for a riderless horse or the inert figure that I felt sure I should find. At last I arrived back at the clearing where I had left him, and there he was—he and the horse, both perspiring freely, L—— hopping on one leg trying to reach the stirrup with the other, swearing volubly the while, whilst Ginger was prancing always just away from the raised foot. The picture presented such an anticlimax to my expectations that I laughed so much I could barely hold Ginger whilst L—— mounted. He had been trying to mount ever since I had left him nearly three-quarters of an hour ago, and he was in a mighty bad temper about it."

Finally, before accompanying the 40th Division to France, we may look at its medical units : "Tweseldown, a few miles from Aldershot, will always bring up memories of the past to those who served in the Royal Army Medical Corps during the war. Here were assembled both officers and other ranks in one huge camp, and at odd moments the Powers that Be would tell off the necessary personnel to furnish field ambulance, hospital ships, or hospitals. And at an odd moment during the latter part of 1915 the field ambulances for the 40th Division commenced to form; they received their numbers, 135, 136 and 137 at first, and little else for a long time, and it was not until early 1916 that equipment was forthcoming to make training a reality. Fortunately, the material in the raw was good, the officers and men were keen and able, and the ambulances were soon in a position to take the field.

"Temporary commanding officers were appointed, and odd numbers of other officers were attached for duty for varying periods, with the result that the little huts provided as orderly-rooms were overcrowded with fully-qualified medical men, some of whom had served in O.T.C. (Officers Training Corps) and were thoroughly acquainted with military life; others, from a quiet country practice, were overawed, and the salutes to the officer commanding had all the varieties from the snap and shake of the Guards to the one finishing with putting gloves and stethoscope inside cap and depositing the lot on the 'Orders of the Day.' Map-reading seemed to come natural to men who had studied location of arteries and muscles, and we all knew what was meant when an officer said he fell off his horse at the 'E' in Eversley Common.

"Equipment was drawn from the Ordnance Stores at Aldershot, and there was keen rivalry between the ambulances to see who could obtain the major portion. One quartermaster attached to 135 was cute enough to obtain papers authorizing claim on an ambulance wagon already horsed and claimed by 137. The ambulance wagon was transferred on demand, and the lucky quartermaster found himself transferred to 137, and had the pleasure of having to go into Aldershot again and draw another wagon. Report had it that the artillery had first choice of horses and the 'remainder,' after every other unit was supplied, was to be portioned to the Royal Army Medical Corps. Luckily the horsey men attached to the Royal Army Medical Corps belonged really to the Army Service Corps, and they had some very smart warrant and non-commissioned officers; so after some of the woolly, untamed steeds were earmarked they were purloined, clipped and exchanged within half an hour, and many a poor animal went through the war with a Royal Horse Artillery prance and a castor oil dragoon on its back. Later on our commanding officers arrived, all Regulars with past war experience (Lieutenant-Colonel Hunt 135, Lieutenant-Colonel Rowan Robinson 136, and Lieutenant-Colonel Dunkerton 137), and they must have been agreeably surprised at the highly efficient state of their units, and under their finishing touches the units were fit for active service.

"It was not until the middle of May, 1916, that a camp was formed at Bullswater and pre-embarkation leave commenced; and at midnight on June 2nd the curtain was rung down on the first act—the camp was struck, and we moved off to entrain for that fair land of France."

CHAPTER II.

THE FIRST SIX MONTHS IN FRANCE.

A HUNDRED years hence—when war will probably be an affair of flying-submarines of some 40,000 tons apiece, capable also of moving across country at sixty miles an hour and belching out destruction by death rays—people reading of the formations of 1915 may exclaim, " What was a ' division,' anyway ?" So far it has been assumed that the knowledge is common to everyone, but the moment is now a good one, while the 40th Division is disembarking in France, to give a brief summary of such unit.

Stated briefly, a division was a formation of all arms forming a self-contained tactical unit and consisting of approximately 20,000 of all ranks, 64 guns, machine guns to the number of 54, a squadron of cavalry, engineers, and the necessary medical, transport and other services. The bulk of the personnel was found by the infantry, which at that time consisted of twelve battalions divided into three brigades. So far for the rough, general idea, and we now come to the more detailed composition of the particular division which is the subject of this History.

First and foremost came the divisional headquarters— the general officer commanding and his staff. The divisional commander when the 40th Division landed in France was Major-General H. Ruggles-Brise, and the officers who formed his general and administrative staffs have been mentioned by name in the previous chapter. Next come the three infantry brigades, numbered 119, 120 and 121, and commanded at that time by Brigadier-Generals Cunliffe-Owen, the Hon. C. S. H. D. Willoughby, and J. Campbell respectively. The 119th Brigade was entirely Welsh, the units composing it being the 19th Royal Welch Fusiliers, the 12th South

Wales Borderers, and the 17th and 18th Welch
Regiments. The 120th was Anglo-Scots, being made
up of the 11th King's Own Royal Lancaster Regiment,
the 13th East Surrey Regiment, the 14th Highland
Light Infantry, and the 14th Argyll and Sutherland
Highlanders. Entirely English in composition was the
121st Brigade, whose units were the 12th Suffolk
Regiment, the 13th Yorkshire Regiment, and the 20th
and 21st Middlesex Regiments. Territorially, therefore, the composition of the infantry of the Division was
one-half English, one-third Welsh, and one-sixth
Scottish. It should be noted that both Brigadier-
General Style and Brigadier-General Pritchard commanded in succession the 119th Brigade during its time
in England.

This list does not, however, exhaust all the infantry,
for there was a pioneer battalion—the 12th Yorkshire
Regiment—forming part of the Division. These
pioneer battalions—though similar units had existed for
long in the Indian Army—were a new feature in the
British service. Briefly, it may be said that they were
fighting troops, whose main duty, however, was to
relieve the Royal Engineers of some of the less
technical problems of military engineering, and in this
capacity they did sterling service in the war. According
to the official "War Establishment, Part VII, New
Armies, 1915," the artillery of a division consisted of
headquarters, three field artillery brigades and one field
artillery (howitzer) brigade. The enumeration of the
artillery brigades in the 40th Division was the 178th,
181st, 185th and 188th. As a matter of fact this
organization did not last for long after the arrival in
France, for at the end of August, 1916, the 185th was
broken up and distributed among the remaining brigades, which were then reorganized. The artillery
commander during the time in England had been
Brigadier-General F. G. Stone, but the first commander
in the field was Brigadier-General H. L. Reed, an
ex-horse gunner, who had won the V.C. in the South

African War in a gallant attempt to recover some guns temporarily lost to us in the fighting in Natal. According to the official establishment, a divisional ammunition column also formed part of every division, but such unit does not appear in the divisional records, the reason doubtless being that the static nature of the war in 1916 rendered other arrangements necessary. The same remark applies in part to cavalry. A division possessed one squadron, chiefly for orderly work. That belonging to the 40th Division was " A " Squadron of the 1st Wiltshire Yeomanry, but almost immediately after the arrival of the Division in France it was transferred to the XV Corps cavalry.

The engineers of the Division were found by the headquarters divisional engineers and three field companies, the 224th, 229th and 231st; then came a signals unit, or, to give it its full title, the 40th Divisional Signal Company. There was also a cyclist company, but like the cavalry squadron this was transferred to another formation shortly after arrival in France, the 40th Cyclist Company going to Reserve Army on June 11th, 1916. Machine guns had by 1916 become a prominent feature indeed of warfare, and this arm was represented in the 40th Division by the 119th, 120th and 121st Machine Gun Companies. Later in the story, when we come to Bourlon Wood, we shall find the 244th Machine Gun Company also coming very much into the picture, and later the 40th Battalion Machine Gun Corps will tell of the new corps organization which was adopted. The transport of the Division —that is to say, the divisional train as apart from battalion transport—was represented by 292-295 Companies, Army Service Corps—the splendidly-earned title of " Royal " came after the war—while the medical service had in the Division the 135th, 136th and 137th Field Ambulances and No. 83 Sanitary Section. In addition to the units already described, there were the 51st Mobile Veterinary Section, and later there was also the 237th Divisional Employment Company.

A formation like a division, which comprised in round numbers 20,000 men, 6,000 horse, 64 guns, and over a thousand vehicles obviously could not be transported overseas all at once, and as a matter of fact the operation lasted about a week, the bulk of the Division being carried from Southampton to Havre between May 29th and June 5th, though certain supply details embarked at Avonmouth. The voyages were without incident, for, in spite of the submarine activity of the Germans throughout the war, the guarding of the Channel was so efficiently carried out by the French and British Navies that not a single man was lost of the millions that were landed on the Continent. As for the actual landing, it might appear superfluous to record an experience shared by millions. Nevertheless, there is this to be said. Of all the impressions garnered by every individual who served in France, there is none quite so sharply etched in his memory as the recollection of the first hours in the theatre of war. It was the feeling which comes after the long weariness of rehearsals when the curtain goes up on the first night. The hour for which all the preparation was aimed has arrived, and success or failure will be quickly registered. It is worth while to turn aside from the main story for a minute and live those first hours in France once again.

"Three a.m.," says one, "and we slowly recovered consciousness in the little cabin, apparently a second charthouse on the boat-deck of the cross-channel steamer *La France,* which had brought 900 of our battalion across from Southampton. We were a small party of five, and had commenced the voyage seated round the table in this deck-house, but we were in almost every other position but seated after the eight-hour crossing—without food or light—and all felt a little peevish. The decks were a sight for the gods, and our sympathies were with the ship's crew who would have to clean these up. At this early hour the harbour was quiet, except for the squeaking of a dredger working overtime deepening some berth, and the cries of the seagulls as

they wheeled about searching for breakfast—five hours
to go before we would find ours. The transport wagons,
horses, mules, and the remaining 100 men had gone
ahead in a larger boat which had more deck space for
the wagons, so that at about 7 a.m. we were able to
disembark without trouble. The town at this early hour
smelled fresh and clean, and everyone looked about with
interest, our attention focussed particularly on details,
as all seaports possess paved quays, railway lines,
cranes, and swing-bridges across the locks; amongst
these details were the length of the French sentries'
bayonets, the turn-back of their greatcoats which they
apparently always wore, the clever way in which the
children kept their feet in their sabots on the
uneven *pavé*.

"We marched on somewhat unsteadily over the railway
lines and *pavé* until we reached a wide avenue, where
a halt was called and we fell out for a smoke. By this
time the inhabitants, especially the small fry, began to
take a certain amount of interest in us, and on all sides
rose the cry ' Bully beeef—Biskeet.' We had now come
to wider streets and better houses, and on resuming our
march we swung on to the sea front and marched north
for about a mile, when we commenced to climb a long
and winding hill, past the headquarters of the Belgian
Government, apparently housed in one large hotel and
a camp of comfortable wooden huts. After climbing
for about two kilometres we reached a rather scattered
camp with a splendid view over the bay and the
Channel. Later, in a stroll through the town, we
inspected our surroundings, and although we liked the
houses they struck us as rather too ornate, with their
curved eaves and different coloured bricks and tiles
accentuated by the brilliant greens or white of their
shutters, and their gardens, too, were small in
proportion."

"We saw no young men in civilian clothes; in
accordance with the Continental custom (and strictly
according to war-time regulations, of course) everyone

on leave apparently wore uniform, even in his own garden or on the beach, and it must be admitted that in a setting of vivid houses, the uniforms—whether soldiers, gendarmerie, sailors with their rather childish red pom-poms on the top of their caps, W.A.A.Cs., nurses, tram-conductors or bathing machine attendants —provided enough variety to satisfy the most enthusiastic devotee of colour. We noticed, too, the small number of children of the better class—presumably they had been sent to the south, to be away from the bombs and other unpleasant reminders of the war. Coming as we did from a town of very modern growth, we were struck by the curious mixture of old and inefficient gear and new and often more modern installations than we had at home. Contrast, for instance, the use of penny tin trumpets for signalling to the shunting trains on the railway with the presence of an up-to-date factory for making liquid air, and the fact that up another long, winding hill to the camp the overhead wires for the trams were supported by a modern steel post and a bent wooden one alternately. So much for our impressions of Havre and its inhabitants in the brief period at our disposal.

" Before returning to camp it occurred to our youngest member to enquire as to what the inhabitants thought of us; he had heard during our march the remark ' *Comme ils sont solides,*' addressed by one spectator to another, which showed that so far as our appearance on parade was concerned we had created a favourable impression. But not satisfied with this, he addressed a man, by appearance a broker in a small way, and more by reason of the latter's knowledge of English than his own knowledge of French, gleaned the information that : Firstly, the British soldiers who arrived early in the war were much too optimistic as to how soon they would smash up the Kaiser's Army. Secondly, he was not alone in his admiration of the quality of our equipment, horses and transport wagons. Thirdly, he told us that they admired the Scottish

soldiers more than the English, because when an
Englishman went into a shop to purchase a certain
article he paid the price asked at once and departed, but
the Scot argued at some length about the price and
generally got a reduction. (Which was a polite way,
one can only suppose, of telling us that we were soft.
This also confirmed our original deduction that our
informant was a commercial man.)

" After our examination of this corner of the town we
clambered up the hill again; here we received our second
shock—the English papers had just arrived, and we
were confronted by the first and far too pessimistic
report of the Battle of Jutland, which, although from
its geographical situation and the fact that the German
Fleet retired to its base after the action, leaving us still
in command of the battle area, we took to be a moral
victory though not a material one. This action formed
the principal topic of conversation as a little later we
wound down the hill again and across the back of the
town to a goods station on the outskirts. On this march
a little girl of about twelve years of age ran out to the
head of one of the companies, which were well separated
out of consideration for the traffic, and, taking the hand
of the officer at the head, walked as far as the station
with us. And so this was Havre. The curtain was up,
and we had our first, brief, wondering look around."

By June 9th the 40th Division had concentrated some
ten miles west of Béthune, the exact area being bounded
by Lillers—St. Hilaire—Rely—Febrin Palfart—Fontaine les Hermans, with headquarters at Norrent Fontes.
Railhead was at first at Chocques, but was subsequently
moved to Lillers. The concentration area was in the
sector of the I Corps of the First Army, and at once
units of the Division were attached to formations of the
I Corps for training. After a week, Divisional Order
No. 1 was issued, by which the Division was moved
forward to a fresh concentration area nearer Béthune,
headquarters being then established at Bruay. Thus
June closed without the Division being actually in the

line, but the attachment for training had taken its toll,
and before the Division had been three weeks in the
battle zone it had suffered over 250 casualties, the killed
including 1 officer and 46 other ranks. This is the kind
of thing which distinguished the condition of being
" out of the line " in a quiet sector in an uneventful
period of the Great War.

The beginning of July was a landmark in the history
of the 40th Division. It was ordered to take over the
right sector of the I Corps in the Lens area, the 16th
Division being on its left and the 47th Division of the
VIII Corps on the other flank.

The country in the Lens area was flat, and
generally uninteresting, covered as it was by numerous
mining villages and disfigured by slag heaps. These
latter offered certain advantages as regards command
and observation, but for that reason received a great
deal of unwelcome attention from the artillery of both
sides. The trench system was on the whole good,
and compared favourably with the protection in the
salient—in the minds of those who had done Ypres—
and with that in the Somme area, which the 40th
Division was soon to experience. Mining operations
were being carried out—not coal mining, gentle
reader, but mining of a more military and murderous
nature. The outstanding features in the landscape
were the Double Crassier in the Maroc sector, and the
mines which had been blown in the sector of Loos.
The Double Crassier was an immense slag heap with
its butt end in the front line of the Division, from
which it projected at right angles towards the enemy.
Under this slag heap the miners worked—again, be
it noted, not coal miners, but the miners who blew
people up sky high when they could—and were in
touch with German miners working from their line.
The removal of the mining excavation was always
a serious problem, as it consisted of very visible
white lumps which could only be cleared up at night.
Carrying parties were therefore freely employed under

cover of darkness; the work was strenuous and imposed
a severe strain on the men. The enemy at this time
were exceedingly active with trench mortars and rifle
grenades, particularly about the Double Crassier. To
counteract this activity it was found necessary to keep
a specially trained party of men of sufficient strength
to supply reliefs to hold this slag heap. These men
were trained at the brigade bombing school in a four-
day course. The result was quite satisfactory, and by
this means the enemy's activity was well kept in check.

Pen pictures of some of those mining towns through
which the 40th Division moved on the occasion of its
first experience of the line will bring back to many the
summer of 1916. Nœux-les-Mines was a dreary-looking
town with wide footways at either side of the main road,
the latter being *pavé* of the usual vileness and the
former simply beaten-down mud and coal dust kept in
place by a narrow whitewashed stone kerb. The mines
and railways were still working, though only four
and a half miles from the front line and exposed to
shell fire of guns of 8in. calibre and upwards. The
monotony of the houses was frequently broken by
estaminets, and occasionally by some big building
having the appearance of an office of one of the mining
companies, and in a big villa on the eastern outskirts
of the town a casualty clearing station had been
established.

Three miles nearer the front was Les Brebis, " and
here we were struck by the fact that the inhabitants
—except those actually engaged about the house—
were carrying gas masks of the flannel bag type then
in vogue." From the outskirts of the town " we caught
glimpses of the trench system, rendered conspicuous by
the strong sun shining on the excavated chalk which
formed the sub-soil here." The land on this side of
Les Brebis was not under cultivation, and as far as the
eye could see was a waste of rank grass, with wonderful
patches of wild flowers—mustard-yellow or red with
poppies, some of the patches being about a quarter of

a mile square. Bully Grenay was " one of the most
extraordinary villages to be found on the whole front."
This was due to the impassivity of the inhabitants, who
were actually in the battle zone. Some of the houses
faced west with their backs towards the line, " and in
most cases they were still inhabited by civilians, although
we had our howitzers literally in their back gardens."
Curiously enough, over half the houses had their
windows still intact, although the place was only
3,000 yards from the line and within range of the
lightest of artillery.

Maroc was a quite modern " model " village, as was
Calonne, the designs being so similar as to suggest
that they had been built by the same architect and
contractor. Across the eastern edge of the latter town
the railway was carried on an embankment some 18ft.
high, pierced by a bridge to let the high street
through. The aperture of the bridge was completely
filled by a huge mound of earth, held in place
by timber and sandbags, thus preventing the enemy
enfilading the street. A certain amount of dead ground
was thus provided, in which working parties, particularly pioneers, were able to carry on in comparative
safety. The only precaution really necessary here
was " to detail one man to stand in a sheltered position,
and on hearing the ' pop ' of an enemy trench mortar
he blew one blast on his whistle and pointed to the
projectile as it sailed aloft; if we saw it was going to
drop near us, we scattered without delay." Life, even
in the dead ground of a mining garden city, was not
without its thrills those days.

The first half of July passed peaceably enough. The
enemy was fairly quiet, although there was, of course,
the usual interchange of hate all along the front. At
6 a.m. on the 6th there is the somewhat startling entry
in a war diary, " a rum jar fell in the trench, completely
blocking it," but the visitor was in no way connected
with liquid refreshment, the term " rum jar " merely
denoting here a projectile from an enemy trench mortar.

The usual trench routine was now in full swing, shells, rum jars, rifle grenades, sniping, and a certain amount of aerial activity being noted. Behind the lines there was the incessant minor campaign waged between the representatives of the Provost Marshal's department and the fighting troops. The *casus belli* was the age-long one—wood, and there is a plaintive record to the effect that " it is difficult to make men understand that a ruined derelict house is still of value to its owner."

At the beginning of this chapter it was deemed advisable to give some explanation of the term " division," for the simple reason that, should the volume be read by descendants of those who made the 40th Division, the term might conceivably by then be obsolete. For a similar reason it is advisable to give some indication as to what was meant by "the trenches." Quite conceivably, in the future, efforts will be made with such success to keep warfare mobile that it will be difficult to realize then that in the Great War of 1914-1918 millions of men faced each other for years from excavations separated sometimes by but a score of yards.

The beginning of what is known as " trench warfare " may be said to date from the winter of 1914. Some civilian writers assert that it was inaugurated at the Aisne in September of that year, but this is sheer nonsense. The real commencement was at the close of the indecisive First Battle of Ypres, when the opposing armies had fought themselves to a standstill, when the various trench barriers had been successively joined up from the Swiss frontier to the North Sea, and when a war of movement and manœuvre had become impossible. To visualize the Western Front the reader of the year 2025 must, therefore, begin by imagining two huge opposing armies interlocked in battle on a frontage of several hundred miles. Exposed flanks there are none, since to the east the neutral state of Switzerland constitutes a barrier, while to the west, as a result of the " race to the sea," the coast affords a natural resting place for the left hand man of the long firing line, without fear of molestation from any turning movement. The battle is essentially one of artillery and infantry, and on the British side the cavalry are in the line, dismounted. This is the end of the autumn of 1914. Then imagine further effort of penetration to be impossible on either side owing to the advent of winter, with its attendant rain and mud, estimated to last at least four months. What is the result? Each side " digs in." The firing line, with its supports and reserves, becomes the outpost line. Piquets are joined up laterally by fire trenches. The supports are joined up to the piquets by communication trenches, and to each other by more fire trenches. Reserves are similarly dealt with, and as these have to be reached on foot, in comfort, by day and night, they in their turn are linked up with supporting formations by more communication trenches, so long as cover from view so demands. And so there results the greatest trench systems ever dug, reaching from Switzerland to the Channel, and facing each other across a debatable territory known as " No Man's Land."

In this system British soldiers began to eat, live and have their being in the winter of 1914. But men cannot live merely in hollowed earth. These excavations have to be drained, revetted, and boarded with floor boards which came to be known as " duck boards." Shelters, rooms, cabins, " dug outs " came into being, some reinforced with heavy concrete iron rods, which provided cover from weather and shell fire. In the latter respect many trenches fell far short of the ideal. It must be remembered that as they were " battle " trenches there never had been much chance of " siting," which meant that some were constantly overlooked, or enfiladed, although as a matter of fact it became rather a fetish never to give up any bit of trench, no matter how ill adapted it might be for defence. In the winter battalions went into the trenches for four days, and in the summer the tour

extended to eight days or more. On a battalion front
two companies generally held the fire trench and its
supporting trenches, one company remained in support
and one in reserve, these changing at half-time.
Company headquarters were linked up to battalion
headquarters by telephone, and so on to brigade,
division and corps, army and General Headquarters.

The defensive power conferred by trenches was
enormous, although this was not at first completely
grasped. It was at one time thought possible to
secure penetration merely by flinging infantry against
them, a method which may be described as the "all
blood" system and one mercifully obsolete before the
40th Division took the field. Then came the "all
shell" era, when it was surmised that by a practically
unlimited supply of gun ammunition a breach could
be blasted in the opposing front line, which could
immediately be exploited by infantry. This method
however, did not realize the expectations founded
upon it. Later the advent of the tank threatened
to revolutionize matters, but the failure to combine
masses of these machines with the element of surprise,
and with a sufficiency of intact troops to pour into the
gap formed, led to a temporary reaction against this
new arm. And then, too, there was a tactical counter-
revolution by the Germans, when fortified zones were
substituted for mere lines of trenches and when a position began to be held in depth rather than by a thickly
manned front line.

This is, however, getting away rather from a brief
survey of trench warfare, to which we now return. By
June, 1916, "the trenches" had become properly consolidated. The communication trenches were all named
and the fire trenches systematically numbered from right
to left of sector. Corps, divisions and brigades had
their allocated parts and defence schemes. Communication between the firing line and the covering field
artillery was instantaneous. Some dug-outs were very
deep and bomb-proof up to a 5·9 shell. A system of

drying-rooms for clothes, trench boots and socks was introduced. Log books were kept and handed over by battalions on relief together with trench stores of tools, horns for warning of gas attack, gongs for a similar purpose and blankets soaked in chemicals for the protection of dug-out doors against gas clouds. Bombs and ammunition were strictly accounted for, together with S.O.S. rockets, Very lights and pistols, for which purpose advance parties proceeded to the trenches by daytime, to take over. Trenches became named after the streets and places of the localities from which the divisions were drawn in the old country, so it became easy to know who first improved certain sectors. By degrees battalions came to write and print their standing trench orders in booklet form.

Sanitation was probably the most important item in trench routine after the cleanliness of rifles and bombs, and it is easy to imagine the havoc which might have been played through an outbreak of typhoid. As it was, a new type of fever, called trench fever, developed, which was traced to infection brought about by the bites of lice. The disease itself was not serious to the individual, but sufficient to cause a casualty. " Trench feet," another enemy more deadly than the Germans in the winter months, was a condition brought about by exposure to wet and mud and want of circulation. To guard against this, " Gum Boots, Thigh " became an article of trench stores and were constantly used in the winter, but they, too, had their disadvantages and " drew " the feet. " Trench feet " was combated successfully by discipline and hard work when in the line, and by certain medical precautions. Some brigades were practically immune from this condition in 1917. Rats, which seemed to come from nowhere in quest of food and infested the front line system of trenches, throve throughout the war and became a regular feature of trench life. In course of time the trench system became everywhere such a maze of fire, support, reserve and communication trenches that it

D

became necessary to issue regular trench maps for each
sector of the line, in order that newcomers might be
able to find their way about the labyrinth. And a
large-scale plan of any sector resembles nothing so
much as two spiders' webs, the constructors of which
used red and blue colouring material respectively.

The comfort of the men came to be the next consideration in the line after defence, and cooking and
carrying food and material came to be reduced to a fine
art, while quartermasters and regimental transport
officers delivered rations nightly to battalion headquarters, from whence ration parties, supplied by the
companies, carried for the remainder of the journey.
Battalion and brigade reliefs were almost invariably
carried out by night, on account of the observation of
the enemy, and became a matter of routine. Battalions
marched in by platoons at intervals, and relieved by
platoons. Company, battalion and brigade commanders
left the line on receipt of a code message, by telephone,
that their commands had handed over.

The state of discipline of a battalion or brigade could
be told at sight by the state of the line and the "atmosphere" in the trench system of that line, while the
fighting efficiency of a battalion could also be told at a
glance by the nightly happenings in No Man's Land.
The first thing a good battalion did, on entering the
line, was to obtain superiority by night in No Man's
Land, and then to raid the German trenches for
prisoners for identification purposes. During this
trench life the gunners and infantry came to know each
other and help each other as never before had been
possible.

The chaplains played a very useful part in the
trenches by arranging cinema shows and concerts to
those in brigade reserve and by visiting the front line
trenches daily with cigarettes, comforts and good cheer.
It has been said that trench warfare made the men
"sticky" for open fighting; "lazy" would be the more
expressive word, perhaps, and then only when laziness

was permitted. After a few days' training the men soon found their surface legs. Many pages could be written regarding trench warfare, which became a habit to the men in France, but it is sufficient to say that the British Army was forced underground, owing to modern conditions, and that the men lived underground for nearly four years, with as much protection as possible from weather and huge shells. At first everything was makeshift, but by degrees became highly organized. Of course it sometimes happened that enemy trenches had to be occupied and held. This called for hard work on the part of the men, as the trench naturally faced the wrong way, and all parapets and dug-outs had to be converted.

The first active operation in which a unit of the 40th Division was engaged took place on the night of July 18th/19th. A paramount necessity all through the war was to obtain accurate information as to the whereabouts of each enemy formation, the creation of new ones and the various movements of all these formations, old and new, in, to, and from each theatre of war. In this way it was possible for the Intelligence department at G.H.Q. to draw up an enemy order of battle, an essential both for the arrangement of an attack upon any portion of his front and no less so in awaiting an attack to be made on his part. The methods by which such information was acquired would fill a volume in itself—a volume which will never be written, as obviously much of its contents would be highly confidential and secret. Briefly, it may be said that secret service agents and spies played a necessary part. Then there was the information gleaned from deserters and prisoners, and from the careful investigation of the dead and wounded on a battlefield. But over and above these sources of information there was a method more simple, primitive and obvious in static warfare, and that was to send over a party, under cover of darkness, into the enemy's trenches, knock one or more Huns on the head, haul them back into our lines, and then send them back to the Intelligence people to deal with. The operation by which this result was secured was a "raid." Not every raid was necessarily for this object, as there were raids to wreck some annoying post, or simply to destroy the enemy's *moral* if that was suspected to be getting a little low. But the majority of raids at this time were frankly for the purpose of getting identification.

The 119th Brigade had the honour of being concerned with the first raid made by the Division, and the personnel conducting it was drawn from the 18th Welch Regiment. Shortly after midnight two parties moved towards the enemy's lines, the object being to "secure identification." It may be mentioned here that a successful raid usually demanded an immense amount of rehearsing and extraordinarily detailed instructions, as well as the fruits of experience gained in previous raids. A first raid was therefore always more or less an experiment. This particular raid failed to secure any identification, and after Lieutenant Salisbury, the officer in command, had been twice wounded, supervision was difficult. The two parties got back with the loss of 1 officer and 2 other ranks wounded, besides 3 other ranks missing. On the following night the 121st Brigade had its turn, in conjunction with the blowing up of six mines. The raid did not succeed in its purpose owing to the heavy resistance encountered, but valuable experience was gained. One of the Division's officers (Lieutenant Larell) was killed in this operation and 10 men were wounded, one dangerously. Although the raiders had been unable to penetrate the enemy line, the actual objective being the German trenches south of the Double Crassier, fortune favoured the enterprise. A German walked on to the Crassier and was shot, and from him valuable information was obtained. How ever he got on to the Crassier was a mystery, as the wire there was particularly thick, but it is thought that he had been sent skywards by the explosion of one of the six mines, and on reaching mother earth, rather dazed, he lost his bearings and walked towards our lines. So much for the first two raids. These became quite normal features of a tour in the front line, and while in this area the 121st Brigade alone carried out seventeen of these operations.

Mention has already been made of mining, and in this sector several mines were blown up, so that all battalions of the Division gained experience in consolidating the craters formed. Mining, of course, leads to counter-mining, and, without going into any technical description of the whole art, it may be said that when mine and counter-mine approached a good deal depended on who got his pyrotechnic display off first. The great thing was to be able to locate by sound the " head " of the opposing mine or counter-mine. So long as noise of tools could be detected, all was well; on the other hand, a prolonged stillness meant that the other fellow's job was finished, and pressing the button would be the next item. The Germans put in a most obliging individual, who used always to chink his tools joyously and advertise his arrival and departure by a generous amount of coughing. This unseen and subterranean labourer soon became known in the Division as " Old Bill." From him our listeners got valuable information, as they could tell accurately the German hours of work and locate the position of the head. The affection for this unknown warrior became so profound that on several occasions when the blowing of a mine was to take place the button-presser would hold his hand until it had been reported that Old Bill was safely clear. But on one black day the officer in charge of these mining operations was seen moving about with an air of deepest dejection; interrogated, he replied sadly, " Old Bill is gone." It appears that mine and countermine had approached so close that it was a question of seconds whether Briton or Hun would press his respective button first. This was no time for ceremony. The matter was urgent. The devil must take the hindmost, and so things went sky high, and with them fragments of Old Bill.

During the remainder of the month nothing of outstanding importance occurred, a state of affairs which
continued through August, that month consisting
merely of the inevitable reliefs and of a concertina process of squeezing in and out to extend or restrict the
front. During the night of the 3rd/4th there were
two minor enterprises—as raids were sometimes called—
to secure identification, carried out by parties of the
12th Suffolk Regiment and the 21st Middlesex. In
neither case, however, was the necessary information
obtained. Some ten days later the 12th South Wales
Borderers were more successful, and out of three raiding
parties one succeeded in entering the German lines. A
German prisoner was captured, and important identification was thus obtained. Captain Pritchard died of
wounds received in this operation, and there were 9
other casualties, including 4 other ranks killed. The
captured prisoner was a Bavarian, wearing his identity
disc and in possession of two documents. He was the
first prisoner taken by the Division, and naturally
the South Wales Borderers were not a little proud of the
fact. Captain Pritchard, although wounded, had
refused assistance, and it was he who, jumping into the
trench, bagged the prisoner. Then, already weak from
loss of blood, Captain Pritchard was wounded a second
time, and handed the prisoner over to Second-Lieutenant
Wood. Captain Pritchard would have been recommended for the D.S.O. had he survived. Second-
Lieutenant Wood was awarded the Military Cross.
After conducting the captured Bavarian to our lines, he
returned at once to the German trenches, and was the
last man to leave after the wounded had been successfully got away under his supervision.

After the first week in September things began to get
rather more breezy. On the 9th, which may be taken as a
typical day of this period, there was a gas alert in the
forenoon which lasted for an hour and a half. In the
afternoon the Division blew a small mine in the South
Crassier, and during the night the enemy retaliated

with a camouflet near Hart's Crater, doing, however, no damage to our work. These were the outstanding incidents, so to speak, and throughout the whole day the trench mortars of the Division and, to a lesser extent, the artillery worried the Germans, whose retaliation on this day was comparatively weak. And so on for the next week or so the trench mortars of the Division kept hard at it cutting the enemy's wire. During the night of the 20th/21st a party from the 119th Brigade entered an enemy sap, after identification as usual, but failed in their object, "since the Huns ran away." Outside the actual front line there is a note of "troops still scrounging wood." The organization of the divisional artillery was now altered, the 185th Brigade being broken up and absorbed. Other administrative items worth a passing mention are the employment of female labour " to repair uniforms when tailors cannot be employed," and towards the end of the month an issue of chewing gum was made, to give staying power in long marches or operations. It is thought, however, that the next entry in a war diary— " Internal relief in the 121st Brigade "—has no digestive significance. More raids took place at the end of the month, in one of which a dead German officer was retrieved and supplied valuable information, a statement which also applies to a Saxon helmet found in a trench drawn blank.

The records consulted make it abundantly clear that the Division had come on very fast in the matter of raids, and there is exultation in the entry " marked increase of success on our side." October 8th was a big raiding occasion, four raids taking place, of which two were made by the 13th Yorkshires and two by the 20th Middlesex south and north respectively of the Double Crassier. There is an angry note of one raid about this time having been " spoilt by a Hun dog." On another occasion gas clouds were launched in connection with gas and raid by the 8th Division on the left, which was said to be " a big thing and biggest yet in the First Army." Over and above these raiding pin pricks, there was the mutual blowing up of each other's lines by British and Germans, the latter scoring on the night of the 15th/16th by gaining possession of seventy yards of the Division's line. On the 15th, the 20th Middlesex Regiment found two guards of honour for the French President during a visit by him to Béthune. Three days later the 17th Welch Regiment suffered the loss of their commanding officer, Lieutenant-Colonel Wilkie, who was killed.

On October 20th orders were received for the relief of the Division by the 24th Division, the destination of the former being unknown except that a concentration near St. Pol was talked about. It was thought that the destination would probably be the Somme area, towards which troops had been drifting for months. While the 40th Division had been learning its trade in the Loos sector, one of the fiercest contests of the war had been taking place by the Somme. It will be remembered that the success of the German Crown Prince's Armies had brought about a position at Verdun full of menace for the French, and it had accordingly been decided to launch a great counter-offensive on the Somme on July 1st. There ensued five and a half months' fighting more desperate and sanguinary than anything that had yet occurred in the war. By the middle of October the struggle was not yet over, though the advent of winter conditions would soon make further operations impossible in the churned-up quagmire of the Somme area. It was into this vortex that the 40th Division was now to be sucked.

The end of October witnessed the necessary relief by the 24th Division, and the usual orders—and counter-orders—for the move of the 40th Division, the latter crystallizing early next month in the issue of Divisional Order No. 28 of November 2nd, prescribing a march to the area round Houvin-Houvigneul, south of St. Pol, whence the Division would head south-west towards Frohen-le-Grand. The march took place in an assortment of weather, the expressions " Fine day," " Very wet," " Blowing a gale," and " Snow " being met with at times, but the significant words " Heavy rain " occur with the greater frequency. Towards the end of the month, when divisional headquarters were at Bouquemaison, north of Doullens, orders were received transferring the Division to the XV Corps of the Fourth Army. Thereupon the 40th Division headed westward towards Abbeville, to undergo a course of training, the dislocation at the end of November being as follows : Headquarters at Ailly-le-Haut-Clocher; 119th Brigade around Bellancourt; 120th Brigade around Gorenflot, and the 121st in the neighbourhood of Vauchelles-les-Domart. The command of the 119th Brigade had been assumed by Brigadier-General F. P. Crozier on the 20th of the month.

For just three weeks training continued in this area, save for the interruptions caused by the inclement weather, until orders were received directing the Division to move forward to the Somme district, its destination being the area just west of Bray. The movement was carried out partly by rail and partly by road, divisional headquarters being established at Chipilly on December 15th. Four days later XV Corps Orders directed the 40th to relieve the 33rd Division on the right sector of the corps front. The usual reconnaissance of the position to be occupied was made next day, and immediately after Christmas the 40th was once again " in the line," between Bouchavesnes and Rancourt. The first-named place marked the end of the sector recently taken over from the French, and the 40th Division had the distinction of being the " right of the line " so far as the British Armies were concerned. Immediately on the right of the Division was the 15th Division of the IX Corps of the French Tenth Army, while on the left the 40th joined up with the British 4th Division. In the 40th Division itself, by the end of the year, the 120th Brigade was on the right, the 119th on the left, and the 121st in divisional reserve with headquarters at Bray.

Now began three months in the most God-forsaken and miserable area in France, bar, possibly, the salient of Ypres. The whole countryside was a churned-up, yeasty mass of mud, as a result of the vile weather and of the battle which even yet had not petered out. The weather was awful. Constant rain was varied by spells of intensely cold weather and some very heavy snowfalls. Mud and dirt were everywhere. The French had been in occupation of the line, and, however gallant our allies may have been, their notions on sanitation were mediæval. Billets in the back area were camps of dirty, wet and decrepit huts. Seen at that period of the year the countryside was bleak, mournful, uninviting and miserable; roads cut up; villages badly knocked about, and everywhere "signs of the advance of large bodies of troops," and French troops at that. So much for the back area, Bray to Corlu. But no pen can do justice to the front region— "line" it could not be called. It just beggars description. It consisted of a mass of shell holes; of a general sea of mud; of lesser lakes and lagoons of icy water. Trenches did not exist, except for short lengths on higher ground; of communication trenches there were none; men had to do the best they could to improve such shell holes "as were least full of water and other more unpleasant relics of the battle." Villages there were in profusion, on the map; but in reality they were but flattened brickwork. Looking back on those days it is hard to realize how human beings could have existed in such conditions. The only cheering thought was that the enemy might be as badly off as, or even worse off than, the 40th Division, for the ground sloped badly for them; they, however, were on ground that had not been fought over, so that, save for the disadvantages of the lie of the ground, they were in comparative comfort.

In the front area of the 40th Division one battalion

headquarters received the significant title of "The Aquarium." It was an old German dug-out, which, therefore, faced the wrong way for us, but some precarious cover had been provided by a trench more than knee-deep with water. After climbing down some steps water level was reached, and the aquarium was here some three to four feet deep. To keep moderately dry the occupants sat on the edges, or lay in the top berths with which the dug-out was provided, or squatted on a table the top of which was just above high-water mark. Pumping was of little avail, for, in the pouring rain, pump and Jupiter Pluvius were about game-all.

In these conditions transport work was a veritable nightmare. All supplies of ammunition, water, rations, clothing, etc., had to be taken up on pack animals, as, owing to the mud, which for the greater part of the distance was seldom less than waist deep, vehicles became obviously impracticable. Nightly a convoy of about eighty animals went up to one battalion. Although the total distance covered from the mule park to handing over the supplies to the battalion was only a very few miles, the return journey lasted from twelve to fifteen hours, owing to the fact that it was necessary to fight one's way through the mud, which at times came up almost to the arm-pits. The men travelled without greatcoats, and did not carry anything which they could conceivably leave in huts. They were mostly dripping with perspiration when they reached their journey's end. Owing to the fact that the ground had been shelled so constantly during the Somme offensive, it was intersected with shell holes long since filled with mud, and when an unfortunate animal or man fell, it was a matter of the very greatest difficulty to extricate him alive. The animals, already burdened with loads, had a most distressing time, and sometimes, owing to a broken leg or otherwise, had to be shot. The supplies were then taken off and distributed amongst the rest of the convoy. It sometimes happened, however, that it was impossible to burden them with the additional pack saddle, and this had to be left until the following night, when an unharnessed animal would be taken up and attempts made to recover the saddle, although in most cases, by that time, it had completely disappeared in the mud and all trace of it was lost. It soon became obvious that the majority of the men were physically unable to continue this nightly strain, and, therefore, in due time reinforcements were procured, so that it was possible to give them one night's rest in three.

The artillery had left the Loos sector somewhat later than the remainder of the Division, and had followed a somewhat different route. On December 16th, however, it reached the destination on the Somme, and at once relieved some French artillery there. Our gunners found the latter " amazingly quick and direct in their methods, and with that power of distinguishing the essential from the unessential in war which has always distinguished this great nation." Their cuisine in the officers' messes also seemed much better than ours, although their rations were not so good. An interesting item is that the French artillery " never seemed to use the telephone—so much a bugbear with ours." The artillery officers' dug-outs of the French fell somewhat short of the accepted British standard of comfort. But a note of cheerfulness was afforded by pictures from *La Vie Parisienne* and " other drawings perhaps peculiar to the French character."

Christmas Day, 1916, was marked by a severe *strafe* inflicted by the German artillery on our guns. It began in the afternoon, just after lunch—a favourite time with the Huns—and was heralded by a ranging round burst high in the air over one of our batteries. This was followed by a salvo of 5·9's, and then single rounds at 30 seconds interval began, lasting for three hours. And in these conditions of *strafes*, mud, wet, dirt, discomfort, cold and trench feet the 40th Division completed its first six months in France.

CHAPTER III.

THE SOMME COUNTRY. THE GERMANS WITHDRAW TO THE HINDENBURG LINE.

THE year 1917 started in a way which distinguished it from its predecessors, and for a time held out hopes of complete and early success. The principle of universal service had been adopted; adequate supplies of recruits were thus provided for; and the number becoming available at any given moment could be accurately gauged. This was an immense advantage in planning operations; and, further, it put an end to the abominable system whereby wounded and shattered men, who had voluntarily enlisted, were hurried out a second or third time overseas in order that others, whose patriotism and courage were less pronounced, might luxuriate in safe and lucrative billets at home. In the Government, too, there had been an important change. Early in December, 1916, the Asquith administration had collapsed, and Mr. Lloyd George had become Prime Minister. He had made up his mind that the Somme had been a costly failure, and was eagerly looking for some short cut to success which would be less expensive in personnel than a war of exhaustion. The year 1917 was, therefore, above all things to be the Year of Victory, and both in England and France loans were floated, and eagerly subscribed to, in the hope that within twelve months Germany would be beaten to her knees. These great hopes were, however, doomed to disappointment.

These high deliberations in Whitehall were naturally unknown to, and outside the ken of, the 40th Division, which had enough to do to keep itself warm and to carry up rations and ammunition through a land of quagmires

and lagoons. The new year was marked by an outburst
of activity on the part of the enemy, for during the night
of January 2nd/3rd the Germans "threw a lot of red
rockets" on the 40th Division, as well as on the
8th Division on the left and on the French
18th Division on the right. Along the 40th Division
front this outburst crystallized into a creeping barrage
from supports to rear, but no infantry action followed.
Probably the enemy was endeavouring to disturb the
system of reliefs, but in this he failed completely. The
next excitement came three days later, when great
aerial activity was displayed on both sides, and
in which one of our 'planes was brought down,
though under control. This was the last occasion of
excitement of this kind for nearly three weeks, weather
conditions militating against air work, there being
several references to " snow " and " snow and thaw."
On the 23rd a thrilling sight was witnessed—a German
'plane being brought down in flames over Le Forest.
The month of January, from the purely military point
of view, had been uneventful. The fighting on the
Somme had so churned up the ground that serious
operations there during the winter months were out of
the question. The 40th Division was concerned
chiefly with the routine of reliefs, and at the end of the
month it moved into corps reserve on being relieved by
the 8th Division.

Amid the mud and slime of the Somme country of
those days "paper" held its own, and not all the
abnormal conditions could divorce some people from
the routine of voucher and receipt. The pack saddles
of the 13th East Surreys were a case in point. Ninety
had been in nightly use for a considerable period.
The time came when the battalion was relieved and
the saddles had to be handed over to the Ordnance
sleuths. Now of the ninety original saddles many
were worn and incomplete, and, further, many more
lay buried in several feet of mud. However, about
thirty were completed by stripping portions from the

remainder of them and assembling the fresh lot " under battalion arrangements." The problem now before the battalion transport officer was to make thirty saddles convey the impression of ninety. Like all mighty achievements, the basic idea which sprouted to success was comparatively simple. As a preliminary the transport officer displayed, with quite justifiable ostentation, before the eyes of the Ordnance lynx, nine wagons sufficient to hold ninety saddles. Wagon No. 1 duly passed that official, ten saddles were counted within it, noted down, and the driver moved on in conscious virtue. Then while wagons Nos. 2 and 3 were keeping the Ordnance officer in play, the driver of No. 1 lashed his mules round some convenient houses, where well-trained myrmidons hurriedly unyoked the team and substituted a fresh one. The driver—with more ostentatious virtue than ever—then cut into the procession, and saddles 1 to 10 now became saddles 31 to 40. A similar expansion of " Now we go round the mulberry bush " soon brought the total to the desired ninety. The deficiency was thus made good. A clear receipt was given, " which apparently satisfied all concerned." It is melancholy to realize how quick the New Army was to imitate the wickedness of the Old.

The weather showed no sign of improvement, and taking it all round the conditions of the winter of 1916/1917 were exceptionally severe. All through November and December it had been cold and wet. In January " the cold was intense, which, combined with a biting wind, made life almost unendurable." There were, in the 48th Casualty Clearing Station, acute pneumonia wards, a significant index of weather conditions. About February 12th a colder spell set in, which lasted a week or so, the temperature at times falling to nearly zero Fahrenheit. During this time it was exceedingly difficult to water the artillery horses, which often had to be led for miles in the search for unfrozen water. Their hair was, of course, left long, and the mud which had adhered to their bellies became congealed "and bales of it hung on them for six weeks, and were impossible to remove." The case of the regimental transport animals was, of course, no better. The animals presented a pitiable appearance, as they had been previously smothered in mud, and, despite the best efforts to scrape it off, they were always coated with an enormous quantity. This had now frozen stiff, and their tails became one solid mass of frozen mud. It was clearly impossible to do any effective good with brushing, and therefore it was necessary to go over from ears to hoofs crumbling the mud between the fingers in order to break it. This was a slow and tedious operation, painful to animal and man. Harness cleaning became practically impossible because the water froze the moment it was put upon the leather, and when flung upon vehicles to wash them it turned at once into icicles. In these conditions it is not difficult to realize that possibly the health and spirits of the troops had never been at such a low ebb as in those terrible months.

When February opened the divisional headquarters were at Corbie. During the night of the 11th/12th the Division relieved the 8th Division in the Rancourt sector, becoming the left division of the XV Corps, the disposition then being that the front line was held by the 119th Brigade, the 121st in divisional reserve, with the 120th chiefly employed on corps fatigues. Three days later the German trenches were subjected to a very heavy bombardment. In this *strafe* the 121st Machine Gun Company co-operated with indirect fire, and during three bursts of fire in the afternoon the guns averaged 250 rounds a minute. Next day—February 16th—the enemy got a little of his own back, for his airmen managed to bomb Plateau dump with such effect that "ammunition was exploding all day." Just before the end of the month there were persistent reports to the effect that a retirement of the Germans in front of the Fifth Army was likely to take place, and speculation ran high as to whether this might extend to the sector held by the 40th Division. Active patrolling now became the order of the day—or rather of the night—and the artillery was directed to pay considerable attention to the roads leading back from the German position. There were many who scoffed at the rumour, but it turned out to be true—so far as the front of the Fifth Army was concerned; but in spite of a heavy bombardment, the Germans showed no inclination to vacate the terrain opposite the 40th Division. An attempt was now made to hurry them up, and on February 28th the Division co-operated with the XIV Corps in an attack against a portion of the German position. The co-operation consisted of a barrage by the artillery and a smoke barrage by the 121st Brigade. The operation was a complete success, the whole of the objective being secured. On the front line and supports of the 40th Division the enemy put down a fairly heavy artillery and machine gun barrage, but for once he was off his shooting, and no casualties ensued.

March came in like a lion, at any rate for the 13th Yorkshire Regiment, for on the very first night of the month a post held by six men of the battalion was the subject of considerable attention by the Germans. First of all a heavy barrage was put down, which was very accurate in effect and contained many lachrymatory shells—an official term which really means those shells that used to make your eyes stream water. The raiding party, when it arrived, proved to consist of twenty-five Germans, led by a powerful, brave and loud-tongued non-commissioned officer. A fierce hand-to-hand struggle took place, during which the enemy non-commissioned officer was wounded and captured, and after this the remaining Germans seem to have had enough of it. The wounded prisoner continued to shout out instructions till the end of the business, and died shortly afterwards. He gave his captors the name of his company and regiment, i.e., the 10th Company of the 104th Infantry Regiment, but quite rightly refused to be drawn further, and died game. In reading some

E

notes of this raid, the present historian was startled
to read the statement, "Three dead hens found," but
hazards the solution that the third word in quotes is
really "Huns" with the initial letter in what printers
term "lower case."

On March 4th the 8th Division, on the right,
carried out an operation the object of which was to seize
a portion of the enemy's position east and north-east of
Bouchavesnes, and, as had been the case in a similar
attack narrated earlier, the 40th Division was told off
to assist with barrage and smoke screen, while the 120th
Machine Gun Company was put at the disposal of the
attacking division. The operation was a complete
success, the objective being secured and held in spite
of repeated enemy counter-attacks. The next night
there fell two inches of snow, a foretaste of the weather
which was to last for well over a month. "This was
the worst weather of all to endure; neither man nor
beast actually suffered much during the extreme cold,
but this was really terrible." Further, rations, and
particularly forage, began to fail owing to the increasing
activity of the German submarines, for Germany had
now embarked upon that unrestricted under-water
campaign which was to bring her an initial temporary
advantage but was to work her eventual ruin, for the
policy dragged America into the war.

Two days after the successful attack round Bouchavesnes the division began to move to the southern
sector of the corps front, the movement being completed by March 9th. The Rancourt sector which had
been held by the 40th was handed over to the 8th
Division, the former taking over its new sector from
the 33rd, with the result that the front of the XV Corps
was now held by two divisions—the 40th on the right
and the 8th upon the left. News of a possible German
retirement was continually gaining force, and on the
13th a conference was held at corps headquarters to
decide upon a line of action in these new circumstances.

To enable the reader properly to understand the situation on the Western Front at this time, in detail, it would be necessary to write several pages of an appreciation of the situation, which would deal at less or greater length with each theatre of the war. This modest' volume does not, however, aspire to be a history of the war, but a narrative of the part played in it by the 40th Division. It is, therefore, merely necessary to state that the Germans had been seriously shaken by. the Somme fighting in 1916. In the neighbourhood of Beaumont Hamel the 63rd Division made an important advance early in 1917. It had become increasingly evident that the German defence was weakening, and with the spring the conditions became relatively favourable for a withdrawal on their part, for the thaw which succeeded the period of exceptional frost had turned the old Somme battlefield into a quagmire once again, while exerting but little effect on the roads elsewhere. As a consequence, the Germans, if they chose to retire, could do so fairly quickly, whereas the Allies, in following up and being confronted first by the quagmire, must do so very slowly; and this takes no account of the artificial expedients which the Germans could employ to delay pursuit still further. A withdrawal by the Germans on a wide scale had therefore been expected, and it had been definitely ascertained that they had been feverishly at work upon a new defensive line in rear.

This was the famous Hindenburg Line of history, which branched off from the original German defences near Arras, ran south-east for twelve miles to Quéant, and thence west of Cambrai in the direction of St. Quentin. The immediate object appeared to be escape from the salient between Arras and Le Transloy, but it was also evident, from the preparations which the Germans were making on a grand scale, that they contemplated an evacuation on much wider lines. The underlying motive of a withdrawal generally was to husband strength. The move back to the Hindenburg system would cause a considerable diminution of the

German front and a consequent increase in the number
of German reserves. It was clearly necessary for the
Germans to take these measures. They had lost very
heavily on the Somme, and they knew perfectly well
that the French were meditating a great offensive in the
" Year of Victory."   There was, too, always the possibility of Russia even yet doing something big, and
America might not always be too proud to fight.

So far as the 40th Division was concerned, March
17th, 1917, was the day when it first passed from passive
to active warfare. Two days earlier the Germans were
clearly retiring in front of the 8th Division, and the
40th had been doing its share of active patrolling,
which, however, merely showed that opposite the Division the enemy was still sitting tight. It was clear,
however, that a general withdrawal of the Germans
was now merely a matter of time, and divisional orders
had been issued containing instructions as to what the
line of action was to be. Briefly the great thing would
be that everyone would push on; the present line was
to be regarded as a defensive line to fall back upon in
case of strong counter-attacks; and every one was to
beware of booby traps. Then came March 17th, when
at long last the Germans in front of the 40th Division
were clearly off. Immediately the 40th got going, and
on the 18th occupied Mont St. Quentin, Péronne, and
Haut Allaines, with patrols out as far as Bossu, where
German cavalry could be seen east of that village. The
abrupt, even though long-expected, departure of the
enemy caused a feeling almost of uncanniness. He had
shelled the Division rather heavily the day before, and
then—silence. The sensation was extraordinary.
" One crept out into places where it would previously
have been certain death to approach, and, finding nothing
happen, the whole thing seemed unreal. It was like a
man who had lived in a caisson below water and at
great pressure suddenly coming to the surface."
Exactly the same sensation was felt, later, on that day
of days—the Armistice, in November, 1918.

The first unit of the British Army to enter Péronne was the 13th East Surrey Regiment, the transport of which had an exciting journey to and through that town. On the morning of March 18th the transport officer was ordered to report at brigade headquarters. He was then informed that the enemy had withdrawn, that the battalion was following up as closely as was practicable, and that he must start forthwith with ammunition and supplies for their requirements. Owing to the rapidity of movement, communication had broken down. It was impossible to ascertain where the battalion was to be found, but it was assumed it was following the general line towards Péronne. The transport, therefore, started and made its way up to the late headquarters, but found that they were vacated, and there were no orders as to where they had proceeded. The transport officer accordingly decided to proceed along the main road to Péronne. It was a matter of great interest to observe the old landmarks which had not been seen by day for many months. Considerable caution was necessary, as there was no knowledge as to whether the next hundred yards would find them with friends or amongst the enemy. Towards dusk the transport came to within sight of Péronne. The convoy was then halted, the men and animals took cover in hedges and ditches which ran along the side of the road, and the transport officer, Corporal Bull and Private Burrell went forward. A British officer was sighted, who imparted the discouraging information that to the best of his knowledge the enemy had not yet vacated Péronne. The position was now one of some difficulty, as it was obviously undesirable to take in the convoy if hopelessly surrounded by the enemy, but it was equally impossible for the battalion to be left without ammunition and supplies.

The transport officer, therefore, decided to run the risk, and concluded that, even if the enemy were still in the town, they would only be there in small numbers. The town presented an amazing sight, as most of the houses had been set on fire by the retiring enemy; household furniture, bedding and the like had been flung out of the windows and were in blazing heaps on all sides.   It was now nearly dark, and it was impossible to ascertain whether the enemy had left, but no interference took place.   A very disquieting moment occurred when cavalry was heard approaching.   Men and animals were, therefore, put into as much cover as possible.   The transport officer went forward to investigate, and was much relieved to find it was a squadron of British cavalry, the commanding officer of which informed him that they had been sent forward to reconnoitre and ascertain whether Péronne was cleared from the enemy.   This officer did not believe, until he saw the entire transport convoy, that the Surreys had come through the town.   It is a matter of interest that up to the last day of the war another regiment claimed that they were the first troops through Péronne, but this is entirely incorrect, as the privilege belongs entirely to the East Surreys.   The officer in charge of the cavalry squadron above referred to was asked whether he had seen anything of the battalion.   He stated that he had seen some troops proceeding towards Allaines, so it was decided to proceed in that direction.

The march continued in the dark, over unknown ground, and with the ever-present feeling that it might be possible at any moment to run into parties of the enemy.   After some considerable wandering, a village was seen in the distance.   The transport proceeded as close as the officer considered it to be wise, and was then halted, and he and Corporal Bull and Private Burrell advanced up to the outskirts of the village. He then halted the little party and explained that he was going into the village to ascertain whether it was held by British troops or the enemy; if he were not back within ten minutes, they were to return to the transport.   Corporal Bull was to take charge, as they could then be satisfied that the village was in enemy hands.   Proceeding with the greatest caution, he got

into the village, and at some distance found a barn
which was illuminated and heard voices, which from
that distance could not be identified by language. He
wriggled his way up towards the door in order to listen,
and then heard what possibly was the most welcome
sound he had heard for a considerable time——a voice
saying, " Where the 'ell have the —— rations gone?"
Doubts being then put at rest, he went into the shed
and found not only were they British troops, but by
the greatest luck they were his own battalion. The
supplies were then delivered, and the transport, after
an extremely long and tiring march, proceeded back to
its own lines. Some of the dug-outs in the village were
lavishly furnished, the walls were covered with polished
wood, and in one instance a table laid with napery,
crockery and cutlery of a nature which infantry troops
had not seen except when on leave.

Nothing of outstanding interest seems to have occurred
during the remainder of the month. The Germans had
made their plans for withdrawal with characteristic
thoroughness, and the records of the 40th Division contain chiefly an enumeration of the positions occupied
each day and the steps to be taken in the event of a
sudden turn at bay by the enemy. On the 21st the corps
mounted troops were ordered to establish outposts on
the line : high ground south of Longavesnes—north-
east of that village—north-east of Lieramont—south
and south-east of Sorel-le-Grand, and a comparison of
this line with that held by the Division before the
German withdrawal will show that steady, if slow,
progress was being made by the British in following
up the enemy. There was, of course, no question of
pursuit—a term which applies an "all out" chase of
a beaten enemy, for here it was entirely a question of a
cautious advance to take possession of terrain voluntarily abandoned by the foe. Towards the end of the
month the Division ceased for the moment to take an
active part in the advance, for it was withdrawn from
the line to work upon roads and railways. This was

the urgent need at the time, for without adequate communications no advance could be maintained, and naturally the Germans had done everything they could, by damaging things, to slow down the Allied advance. Captain Cowtan, staff captain of the 121st Brigade, now became D.A.A. and Q.M.G. of the Division.

The Division was not, however, entirely immobile during this period. On the 21st a "mobile" or "flying" column had been formed, under the command of Brigadier-General F. P. Crozier, of the 119th Brigade. It consisted of the corps mounted troops; a section of 18-pounders with a quota of ammunition column; one battalion of the 119th Brigade; a platoon of the 12th (Pioneer) Battalion Yorkshire Regiment, and a bearer sub-division. The trouble about this flying column was that it did not fly. It wanted to, badly—but just wasn't let. It resembled very much those tired-looking sea birds one sometimes sees on the beach of southern England. They would give anything to soar, but their wings are coagulated with waste oil from oil-burning vessels. The oil in this particular case was Superior Authority. This Power in the background would not let the column spread its wings too much; it laid down a daily "line"; and the flying column became one merely of diurnal jumps or waddles, a dismounted thrush rather than an eagle. When the commander first received his appointment, visions of dashing through a gap at night and exploiting the gain at once floated through his brain. Verbal instructions were forthwith issued to his various subordinates. "But all that was washed out" is his wistful comment. But the column did valuable work and suffered its share of casualties from the Hun booby traps of all sorts.

If the reader now thinks that he is going to accompany the 40th Division to a land of milk and honey he may as well slough off the misunderstanding herewith. The actual slime and shell holes may have been left behind, but the Hun had seen to it that the advancing

Allies should not lie on beds of roses. Quite rightly
the less unhabitable dwellings are allotted, when possible, to medical units and formations. But even here
there was not much of the " home from home " idea.
We read of a medical headquarters billeted in a village
" which was practically a heap of bricks." There the
personnel managed to find a house " with only the roof
blown off," as the narrator gratefully remembers. In
this the medicine men made themselves at home. A
good deal, of course, depended on the weather, but
" luckily it only rained once, and then we had to wrap
our blankets up and stand against the wall." The
stay was not without some real excitement. An Irish-
man belonging to the ambulance came in with a box of
detonators one morning, and proceeded to display these
useless trophies with the triumph of the confirmed
looter. Almost immediately a detonator went off,
removing one thumb and two fingers from the Irish-
man. So like a detonator. The narrator of the
incident, an orderly of the ambulance, was " splintered
with little bits and also received a black eye from the
concussion." Did his name go down to glory as
among the wounded in action? Not a bit of it. He
just got " ' medicine and duty ' and a ' choking off '
from the colonel." As the victim pathetically adds,
" wholly undeserved, as I was only an interested
spectator." War is full of hard luck, and this is a
striking example of the fact.

CHAPTER IV.

FIFTEEN RAVINE. VILLERS PLOUICH AND BEAUCAMP.

GENERAL JOFFRE'S plan for ensuring that 1917
should prove to be the year of victory was based
upon a policy of following up the Somme victory by a
campaign in which the British should gradually come
to play a larger, if not a preponderating, part. The
underlying idea was that the French had practically
reached high-water mark as regards man-power, while
the British strength was still growing and would
continue to do so. No sooner, however, had General
Joffre's plans been completed than circumstances
occurred to render them to some extent nugatory.
Political intrigues in France led to his virtual retirement; at a conference held at Calais in February, 1917,
the British Army was placed under the command of
General Nivelle, General Joffre's successor, a decision
which was the cause of immediate friction. Then the
Germans, by their withdrawal to the Hindenburg Line,
upset the plans which General Nivelle had drawn up
for his great battle. In the altered circumstances
grave doubts arose in the minds of the senior French
commanders as to the feasibility of the plan, and on
the very eve of the offensive the French War Minister
assembled a Council of War in which the operation
was severely criticized. It was, however, decided to
proceed, and on April 9th the spring campaign began
with an attack by the British Third Army east of Arras
and by the Canadian Corps and one brigade of the
5th Division on Vimy Ridge. Immediate success
awarded this effort. The second of General Nivelle's
blows was delivered by a group of armies near St.

Quentin, but dwindled to a mere demonstration. His main attempt, in the neighbourhood of Rheims, began on April 16th, but, in spite of initial success, fell far short of expectation. The *moral* of the French became profoundly depressed, and it became necessary for the British to keep up the pressure east of Arras as long as possible.

That portion of the British Armies which stood at the time between St. Quentin and Arras was therefore clear of the main tide of the offensive, but it was far from being in a back-water. It was essential to keep the Germans busy during their withdrawal to the Hindenburg Line, and the ground recovered had to be made good, communications restored, and defensive lines prepared in case the Germans might surge forward again. The first three weeks of April represent, therefore, a methodical step-by-step advance by the XV Corps—in which was the 40th Division—and other corps, without any actual battle or engagement, but with a continual clash with German rear-guards and a steady drip of casualties. The headquarters of the Division moved forward to Manancourt on April 6th, and upon the 8th the German line was heavily bombarded by the XV Corps, supplemented by some minor operations. The weather still kept up its spiteful treatment, and there was a fairly heavy fall of snow as late as April 10th. The disposition of the XV Corps now was that the 8th Division was on the right, the 40th in the centre, and the 20th on the left. During the night of the 12th/13th the 8th Division captured Gouzeaucourt, and this operation was in connexion with an advance of the outpost line by the 121st Brigade. The latter met with no opposition, except upon the right, where a sharp machine gun and rifle fire imposed some delay. And thus it came about that by April 20th the 40th Division had worked its way forward to the strip of front between Gouzeaucourt and Gouzeaucourt Wood. Eight miles or so to the north-east could be descried the roofs and spires of a city. It was Cambrai. And slightly west of it might

have been observed a wooded ridge. That was Bourlon
Wood, and the 40th were to know much of that wood
ere the year was out.

At the moment, however—and eliminating other
corps—the situation may be described by saying that
the XV Corps was now knocking against the outer
works of the Hindenburg Line. The enemy resistance
was stiffening, and it was now no longer a question of
avoiding booby traps, but of throwing the Hun out of
his strong places by violence. Consequently, on
April 20th, we find attack orders issued by the Division
for an important operation on the following day. The
8th Division, on the right, would attack Gonnelieu,
while the task of the 40th was to make good the spur
north-west of that village, Fifteen Ravine, and thence
still north-westwards until touch was secured with the
20th Division on the left. The 40th Division had two
brigades in the front line, of which the 119th was on
the right, and in its sphere was the ravine. The 120th
was on the left. The 121st Brigade had been at this
time withdrawn from the front and was resting and
refitting at Etricourt.

The terrain over which the attack was to take place
was open and undulating, but intersected by numerous
so-called ravines characteristic of this sector of the
front. There was little or no cultivation, but the grass
was thick and high. The villages were mostly
standing, as the enemy was using them as strong
points, while the ground was fairly free from shell
holes and remained so for a considerable time afterwards. A narrative informs us that "partridges were
plentiful, and there were many nests of young birds
and subsequently coveys." As for Fifteen Ravine,
it derived its name from fifteen trees which had
bordered it until destroyed by the Germans, who
doubtless realized their value as ranging marks for the
British artillery. In reality, the ravine was more what
those with experience of South Africa would call a
"donga," and was nowhere more than ten feet deep.

All cross roads had been "cratered" by the enemy.
Taken as a whole it was good fighting country, with
natural cover and good observation. No Man's Land
was very wide in places, "and extremely interesting,
owing to the long grass," as one idealist puts it.

So far as the left brigade was concerned the operation was destined to be practically a bloodless one.
The 13th East Surrey Regiment was on the right, and
shortly after midnight it sent forward patrols to have
a look round. Cautiously advancing, these patrols
actually reached the objective without opposition and
found no sign of the enemy at their goal. The
remainder of the battalion followed in due course, and
a series of strong posts was held along the new front
by portions of "A," "C" and "D" Companies.
The remainder of these companies held the line of
resistance along the north-east border of Gouzeaucourt
Wood, "B" Company remaining in reserve. Three
men were wounded during the day. To the left of the
East Surreys the 11th King's Own had almost as easy
a task. The barrage opened at 4.15 a.m., and an hour
later the battalion was able to report that the objective
had been gained and that ten prisoners had been
secured; the left company was held up for a time by
machine gun fire, but reached its objective eventually,
although a post on the right had to be withdrawn
owing to heavy bursts of machine gun fire from
Trescault. Three platoons of the King's Own pursued
the Germans as far as the ridge west of Beaucamp, but
were then recalled.

Opposite the 119th Brigade the Germans put up a
stiffer fight. Prior to the assault the 119th Brigade
was disposed as follows: The front line was composed
of the 19th Royal Welch Fusiliers on the right and
the 12th South Wales Borderers on the left, the 18th
and 17th Welch being in brigade support and reserve
respectively. At Zero hour the artillery barrage
opened, and the front line battalions, already formed
up on a line parallel with the objectives and in front

of our main position, moved forward. Immediately the Germans put down a nasty barrage of shrapnel and high explosive, but the 119th Brigade pushed on quickly, and the Fusiliers on the right got to the position assigned to them by 5.15 a.m. with little difficulty. Patrols and covering parties were at once sent out, and in response to a request for assistance from a battalion of the 8th Division a successful raid was carried out upon an enemy strong post north-west of Gonnelieu, and, in addition, a company was deployed to bring covering fire on the ground east of that village.

In the sector allotted to the 12th South Wales Borderers was the Fifteen Ravine, and it was in this part of the field that the resistance was the most severe. Machine gun fire was opened from snipers' posts along the front of the ravine, and the Germans plastered a cross-roads just north of the western end of Gouzeaucourt with all manner of artillery projectiles. The Borderers had moved forward at 4.20 a.m. when the barrage was put down, but were checked about five o'clock by sniping fire. This nuisance was suitably dealt with, and by 5.15 a.m. the ravine was in the hands of the South Wales Borderers. The Germans held on to it until the last moment, and, although the statements of prisoners varied, it seems that the ravine had been held by a company of 150 men, supported by machine guns and with snipers' posts in front. By 5.45 a.m. all opposition had been disposed of and consolidation was begun. The moppers-up on the flank searched all shelters and dug-outs, two deep mined dug-outs being discovered. The moppers-up failed, however, to discover three strong points between the brigade's former outpost line and the ravine, and the garrisons of these posts opened fire in rear of the left flank of the Borderers and upon carrying parties going forward. These Germans were, however, dealt with by a platoon from the 18th Welch, under the intelligence officer of the 12th South Wales Borderers.

The enemy's rifle and machine gun fire continued till the afternoon, and it was clear that he had many sniping posts still in working order. In this attack by the South Wales Borderers particularly good work was done by the carrying party from the 119th Trench Mortar Battery which, under a sergeant, carried material from the brigade dump to forward battalion dump all day without stopping; during the earlier part of the day under severe artillery, rifle and machine gun fire.

In this action the 119th Brigade had 157 casualties, 10 being officers. Forty prisoners were taken, and, compared with our own, the enemy's casualties were heavy. The South Wales Borderers counted 34 dead Germans, exclusive of others seen to fall and carried away. Undoubtedly many casualties were prevented in the Division by the assaulting troops forming up in the dark ahead of the forward line of defence, for when the enemy barrage fell it was on the defensive line, and thus over the heads of the assaulting troops. Our barrage was very accurate and well timed. On the whole the operations were carried out with steadiness and precision, and well-deserved congratulations were received from corps and army.

This attack was, however, merely the preliminary to a much larger operation which in any other war would have merited the title of a battle. Facing the 40th Division there now stood the strong villages of Villers Plouich and Beaucamp, the reduction of which was now to be carried out. Accordingly, by Divisional Order No. 74, which was issued at 4.30 p.m. on April 22nd, the details of the operation were set forth. The Division was to capture by assault the two villages named, on the 24th, and was also to gain a footing on the higher ground beyond. As before, the 119th Brigade was to be upon the right, with the 120th on the left, whilst the 121st was to hold two battalions and a machine gun section in readiness to support either brigade as required.

So far as regards the general outline of the operations which were to ensue; it is now possible to describe the doings of the two front line brigades in greater detail. To take the 119th Brigade—which was upon the right—first in order, its objective was to be, practically speaking, the line of low spurs just beyond Gonnelieu and Villers Plouich, but exclusive of those villages. Strong points were to be established at certain detailed spots, and patrols were to be pushed forward from the northern end of the new line when it should be gained. Prior to the attack the disposition of the brigade was that the 18th and 17th Welch Regiments were in front on the right and left respectively; the 19th Royal Welch Fusiliers were in support, and the brigade reserve was found by the 12th South Wales Borderers. Brigade battle headquarters were hard by the road between Fins and Gouzeaucourt and rather nearer the former village. As for the actual attack, the 18th Welch upon the right were to make a start by establishing four strong points with a company on the spur which marked the right of the brigade objective, north of Gonnelieu, each post to be garrisoned by a platoon with two Lewis guns. On the left the 17th Welch Regiment was to attack with two companies in line of column of platoons and two companies in support. All positions, once gained, were to be immediately consolidated. The two leading battalions were each to have four guns from the 119th Trench Mortar Battery, while the guns of the 119th Machine Gun Company were to be employed chiefly in supporting the attack by direct fire.

The ultimate objective of the 120th Brigade upon the left was a line which started where the objective of the 119th left off and then ran north to the railway line, whence it bent back sharply to the west, keeping north of the villages of Villers Plouich and Beaucamp. The two villages were therefore in the sector of the 120th Brigade, and each was the subject of a separate attack. For the capture of Villers Plouich there was detailed the 13th East Surrey Regiment, which was to be supported by the 14th Highland Light Infantry, while Beaucamp was earmarked for the 14th Argyll and Sutherland Highlanders. The brigade reserve was to consist of the 11th King's Own, less one company placed at the disposal of the Highlanders. The bulk of the guns of the 120th Machine Gun Company were allotted to assist the two attacks, eight, however, being kept in reserve at Gouzeaucourt Wood, which was to be the line of resistance in case the Germans should pass to the offensive and counter-attack. The task for the 229th Company Royal Engineers was to establish forward dumps and to be ready to send forward parties to aid with their technical skill in the all-important work of consolidation. The battle headquarters of the 120th Brigade were to be just in rear of Gouzeaucourt Wood.

As for the 121st Brigade, it will be remembered that it was resting and refitting, and that its task was to have two battalions detailed in readiness. Accordingly, the 21st Middlesex were ordered to leave Equancourt at 5.15 a.m. on the 24th and to proceed to the western end of Dessart Wood, where they would come under the orders of the brigade commander of the 120th Brigade. Similarly the 13th Yorkshires, leaving Etricourt for Fins, would come under Brigadier-General Crozier, of the 119th.

From the general lay-out of the battle, as set forth in divisional and brigade orders, we may now pass to a detailed description of the actual fighting. In the 119th Brigade the 18th Welch, on the right, advanced just before midnight of the 23rd/24th and occupied its objective with practically no resistance. Here, by five minutes past two on the morning of the 24th, consolidation was complete and four strong points had been established. When dawn came two posts were pushed forward and touch gained with the left battalion of the brigade. So far the 18th Welch had had practically no fighting, but shortly before 10 a.m. a number of

F

Germans were observed in a ravine in rear of the battalion. A patrol was at once sent to deal with these stranded Huns, 27 prisoners and a machine gun being the resultant bag. During the forenoon the right support was rather heavily shelled, the Germans evidently expecting an attack from that direction, but, after that, things generally quieted down.

Upon the left of the 119th Brigade the 17th Welch formed up, before the flag fell, on a tape in advance of the front line. Once again this proved advantageous, for when, in reply to the British barrage, the German guns quickly replied, the enemy's shells did little damage, passing over the heads of the Welshmen. The 17th lost no time in advancing to the attack, but were soon held up by wire. In most places the wire was one belt of some twenty-five feet in width on screw pickets, though for about 500 yards a second belt, ten yards behind the first, had been constructed. The barrage supporting the attackers had, however, been well sustained and accurate, with the result that a gap was found, through which the 17th Welch Regiment made its way and then proceeded to bomb the enemy trenches. By 7 a.m. all the objectives of the battalion had been secured and consolidation put in hand. And thus the morning thereafter wore away in comparative quiet, until shortly before ten o'clock, when reports came in as to a check to the brigade upon the left. A warning was now received by telephone from divisional headquarters to say that possibly the 119th Brigade might be required to wheel inwards and attack Beaucamp, and, accordingly, arrangements were provisionally made for the 19th Royal Welch Fusiliers and the 12th South Wales Borderers to move to the east of Villers Plouich, and for the 13th Yorkshires to come up from the main line of resistance in rear.

As a matter of fact it was not found necessary to put these orders into execution, and the task of the 119th Brigade was over for the day. It had been a smart and well-managed attack. The artillery barrage was well timed and accurate. Brigade headquarters were throughout in constant communication by telegraph with battalion headquarters, and although telephone communication was constantly being interrupted it was always promptly restored. The machine guns had been dug in the previous night and great care taken to camouflage them. Though they fired throughout the operations the guns were never spotted by the Germans, and they managed to get off 27,000 rounds in all. The casualties sustained by the brigade were 8 officers and 79 other ranks. Sixty-one prisoners were taken, and it was obvious that the enemy had suffered very heavily.

It will be remembered that the task of the 120th Brigade, on the left, was to include the capture of the two villages, Villers Plouich and Beaucamp, the former operation being entrusted to the 13th East Surrey Regiment—who were to be supported by the 14th Highland Light Infantry, while the 14th Argyll and Sutherland Highlanders were to make themselves masters of Beaucamp. At 2 a.m. on the 24th the 13th East Surreys, with a strength of 24 officers and some 600 other ranks, under Captain L. B. Mills, moved forward and occupied a new trench running north-west from Fifteen Ravine. The order of attack was that " B " and " A " Companies should be in the front line (working from right to left) supported respectively by " D " and " C " Companies. Every man carried two sandbags and two bombs, while one platoon of each of the support companies carried entrenching tools in the proportion of three shovels to one pick. Zero hour came at 4.15 a.m. The artillery barrage burst out, and immediately the 13th East Surrey Regiment crept forward in four waves towards the enemy's wire. The German guns answered almost at once, but did little damage to the East Surreys; the 14th Highland Light Infantry, who had formed up in rear, were, however, not so lucky—they received the " overs," and eight men were knocked out immediately.

Within seven minutes the nearest German trenches
were entered and captured, and the advance against
the village of Villers Plouich was at once continued.
It speaks well for the communication arrangements—
and those whose experience is confined solely to 1914
will appreciate the fact—to find that within eight
minutes of the capture of the trench the fact was
announced to the commanding officer of the 14th
Highland Light Infantry, in support, by telephone.
Meanwhile, the East Surreys were making their way
through the gloom to Villers Plouich, and during this
advance a good deal of trouble was caused by the
enemy's strong points and machine gun emplacements,
but this was overcome by the concentrated fire of Lewis
guns and by daring attacks made by the battalion
bombers.

At half-past five Villers Plouich was reached and
the 13th East Surrey Regiment was then divided into
three parties, the right under Captain Crocker, centre
under Second-Lieutenant G. R. Alexander, and left
under Captain Naunton. The right party met with
strong opposition, but reached the ravine about 700
yards north-east of the village. Here Captain Crocker
was killed, and the command of the party was taken
over by Lieutenant F. J. T. Hann. And now there
took place an act of outstanding gallantry. Two of the
enemy machine guns were holding up the advance of
the right party of the East Surreys. Corporal E. Foster
was in charge of two Lewis guns, assisted by Lance-
Corporal J. W. Reed. These two non-commissioned
officers attacked the German machine guns, put them
out of action, and then captured the teams, a feat which
earned for Corporal Foster the Victoria Cross and the
Distinguished Conduct Medal for Lance-Corporal Reed.
As for the centre and left parties, the former managed
to get through the village apparently without much
difficulty, and took up a position on the high ground
known as Highland Ridge. The left party, after
storming a German strong point on the sunken road

between Villers Plouich and Beaucamp, captured the German position after a sharp fight, and made 100 prisoners. It was now found that Beaucamp had not yet fallen to the 120th Brigade, and any farther advance by the left party of the East Surreys was impossible. The captured strong point was therefore consolidated, and a defensive flank thrown out to command Beaucamp and the high ground to the north-east of that village.

The capture of Villers Plouich had been promptly reported to the officer commanding the 14th Highland Light Infantry, in support. In response to a request for reinforcements the latter battalion had been moved forward to the fork in the road west of the village, fortunately arriving before the Germans started plastering the way up with shells. As Beaucamp was still in German hands, Lieutenant-Colonel Dick made his dispositions to hold the roads leading to Villers Plouich. It was clear that in the ravine north-east of the village the East Surreys were meeting with considerable opposition. When Captain Crocker was killed the advanced platoon was apparently withdrawn, and Second-Lieutenant Carmichael, with " A " Company, 14th Highland Light Infantry, was sent up to reinforce. The situation was soon restored, 20 Germans being taken.

At 6.30 a.m. the covering barrage shut down and the work of consolidation around Villers Plouich was continued. Ten minutes later, however, the enemy opened a very heavy artillery fire on the centre and right parties of the 13th East Surrey Regiment. The defences which these parties had been able to throw up were, of course, flimsy and incomplete, and a temporary withdrawal was therefore decided on to such cover as was available on the eastern outskirts of the village. This withdrawal was carried out simultaneously by the centre and right, while the entrances to the village were secured by Lewis guns. Meanwhile, the 14th Highland Light Infantry had come up to reinforce, and the line was again advanced by the East Surreys some 300 yards

beyond the village. About nine o'clock Captain Mills
was wounded, and Captain Naunton assumed command
of the battalion. Strong posts were established on the
line now occupied, and although the enemy opened a
very heavy fire at 8.30 a.m., which continued for six
hours, the line was firmly held. The bombardment
slackened at 2.30 p.m., but the enemy kept up an occasional fire on Villers Plouich and the entrance to it.
Lieutenant-Colonel Dick, of the 14th Highland Light
Infantry, was now the senior officer on the spot, and
as evening came he was able to adjust the companies
of the two battalions. The bulk of the defensive work
was allotted to the Highland Light Infantry, in view
of the fact that the 13th East Surrey Regiment had
borne the brunt of the fighting during the day. The
casualties in that battalion were just under 200, of
which number 29 were killed, including 3 officers—
Captain E. Crocker, Second-Lieutenant G. R.
Alexander (attached from the Royal Sussex Regiment)
and Second-Lieutenant R. N. Goodyear.

The capture of Villers Plouich was a fine piece of
work. Although the brunt of the fighting fell upon the
East Surreys, the Highland Light Infantry rendered
valuable assistance in support, and there is a soldierly
appreciation in the official narrative of Lieutenant-
Colonel Dick, who paid a generous tribute to "the
rapidity and dash with which the East Surrey
Regiment, most capably commanded by Captain Mills,
captured the village." The price paid by the victorious
battalion was high, but on the other side of the account
are the items of 4 officers and 300 other ranks of the
Germans taken prisoner. Also ten machine guns and
some five hundred rifles formed part of the East Surreys'
trophies. A Victoria Cross had been won by Corporal
Foster, who was also awarded the *Médaille Militaire*.
And, in addition to the Distinguished Conduct Medal
conferred on Lance-Corporal Reed, five Military
Medals were won by the battalion. In memory of this
feat of arms, and to perpetuate the connexion between

Wandsworth and the 13th East Surrey Regiment, that
borough subsequently adopted Villers Plouich under
the scheme of the British League of Help in 1920.

The sterling success against Villers Plouich was to
a certain extent offset by a set-back upon the extreme
left. The 14th Argyll and Sutherland Highlanders
had been detailed to capture Beaucamp, and at
3.45 a.m. that battalion silently lined up along the tape
laid down at its jumping-off position. Half an hour
later Zero hour came; the barrage opened, and the
Highlanders immediately moved forward in the darkness through the enemy's shells, which were now
falling thick and fast. A thick belt of wire was the
first obstacle encountered, and the Argyll and Sutherland Highlanders experienced much difficulty owing to
enemy machine guns enfilading them from the left
front until these were dealt with by bombing and Lewis
guns. After a brief fight the German resistance was
overcome and the first enemy position was seized, some
moppers-up from the 14th Highland Light Infantry
and the 11th King's Own being left to complete
things. A large number of prisoners had been secured,
and these were promptly sent to the rear under escort,
one batch being, however, caught in the German
barrage and wiped out.

It was still dark when the Highlanders actually
reached Beaucamp about twenty minutes to five.
Scouts were sent forward, but, contrary to expectation,
practically no resistance was encountered, and the
village was soon in the hands of the battalion, which
picked up a few more prisoners. It was quite a
different story, however, when the two leading companies emerged from the main street and began
deploying right and left. Immediately a sustained
machine gun fire came from the left, and particularly
from the direction of Bilhem. In the gloom it was
impossible to locate the opposition, but a message was
sent back to the artillery to pay attention to Bilhem,
and this was done. The left flank of the battalion was,

however, still under a hot fire, and the reserve company
came up to strengthen it. Every available Lewis gun
was brought into action, but it was impossible to beat
down the German machine guns.

By half past six the situation was serious. The
commanders of the three leading companies had become
casualties; progress was impossible; no useful purpose
could have been served by keeping the battalion
exposed to the murderous enfilade fire, and it was
determined accordingly to withdraw through Beaucamp
and to consolidate a couple of hundred yards south of
that village. A kind of stalemate now ensued, but with
daylight it was possible to locate the enemy more
easily, and about nine o'clock the 14th Argyll and
Sutherland Highlanders were able to send back a
message indicating the position of the enemy's
machine guns. Our artillery was promptly switched
on; the Lewis guns of the battalion joined in, and the
effect was very marked. It was shortly after this that
word was sent by telephone to the 119th Brigade,
warning it that possibly it might be required to throw
its weight against Beaucamp.

Somewhere about eleven o'clock it was thought that
the Germans were about to make a counter-attack, for
they put a box barrage round Villers Plouich, but
nothing came of it, and shortly afterwards the Argyll
and Sutherland Highlanders sent forward patrols and
snipers into Beaucamp. These were, however, quickly
driven out, showing that the Germans, under cover of
their intensive machine gun fire of the morning,
must have reoccupied the village shortly after it had
been evacuated by the 14th Argyll and Sutherland
Highlanders. A further attempt was made about
2 p.m. to gain a footing in Beaucamp, but with no
better success, and this was apparently the last effort
made. It was now realized at corps headquarters that,
unless Bilhem should be taken, Beaucamp would
continue to be a very difficult nut to crack. It was
decided, therefore, that Bilhem should be attacked

during the night by the 20th Division, and that, in
case of success, a further attempt should be made
against Beaucamp at 4.15 a.m. on the 25th. This
attack would be carried out by the 11th King's Own
Regiment, which during the night would relieve the
14th Argyll and Sutherland Highlanders.

While the relief was actually in progress the welcome
news arrived that the 60th Brigade of the 20th Division
had seized Bilhem; with the result that when the
King's Own advanced, protected by the usual barrage,
the patrols sent forward found Beaucamp once more
evacuated. This time there was no reception by
intense machine gun fire on emerging from the village,
and the King's Own speedily established posts on an
arc round Beaucamp. Consolidation was immediately
begun, and although it was interrupted now and then
by shell fire the work was not seriously delayed.

The task allotted to the 40th Division had now been
successfully accomplished. The fighting had been
severe, especially on the left, and of the total casualties,
which amounted to 664, about five-sixths were suffered
by the 120th Brigade. The number of killed was 133,
of which 107, including 8 officers, were lost to the
120th. In prisoners the Division had taken 4 officers
and 341 other ranks, as well as 8 machine guns.
The set-back at Beaucamp had protracted the operation into a second day, but, in contrasting the attack
upon that place with the quicker victory at Villers
Plouich, one important fact must be borne in mind.
It does not belittle the success of the 13th East Surrey
Regiment to point out that in its attack both flanks
were protected—the right by the 119th Brigade on the
farther slope of the valley in which lay Villers Plouich,
and the left by the 14th Argyll and Sutherland
Highlanders, who were all the time either in Beaucamp
or so close to it as to " pin " any Germans there from
counter-attacking Villers Plouich. The Highlanders,
on the other hand, had their left flank much exposed,
and suffered severely from enfilade fire. Further,

there was greater support available for the attack on
Villers Plouich.

After the strenuous period of attack from the 21st to
the 25th, the closing days of April were, comparatively
speaking, of halcyon calm.   During the night of the
24th/25th the 121st Brigade had relieved the 120th,
the 13th East Yorkshire Regiment taking the place of
the East Surreys.   Energy was now concentrated on
further consolidation of the new front.   La Vacquerie
was to be the next problem, and on the 30th the
artillery gave it a preliminary hammering.

CHAPTER V.

La Vacquerie. The Summer of 1917.

THE spring of 1917 showed promise of making up for the horrors of the winter on the Somme. Every narrative consulted talks of fine weather and flowers. Whatever diversity exists between various narratives as to the actual operations, when it comes to a question of weather there are no two opinions. If it rained a good deal the historian soon knows all about it; if it was very cold the historian is not allowed to forget it; if it was muddy the historian comes to loathe the very word " mud "; and now the historian sometimes feels he can have enough even of flowers and sunshine. The pleasure was not, however, unalloyed to all. As one sardonic narrator puts it, " This was on May 3rd, and well we knew it—no time to pick May flowers." This writer was soured by a certain little incident : " When we arrived at Gouzeau-court there was no shelter for a first-aid post, so we had to make some in a sunken wood. While we were doing this we had not noticed an observation balloon, but they had noticed us, as just when we thought we had made a creditable bivvy and one that would not be noticed, we received a halo of shells which made the vicinity very unhealthy." And that was the reason why one member of the Division had " no time to pick May flowers."

The month of May actually opened with an operation in which the bulk of the Division was engaged. La Vacquerie, just off the Cambrai road, was practically the only village in the immediate front still in German hands, and it was decided to round off the series of successes already achieved by the capture of that place.

This decision was, however, soon altered, and the attack was to be replaced by a raid on a wide front, in which both the 8th and 40th Divisions were to be concerned. In the latter the 119th Brigade was to be on the right, with the 121st Brigade on the left, covered by the guns of the Division and those of the 25th Artillery Brigade of the 1st Division. The 120th Machine Gun Company came under the orders of the 121st Brigade, and the 4th Guards Machine Gun Company relieved the 120th and covered the front of the 120th Brigade, which was on the left of the Division. The objective of the raid was, roughly speaking, the village of La Vacquerie and German trenches north-west of it, part of the 8th Division raiding Sonnet Farm, just south of La Vacquerie, at the same time. Zero hour was fixed for 11 p.m. on the night of the 5th, and withdrawal was to take place at 1 a.m. on the 6th.

The objective of the 119th Brigade was the small village of La Vacquerie and the ground just beyond, and the *motif* of the raid was that usually at the bottom of these operations, namely, to inflict loss upon the enemy; to damage his defences; and, above all, to obtain identifications. The disposition of the 119th Brigade was that on the right were the 12th South Wales Borderers, with the 17th Welch—who came up from Dessart Wood during the evening of the 5th— on the left. Brigade support and reserve were found by the 19th Royal Welch Fusiliers and 18th Welch respectively, the reserve battalion taking up its position in a sunken road on the northern outskirts of Gouzeaucourt. The machine gun company of the brigade dug in and carefully camouflaged sixteen guns, with the object of being ready to support the assaulting troops. Four guns of the 119th Trench Mortar Battery were to be brought into action, and the 224th Company Royal Engineers was to follow the infantry and destroy all cellars and defences which the infantry might be unable to deal with effectively.

As for the two assaulting battalions, these were ordered to raid with two companies in front line, one in support, and one in battalion reserve. The assaulting waves were to push on till the objectives were reached, and then hold on as a covering party till 1 a.m., while the moppers-up were destroying dug-outs and " cleaning up " things generally. In raids the great difficulty was the arrangements for withdrawal, and in this case the supporting companies were to form a kind of rear-guard while the moppers-up, trench mortars and covering party fell back in this order. Each platoon commander took with him a shell case as a gong with which to give the signal to withdraw. An order had been issued that no dead of the Division were to be left upon the ground—a directive extremely difficult to fulfil upon a dark night. Major R. J. Andrews, of the 17th Welch, was placed in command of the forward operations and ordered to supervise the withdrawal.

By five minutes to eleven all the units of the brigade had reported by code that they were ready to advance. Sharp at 11 p.m. the barrage fell and the troops moved forward. The moon was nearly full, but the night was cloudy, and, immediately after the barrage opened, rain fell, though not heavily. The right of the 12th South Wales Borderers was hung up by wire some distance short of the objective, but forced its way through, though under heavy artillery and trench-mortar fire. The left of the battalion met with no opposition till the village was reached, but here there was a great deal of wire, which delayed matters for a bit. Only a few of the enemy were encountered, but " such as were met were suitably dealt with," and a few prisoners were made.

The South Wales Borderers on the left of the 119th Brigade likewise met with but little opposition until La Vacquerie was reached, but about 11.20 p.m. the battalion came under heavy machine gun and rifle fire from the north-west of the village. Also at least two aerial dart throwers were in action. A great deal of uncut wire was found in the village, but the battalion made its way through it, though with difficulty, and reached its objective. The darkness also imposed delay, but the church in the village was fortunately still standing, and it provided a most useful landmark. Owing to the heavy fire which kept coming from the left, it was clear that the 121st Brigade must be encountering a particularly stubborn resistance. Major Andrews therefore ordered two platoons to form a defensive flank. Three patrols were also sent out on the left, but, encountering heavy fire, were forced to withdraw.

Although the enemy's wire had been the target for our artillery for several days before the attack, the gaps were insufficient. Delay was thus caused; and in a raid delay is a serious thing, especially when the troops moved off only at 11 p.m. and had to begin withdrawing at 1 a.m., so as to be back before daylight. Consequently, the mopping-up was not as complete as had been hoped. To begin with, on several occasions the moppers-up found themselves in the actual battle, owing to the assaulting troops being delayed by wire. This was also the case with the sappers, one of whom was shot at a range of three yards. The engineers did, however, manage to blow up several houses and to destroy two dug-outs. Outside the village also a house was wrecked which had " two dead Germans hanging out of the window of an upper story."

At 1 a.m. all the gongs were sounded and the withdrawal was begun in exact accordance with the orders previously issued. Each party, as it passed the supporting line, which had moved into position as a rear guard, reported to Major Andrews, who had taken up his post at the cross roads south of La Vacquerie. The retirement was unmolested, and was carried out with great exactitude and steadiness. When the bag was counted it was found that 8 prisoners had been captured—all of them by the Borderers. The casualties sustained by the brigade were 4 officers and 101 other

ranks, including 10 missing. The supporting battalion
—the 19th Royal Welch Fusiliers—came off worst,
suffering 40 casualties.

The 121st Brigade had the 20th Middlesex on the
right and the 12th Suffolks on the left, these two
battalions forming the front line. The Middlesex
advanced under our barrage and soon came under that
of the enemy, several casualties ensuing, among which
were 3 officers and 2 platoon sergeants. The advance
was, however, continued, but by twenty minutes after
midnight so little progress had been made that, in view
of the order to withdraw at 1 a.m., it was decided not
to press on farther, and, accordingly, by 2.30 a.m. the
battalion was back in its original position. The
Suffolks, on the left, had their left flank covered by
two guns of the 121st Trench Mortar Battery. When
the two leading companies approached the German
trenches it was found that a gap had been satisfactorily
cut in the wire by our guns. Soon, however, the right
company was in difficulties owing to a further belt of
wire which was intact, and to fire from an enemy trench
just beyond. The left company now wheeled inwards
to assist the right, but the hornets' nest was buzzing—
and stinging—angrily, with the result that further
progress was out of the question. Some damage had,
however, been done to the enemy's trench system; in
particular, two dug-outs " from which the enemy
refused to emerge" were destroyed. The signal to
withdraw was now made, but in the darkness and confusion many of the battalion moved forward and were
lost, although seven rejoined later.

Thus ended the operation generally known as "La
Vacquerie," the results of which fell short probably of
expectation. But the fact was that, now that the
Germans were bedded down on their famous
Hindenburg Line, they were not prepared to suffer tres-
passers gladly. Their defensive organization was in
thorough working order, and " soft " sectors in their
front had been stiffened by the introduction of class

troops. As we shall see in the further narrative contained in this chapter, not only were the Germans now very wide awake to nip any of our raids in the bud, but they could—and did—try the raiding game themselves. The Germans were no longer doing little rearguard actions, but were committed to the defence of a splendidly organized system, which they were prepared to hold obstinately to the end. La Vacquerie was a foretaste of this resolution, and in the operation the 40th Division had 257 casualties, including 31 killed. In the latter number were 2 officers, one from each of the brigades taking part. As showing the "punch" required in these so-called "minor affairs," it may be mentioned that the machine guns of the division got off over 330,000 rounds.

For about a fortnight after the La Vacquerie business there was comparative peace and quiet. It was decided from above that a generally defensive policy should now be adopted in this sector of the British front, and, accordingly, there was nothing more exciting for the moment in the Division than a readjustment of its line, the routine of reliefs, with of course the inevitable patrolling and the incessant mutual pin-pricking of minor artillery strafes and dog-fights in No Man's Land. On the 13th the 120th Brigade, on the left of the Division, was relieved by a brigade of the 20th, and went back, to become for a time divisional reserve to the 8th Division, this movement being part of a kind of "general post" in which the 8th, 20th and 40th Divisions were concerned.

The quiet was interrupted by a couple of raids on' the 19th and 22nd. The former was carried out by the 17th Welch, between 9.45 p.m. and 10.15 p.m., and was composed of 2 officers and 30 other ranks, with the battalion intelligence officer attached. The objects were, first, to secure identification; secondly, reconnaissance of the German wire and trenches; and thirdly, to search the "Barracks," a building on the Cambrai road on our side of La Vacquerie. Six groups

were formed, and the job was done very neatly. The
"Barracks" was drawn blank, but the 17th Welch
killed 7 Germans and bagged 2 prisoners before they
broke off, returning without a scratch themselves. The
other raid fell to the lot of the 121st Brigade, a party
of 2 officers and 67 other ranks of the 12th Suffolks
being entrusted with the task. Besides identification,
the party was to destroy enemy dug-outs and to cut
gaps in the enemy wire with Bangalore torpedoes. The
night of the 22nd was very dark and rainy, a circumstance probably in favour of the raiders. Identification
was secured by the capture of a wounded German, and
three gaps were blown in the wire. Six of the raiders
were wounded, one so severely that he died later. After
this there was another lull, broken merely on the last
night of the month by a small raid carried out by the
11th King's Own, in which a wounded German was
brought in.

On June 2nd the Division became part of the III
Corps. A reference to the divisional war diary for
that month shows that out of the total thirty days of
that month, twenty-five are dismissed with the laconic
entry "quiet day," and a typical narrative dealing with
the transport of a certain battalion mentions "one of
the best camps in its history." There is talk, too, of
tents; of fine weather; and of "luxuriant vegetation"
(which is transportese for "flowers"). It is true that
"a certain amount of inconvenience was always caused
by the shelling of the main roads, and by gas shells,"
but this served rather to throw up the general quietude
into sharper relief. At the same time it is very important to remember that "quiet" in a world war is
distinctly a relative term. The quiet enjoyed by the
Division in that gorgeous June of 1917 was not exactly
the quiet experienced lying in a punt in a shady back-
water on the Thames; nor the ease felt on a sunny
afternoon in watching Surrey v. Middlesex at the Oval.
When your battalion was in reserve, or otherwise out
of the line, the days seemed sunny and peaceful

G

enough; the flowers bloomed; the birds sang. But your battalion was often in the line, and the sun did not shine when you were patrolling No Man's Land at night and the song of machine guns reminded you that even in a quiet period people get killed. And of course there was the inevitable shelling and sniping, in greater or less amount all and every day. What quiet generally amounted to on the Western Front during the Great War was simply this : you knew any given morning that it was " odds on " your turning in that night unwounded and alive. And that means a great deal in war.

July was quiet, too, but the war diary got less enthusiastic in its entries, particularly after logging the fact that, on the 13th, divisional headquarters were shelled for three quarters of an hour during the morning by an 8-inch high velocity gun—just the kind of thing to make a war diarist peevish. In Gonnelieu, too, a heavy trench mortar was destroyed by a bombardment of 5'9's which registered ten direct hits. Towards the end of the month the German artillery is described as being " rather active." Raids were tried several times by the Division, but the Hun was now prepared for this kind of thing—so much so that within little more than a week five of our raids are noted as having " proved unsuccessful." In fact, the Germans now felt sufficiently settled to take a hand in this game themselves, and at 6 a.m. on the 26th they brought off rather a *coup*. The raid was made against the 13th Yorkshires, and was accompanied by a really thorough barrage and box barrage. The operation had evidently been very carefully planned, and was certainly carried out with smartness and dash. Twenty-five of the 13th Yorkshires were taken prisoner, but the battalion, after the first surprise, got down to it with great resolution and deprived the Germans of the greater success for which they had probably hoped.

The comparative quiet lasted into August, but there were the usual pin-pricks and wrangling in No Man's

Land. The raids carried out by the Division now began to reproduce their original successes, and on the 13th one of these enterprises, carried out under orders of the 119th Brigade, resulted in very important identification being obtained by the capture of a prisoner from the 6th Bavarian Infantry Regiment of the 10th Bavarian Division, and a similar bag a fortnight later was also of great value to the Intelligence people.

An innovation in the transport of rations to the front line was now tried. To save the carrying parties the long distance from company to battalion headquarters, it was arranged that supplies should be taken right up to the trenches by pack animals. This was done constantly, at least in one battalion, and by moving the animals one at a time, and without noise, the Germans never jumped to the fact that animals were moving thus freely over the tops of the trenches.

In this month a change took place in the command of the Division, Major-General H. G. Ruggles-Brise— who had been promoted to substantive major-general on June 3rd—proceeding to England on the 24th to take over command of the 3rd Division of the Home Forces. He was succeeded by Major-General J. Ponsonby. Like his predecessor, General Ponsonby was a Guardsman—a Coldstreamer, General Ruggles-Brise on his part having done his regimental soldiering in the Grenadiers.

It has been mentioned that reliefs were part of the usual routine at this time, and it follows that the exact disposition was constantly changing. It is necessary, therefore, to select an arbitrary date and to state how the Division was then disposed. It so happens that the records consulted deal more in detail with August 22nd than any other date examined, and the position of the Division can be given with the maximum of exactitude on that day. All three brigades were then in line, the 121st being on the right, the 119th in the centre, with the 120th Brigade upon the left. Generally speaking, the line ran—not straight, or on a regular arc, but with kinks here and there—from just north of Villers Guislain, by Gonnelieu, to Villers Plouich, and each brigade had two battalions in front, one in support and one in reserve. Of the artillery, the 178th Brigade was behind Villers Guislain and the 181st behind Gouzeaucourt, with the 40th Division Ammunition Column at Nurlu, near which village was also the divisional train. The trench mortar batteries were at Fins, and the engineers, true to their motto, were everywhere, being scattered wherever there was a job which required doing. The headquarters of the Division were near Sorel-le-Grand.

Mutual raiding and counter-raiding, mutual pin-pricking, and mutual killing and wounding, whenever a chance occurred, characterized September. On the 17th a raiding party from the 19th Royal Welch Fusiliers bumped into an unsuspected belt of wire and suffered rather heavily, losing 2 killed and 19 wounded, in the latter number being 2 officers. All the casualties were brought in. A week later a British aeroplane was brought down in flames, falling upon the line of the 40th Division, but fortunately both pilot and observer were unhurt. There is a note of Villers Plouich and Villers Guislain having been shelled on the 20th. The month closed with two highly successful raids, the first of which was carried out by the 14th Highland Light Infantry. In order to confuse the enemy, a smoke barrage was employed and dummies were ostentatiously displayed on the left of the real attack. The enemy were apparently deceived by this slimness, and suffered many casualties, the Highlanders blowing in a dug-out and getting back with 10 prisoners at a cost of 20 casualties to themselves, 1 officer being killed and 2 wounded.

The raid which took place three days after this —on the 25th, to be exact—was quite a big affair. It was entrusted to the 12th Suffolk Regiment, and the raiding party was 200 strong. The engineers did

MAP ILLUSTRATING THE ATTACKS ON FIFTEEN RAVINE; VILLERS PLOUICH;
BEAUCAMP; AND LA VACQUERIE. APRIL & MAY 1917. 40TH DIV.

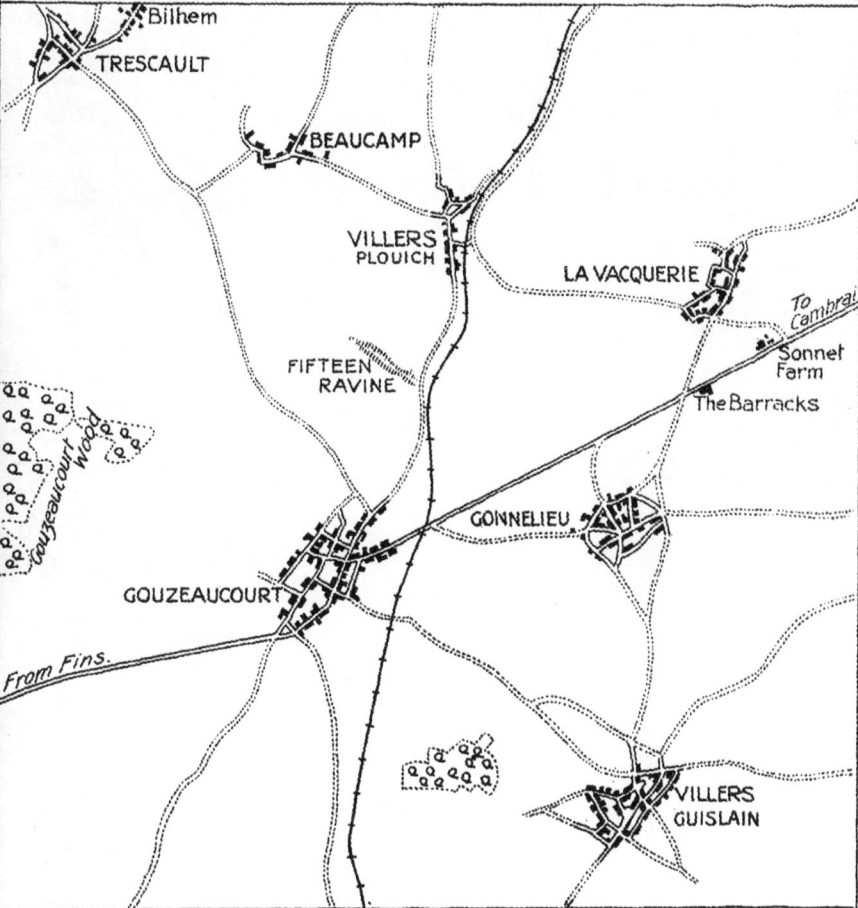

Bilhem
TRESCAULT
BEAUCAMP
VILLERS PLOUICH
LA VACQUERIE
To Cambrai
Sonnet Farm
FIFTEEN RAVINE
The Barracks
Gouzeaucourt Wood
GONNELIEU
GOUZEAUCOURT
From Fins.
VILLERS GUISLAIN

Roads 1ST CLASS
" 2ND & 3RD CLASS
Railways

Scale

To face page 84

Yards 0 250 500 1000 2000 Yards.

splendid work with a smoke screen and with thermit
—"a very valuable incendiary agent" as the
Encyclopædia Britannica puts it. Dummies were
again used, and drew a good deal of fire, but the
Germans were not caught napping this time. They
put down a barrage at once, but the Suffolks made their
way through it to the enemy's trenches, which were
entered. On pushing on, however, a very stubborn
resistance was met with, and although the Suffolks
brought back 5 prisoners and a machine gun they
had paid pretty dearly for their bag. Six were killed,
3 officers and 71 other ranks were wounded, and the
missing—all doubtless killed—were 1 officer and 21
other ranks. In other words, the raiders had over
fifty per cent. of casualties. In any other war such a
butcher's bill would have caused the day on which it
was incurred to earn the title "Mournful Monday" or
"Terrible Tuesday" or "Woeful Wednesday," but
in this contest such an operation was quite normal
during a "quiet" time in a "quiet" sector.

By the beginning of October the 40th Division had
been for six months almost continuously in the line, and
the time had now come for a long-needed rest. On the
1st of the month orders were issued to the effect that
between the 6th and the 11th the Division would be
relieved and proceed, via Péronne, to the VII Corps
area, and, accordingly, by October 12th the 40th
Division was concentrated in the Fosseux area, where
training was soon in full swing. Just before the month
closed a move was made farther west to Lucheux, the
artillery of the Division having gone to Nurlu, where
it was attached to the III Corps. Lucheux, a few
miles north-east of Doullens, lies in a junction of
valleys, the slopes of which are thickly wooded.
Training in wood fighting was a welcome relief after
the months of trench warfare in open ground, and the
instruction was to bear splendid fruit in a few weeks
time. On November 16th the 40th Division was on the
move again—to the front this time, to take part in what
proved to be one of the finest episodes of the war.

CHAPTER VI.

BOURLON WOOD.

TOWARDS the end of 1917 the outstanding feature
was that success was apparently no nearer than at
the opening of the much-trumpeted " Year of Victory."
The extravagant anticipations voiced by the British
Prime Minister had not been rounded off by fulfilment,
partly from causes outside his control and partly from
decisions on matters in which he was able to intervene.
Russia had passed from collapse to defection, and the
envoys who spoke in her name were actually engaged
in peace negotiations.   The Italian Army was defeated.
In Macedonia there was practically a stalemate.
Rumania was cut off from the Allies.   Narrowing down
the survey so as to include only England in the field,
the view was hardly more reassuring.   The financial
situation was graver than ever it had been during the
war; the submarine peril had reached a point that for
some time justified serious alarm; the indecisive Battle
of Jutland of 1916 had left the English rulers in such a
state of timidity that, even eighteen months later,
300,000 men were locked up at home to guard against
" a possible invasion "; the Germans were known to be
transferring troops from the east to the west.   There
were, however, patches of blue in a sky which was
otherwise heavily surcharged with clouds.   British
victories in Mesopotamia and Palestine, though to a
certain extent of the nature of side-shows, were at any
rate wearing down one of the allies of the Central
Powers.   And far above these in importance was the
fact that American troops were now beginning to
arrive, and even the German Supreme Command had

been forced to envisage the possibility of the arrival of
450,000 soldiers from the United States before the
following summer.

In the northern sector of the Western Front the Third
Battle of Ypres had continued until the ridge and
village of Passchendaele had been captured on
November 3rd. The continued bad weather and the
slowness of the progress made by the British troops had
caused the abandonment of the combined attack against
the Flanders coast-line. Nevertheless, the operations
had not been without important result. The *moral*
of the Germans had been appreciably shaken, and they
had been compelled to transfer large forces to Flanders
at the expense of other portions of the line. The
initiative was still with Sir Douglas Haig, and by a
prompt and correct use of it the partial success in
Flanders might be turned to good account. His scheme
was to deliver a sudden blow at another and drier
portion of the front. The sector opposite Cambrai had
been carefully reconnoitred, and had been selected as
the most suitable. In marked contradistinction to the
mud of Flanders, the terrain now chosen was favourable
for the employment of tanks, which were to play an
important part in the enterprise; and as the sector had
been a " quiet " one it was not churned up with shell
holes.

The underlying object was to gain a smart local
success at a point where the enemy did not expect attack
and on a front which had been already weakened by the
demands from elsewhere. The objective was not
Cambrai itself, for the capture of that town was entirely
subsidiary to the fracture of the Hindenburg Line at an
important nodal point. If successful, the whole
German scheme of defence might be disorganized, for
by the capture of Bourlon a defensive flank might be
formed facing east, while the situation might then be
developed, according to circumstances, towards Lille
and the north-west. The essentials were speed and
surprise. Speed was called for owing to the necessity

of anticipating the further heavy reinforcements of German divisions from Russia and of hampering the enemy in their Italian campaign. Surprise was to be achieved by a striking departure from the conventional in two respects : there was to be no advertising preliminary bombardment, but reliance was to be laid upon tanks, of which about 500 would be available; and, secondly, the number of troops engaged was to be relatively small, and from this virtue of necessity the publicity of a large concentration of men and *matériel* would be avoided. Artillery would, in spite of the fact that a prolonged preliminary bombardment would not take place, of course have an important rôle to play, and the artillery of the 40th Division was to cover a portion of the advance of the 6th.

The German defences on the selected front between Vendhuille on the Scheldt and the River Sensée comprised the three systems constituting the famous Hindenburg Line (greatly improved during the course of the year) with fortified posts in advance such as La Vacquerie and the north-eastern corner of Havrincourt Wood; behind this again came two other defensive lines. The front actually to be attacked extended from Gonnelieu on the right to Havrincourt Wood on the left, and the force entrusted with the duty consisted of the full force of tanks with five divisions, namely, the 12th, 20th, 6th, 51st, 62nd and 36th, in part. Two divisions were held as a reserve, and a large force of cavalry was at hand ready to exploit a success toward the north and to turn the enemy defences from the rear. The whole conception was a bold one, especially in view of the fact that the great British losses earlier in the year had not been wholly made good and that eleven French and British divisions had been detached to Italy. Nevertheless, it has received striking tributes from those whose opinions on modern warfare are worthy of respect.

The initial success achieved was considerable. At 6.20 a.m. on the morning of November 20th the barrage opened and the tanks and troops moved forward. The Hindenburg Line was rapidly overrun. The surprise was complete and the enemy surrendered in large numbers, although a particularly gallant resistance by the Germans on Flesquières Ridge seriously hampered the British plans. On the morning of the 21st the attack was resumed, and by nightfall the British had gained possession of the Bonavis spur, Masnières and Noyelles, which provided a bridgehead over the Escaut Canal; the whole of the Flesquières ridge; and the ground north up to Bourlon Wood, including Cantaing and Fontaine-Notre-Dame.

It has been related in the previous chapter that the infantry brigades of the 40th Division were away training and fattening for the kill west of Arras, and that on November 16th they had left Lucheux, heading for the area of operations. By the 22nd Beaumetz was reached, and now the Division began, so to speak, to come into the picture, the disposition of the Division being as follows : Divisional headquarters and 121st Brigade at Beaumetz; 119th Brigade at Doignies, and 120th Brigade at Lebuquière. At 1.30 p.m. on that day a conference was held at Beaumetz, when a general outline was given as to an attack to be made on Bourlon Wood, a preliminary step being to take over the line held at the moment by the 62nd Division. Orders for the latter operation were issued at four o'clock, the gist of them being that the 119th Brigade would be on the right, the 121st Brigade on the left, with General Willoughby's 120th Brigade in reserve. Yet another change in the allocation of the 40th Division had now occurred, for on this day it found itself transferred to the IV Corps, under Lieutenant-General Sir C. L. Woollcombe.

The Division accordingly pushed on, the headquarters moving to Havrincourt, while the brigade headquarters were at Graincourt in the case of the 119th and 121st, and at Havrincourt for the 120th, or reserve, Brigade. General Crozier had taken the opportunity, on the afternoon of the 21st, of riding forward with his staff, battalion commanders, seconds-in-command, adjutants and others, for a brief reconnaissance of the terrain where his brigade was to attack. This cavalcade, over 60 strong, moving at speed and, until the necessary crawling stage began, in full view of Bourlon Wood, seems to have led the Germans to believe that a cavalry break-through was about to begin. The actual reconnaissance was necessarily hurried, but the general "look round" was to prove of enormous advantage on "the day." All three brigades experienced considerable difficulty, for the road was very bad; many trenches had to be crossed, and considerable difficulty was experienced in getting limbers forward. By the time the trenches of the 62nd Division were reached the men were very tired after their trying march. At Graincourt use was made of the catacombs under the church as headquarters, as had been done by the Germans while they were in occupation of the village. This underground habitation was exceedingly comfortable and well furnished, and lit by an electric light plant run by an oil-engine. On taking over the catacombs it was found that the engine room was locked, and when the door was forced three Germans were discovered. As it was highly probable that the place was mined, the prisoners were informed that they would have to work the electric plant, an order which brought a prompt gush of information from the Germans as to the location of their minefield. A good number of mines were thus revealed, many of them being most cunningly concealed.

The two front-line brigades carried out their task of relieving the 185th Brigade of the 62nd Division during the hours of darkness, and their position will be understood by a reference to the photograph facing page 96 and the map which accompanies this chapter. To take the photograph first, the block of buildings to the right is that marked Anneux Chapel on the map. Immediately in front of the other (*left*) block of buildings is

a quarry, and from it, in the direction of Bourlon
village—clearly seen in the picture—leads a sunken
road. Let the reader imagine he is walking up this
road, leaving the quarry on his right—remembering,
should he have a passion for accuracy, that what the
map makers have called " quarries " are really chalk
pits. Very soon he will come to an intersection of
routes, and he will be in exactly the position of a rivet
in an open pair of scissors. This rivet point, which is
clearly seen in the photograph—in the barbarous jargon
of the war " the cross-roads at E.24.c "—marked the
dividing point of the 119th and 121st Brigades of the
Division.

Still looking at the photograph, let the reader
imagine he sees the right-hand man of the 20th
Middlesex Regiment standing at this euphemistically-
termed " cross roads." Two companies of that battalion
are in the front line, and they are holding the sunken
track which disappears on the left-hand side of the
photograph. Beyond them were the 13th Yorkshires,
also with two companies in the front line. Their position is off the photograph, but a reference to the map
will show that they were bent back until the left-hand
Yorkshireman found touch with the right-hand man of
the 107th Brigade (of the 36th Division) a short distance
in front of the Sugar Factory. The two remaining
battalions of the 121st Brigade were thus disposed :
the 21st Middlesex were in support in some trenches
behind the Sugar Factory, south of the high-road,
while still farther back (but north of Graincourt) was
the 12th Suffolk Regiment, which was the brigade
reserve.

Returning now to the intersection of the " scissors "
and looking to the right from it, will be seen the left
battalion of the 119th Brigade, which carried on the
line to Anneux Chapel. From there this brigade bent
back towards Anneux village (the road to the village
can be seen in the picture), and from the outskirts of
the village it swung forward again—as shown on the

map—until it touched the 51st Division, whose line
made an immense bulge towards Fontaine-Notre-Dame,
whence it fell away sharply towards the south. The
first line was held by the 12th South Wales Borderers
from the " rivet" cross-roads to Anneux Chapel, the
19th Royal Welch Fusiliers carrying on the line to
Anneux village. The 17th Welch were in support in
the sunken road running north from the cemetery
between Graincourt and Anneux, while the 18th Welch
were in reserve, similarly sheltered in the hollow road
between Graincourt and the Sugar Factory.

With the illustration in front of him the reader can
thus visualize the terrain of the Bourlon Wood battle,
and by a reference to it and the map can clearly understand the initial disposition of the 40th Division
preparatory to its historic attack upon the wood and
village. He must, however, remember that the view
afforded him was by no means vouchsafed to the soldiers
of the 40th until shortly before the battle opened. The
relief of the 62nd Division was necessarily carried out
under cover of darkness, and, until morning broke,
nothing was visible, except what could be discerned by
the light of a half-hearted moon.

While the two front-line brigades were taking over
their positions, the General Staff of the Division were
busily engaged drafting the necessary orders for the
attack which was to take place upon the morrow. These
orders were issued shortly before midnight of November
22nd/23rd. The gist of them was that on the 23rd the
51st, 40th and 36th Divisions were to push forward and
gain the line: high ground north-east of Fontaine-
Notre-Dame—railway line north of Bourlon Wood—
Quarry Wood—Inchy. In this advance, Bourlon
Wood and Bourlon village were to be taken by the 40th
Division, whose boundaries are shown upon the map.
So far as that division's task was concerned, the 121st
Brigade, under Brigadier-General John Campbell, was
allotted the task of storming and capturing Bourlon
village, while Brigadier-General F. Crozier was ordered

to make a simultaneous attack upon the wood, Brigadier-General the Hon. C. S. H. D. Willoughby's 120th Brigade being held in reserve at Havrincourt. The operation of the Division was to be assisted by tanks, of which thirty-two had originally been placed at the disposal of the divisional commander, who had allotted twelve to the 119th Brigade and twenty to the 121st upon the left, though, as a matter of fact, some were not available when the flag fell. The dividing line between the two leading brigades was, practically speaking, the western edge of Bourlon Wood, which ran generally in a north and south direction. Anneux Chapel had been assigned by divisional headquarters as the initial "boundary stone" between the two brigades, but the two brigadiers, on consultation, agreed to observe the "cross-roads," which have already been mentioned, as the limit to their respective spheres of action. The inter-brigade boundary in the map represents, therefore, the instructions of Division and not the boundary which really existed.

Zero hour was fixed for 10.30 a.m., at which hour the first "lift" of an artillery barrage along the southern edge of the wood, and thence along the German front line, was to take place; a subsequent "lift" of 200 yards taking place every ten minutes. Here it will be convenient to give the disposition of the artillery as arranged and carried out. The 119th Brigade, on the right, was to be supported by a right group, under Lieutenant-Colonel Palmer, and consisting of the 5th Brigade R.H.A., the 77th A.F.A. Brigade (these two attached) and the 181st Brigade R.F.A. These units were to be disposed, generally speaking, from Graincourt to Flesquières, but west of those villages. A left group, under Lieutenant-Colonel Parsons, was to support the 121st Brigade. It consisted of the 178th Brigade R.F.A. and the 310th and 312th Brigades from the 62nd Division, and was to take position parallel to the right group, but closer to the villages named. The group headquarters were in the

catacombs at Graincourt, and the wagon lines in each
case from Havrincourt to Flesquières. In addition, the
87th Heavy Artillery group, under Lieutenant-Colonel
Brancke, was to lend assistance to each brigade. It
consisted of two 6-in. howitzer batteries and two 60-pr.
batteries. In all, 158 guns were to support the 40th
Division.

To return now to the orders for the attack. At
10.50 a.m. the tanks were to pass through the infantry
and advance, being followed by the latter 100 to 200
yards in rear and assisting with rifle fire. This advance
of tanks and infantry was to be supported by the guns,
which were to keep up a mixed smoke, high explosive
and shrapnel barrage. Bourlon Wood and village,
though necessarily prominent features of the attack of
the Division, were not the actual objective, which was
to be the capture and consolidation of that sector of
the line to be gained along the railway line north of
the wood to, or near, the mill on the road to Sains-les-
Marquion. The tanks were not to withdraw until the
infantry had consolidated on the objective assigned
to them, and included in the orders were instructions
to the infantry as to the means of conveying their
situation to our aeroplanes.

Bourlon Wood, with which the 40th Division is
imperishably connected, might justly be named the
key of the whole position. Thickly timbered, some
600 acres in extent, it was situated on a ridge, the
highest point of which rises 150 feet above the level of
the Bapaume—Cambrai road. From the road the
ground slopes gradually upward with a gradient of
1 in 20, so that the wooded ridge stands out promi-
nently above the surrounding landscape. The trees,
principally fir, but with occasional oak, were large in
size, and the wood, especially the lower part, was filled
with a thick undergrowth of hazel and large aspens,
which made progress very difficult. Inside the wood
were many tracks, of which the principal was one running almost east and west across it. In many respects

these were not unlike the drives in an English woodland, but in places their sunken formation afforded
them a special tactical value. The wood did not cover
the whole of the ridge, for, from the western side, there
projected a spur in continuation of the tree-covered
high ground. This spur, being outside the wood, was
within the sphere of operations of the 121st Brigade.

The night of the 22nd/23rd passed fairly quietly, but
the roads leading to the front were sorely congested
with traffic, with the result that petrol for the tanks
arrived only just in time, while the smoke shell which
was to be a feature of the barrage did not come up
at all. By half-past ten on the morning of the 23rd
a slight mist was covering the countryside—a feature,
on the whole, in favour of the attackers. Punctually
to the moment the artillery barrage was put down on
the southern end of the wood and further west. The
absence of smoke shell was to be regretted, but against
this was the fact that the divisional artillery commander had taken steps to see that the bulk of the
ammunition column was passed through the congestion
about Havrincourt, and, except for the smoke shell,
the supply of ammunition was adequate throughout
the day.

A few minutes before eleven o'clock the ground
depicted in the photograph illustrating this narrative
had exchanged its normal stillness for one of movement
and activity. The shells from the Division's guns
were bursting within the wood, and the two leading
brigades were streaming across the open in rear of the
tanks, which were either plunging into the wood or
working up towards the spur on the west of it. General
Crozier's brigade quickly reached the southern edge of
the wood, and in a sunken road at once captured a
number of prisoners and machine guns. The two
leading battalions immediately pushed on, and from
now onwards the guns could do little more than
maintain a protective barrage along the northern edge
of the wood, for the situation in the dense undergrowth

was so fluctuating, and communication became so difficult that any close artillery support was impossible. Meanwhile, General Campbell's brigade was advancing across the open west of the wood, keeping close touch with the 119th on its right, and about this moment the Germans put down a heavy barrage on Anneux and Graincourt to block the advance of reinforcements. Such, in a few words, is a rough picture of the situation about eleven o'clock that famous November morning, and it is now necessary to leave this general description and to follow each brigade in turn.

The early hours of the 23rd were spent by General Crozier and his staff in the catacombs of Graincourt drawing up the attack orders for his 119th Brigade. They were issued at 4 a.m., and were to the following effect : The 19th Royal Welch Fusiliers were to attack upon the right, with the 12th South Wales Borderers on the left. In support was to be the 17th Welch Regiment, near the cemetery on the north-eastern outskirts of Graincourt, while the brigade reserve was to consist of the 18th Welch, under cover south-east of the village. The attack was to be assisted by tanks, of which twelve had been allotted to the brigade. Of these, three were to proceed along the road which runs past the quarry just north of Anneux Chapel; this road will be clearly seen in the photograph of the wood. Another trio was to enter the wood by a ride near the right-hand corner, just off the photograph, and to "splay out as necessary." The remaining half-dozen tanks were to cruise about between these two lots, crushing wire wherever it was to be found and prepared to render any other assistance required. The tanks were to pass through the infantry at zero. The assistance which they would render was clearly very great, but in his orders General Crozier was careful to point out that "tanks were a luxury." The infantry were not to depend too much on them. Tanks would probably be damaged, and, if so, the infantry were to press on unless specifically asked to help.

BOURLON WOOD.

[From photographs kindly lent by the Imperial War Museum.

The plan of attack was that the leading battalions
were to advance on a two-company front in depth and
maintain artillery formation as long as possible,
following 100 to 200 yards in rear of the tanks. The
support battalion was to be ready either to reinforce or
to throw out defensive flanks. Three sections of the
machine gun company were placed in echelon to
protect the right flank, and were to move forward con-
forming to the advance of the tanks, the intention
being that, if the 51st Division was able to push ahead
on the right, these sections would take up a position
north of the wood on both sides of the railway. The
remaining section was to be at the disposal of the front
line, to be used as occasion demanded. No definite
task was assigned to the trench mortars beyond the
conventional instructions to be in readiness. The orders
also contained instructions as regards the barrage,
which would first be put down along the southern
edge of the wood, and communication was to
be ensured by a party of Second-Lieutenant Daniel
and four other ranks, who were to follow immediately
in rear of the leading battalions and to report direct to
brigade headquarters by runner.

" It is now daylight and everything is quiet, just a
few birds singing now and again "—such was the dawn
of November 23rd as it struck a simple Welsh soldier.
To come down to hard prose. In time-table form tanks
were to move in front of the infantry at 10.15 a.m.
Ten minutes later the guns would open with smoke
shell to screen the advance, and at half-past ten
artillery would open with high explosive on the
southern edge of the wood, lifting 200 yards every ten
minutes. Unfortunately, the smoke shells were
" napoo," but on the stroke of 10.30 the guns opened
a three minutes' intense bombardment with high explosive on the southern edge of Bourlon Wood. This
had, apparently, been preceded by an incident which
gave huge joy to the Welshmen—" aircraft appeared
overhead, and one airman went straight for a tree and

H

dislodged a German sniper." At twenty minutes to
eleven the barrage lifted, and immediately the 119th
Brigade advanced to the attack.

In the minds of all those following was working the
absorbing question, " What's going to happen now?"
What volume of fire would burst from that forbidding
belt of trees? How many of those who now breath-
lessly advanced would ever cover those few hundred
yards of intervening ground? The task, indeed, was
a tremendous one. To win through the key position of
Bourlon Wood, to which the Germans attached, and
rightly, such importance, would try any body of
troops; and it is a matter of history that the odds at
General Headquarters had hardened to six to one
against. Nevertheless, even to those whose experiences
had counted High Wood, Trônes Wood, and other
places, no thought of failure occurred. " I never
thought of failure," said one battalion commander,
" I had such faith in my officers and men," and a
similar trust in his brigade animated the brigade
commander.

As regards the initial opposition encountered, the
first impression conveyed to the historian was that it
was surprisingly small. The many personal narratives
give little information of those momentous few hundred
yards. But this silence is due entirely to the fact not
that the peril undergone was slight, but that it was
mercifully much less than had been expected. As a
matter of fact the German guns were, and had been
for some time, very busy. As early as 9 a.m. the
second-in-command of the 19th Royal Welch Fusiliers
had been knocked out, and, before the advance began,
German shells were plastering the terrain to be
crossed. The leading platoons had to push through
this barrage, but " though suffering many casualties
they never faltered." The first to enter the wood were
the 19th Royal Welch Fusiliers, who crossed an enemy
trench parallel to the southern face and then made
straight for the wood, followed on the left by the South

Wales Borderers. It was the right company of that battalion which was the first to put up any Huns, who were at once forced back. Everything was moving in quick time and according to plan, but the pace was slowed a bit on reaching the southern sunken road which zig-zags across the wood roughly from east to west.

This was a defensive line of the Germans, full of dug-outs and machine gun positions. Lieutenant-Colonel Plunkett received a message by visual of this fact. He immediately hastened to the wood, and, as senior officer immediately gave orders for the whole line to attack. It did, and used the bayonet with such purpose that the line was quickly mopped up, many prisoners being made. The two battalions of the 119th Brigade lost no time in pressing on, constantly encountering machine guns in carefully prepared positions, which were invariably put out of action by employing Lewis guns against both flanks, once the machine guns were located. Meanwhile the din of battle within the wood was awe-inspiring. In front, trees were falling wholesale from the shells of our guns, while, around and behind, the German projectiles were crashing everywhere. The roar was supplemented by the ceaseless chatter of enemy machine guns, and of our own Lewis guns which played a splendid part. On reaching the straight east-and-west drive the enemy resistance again became strenuous. "Once more our men charged and got there; the bayonet did the rest." The South Wales Borderers on the left were now under very heavy fire from machine guns, and the left company particularly suffered severely. In "A" Company, No. 4 Platoon found itself completely cut off near a small factory at the end of the wood. "We were now being paid considerable attention by the Prussian Guards, but could give as good as we got." The situation was relieved by the opportune arrival of a tank, which rendered useful assistance at the critical moment.

H 2

The battalion intelligence officer, Second-Lieutenant Morgan, at this moment came up to ascertain what was taking place; while the tank was halted he took cover by it, and was observing through his glasses when he was killed outright by a German sniper.

By midday the situation, apparently, of the Borderers was that one company had reached the outskirts of Bourlon village, but had lost touch with both flanks and could advance no farther. Another company, reinforced by one company of the 17th Welch at 12.45 and by a second company at 1.25, continued to push forward, but was held up inside the wood by heavy machine gun fire. By half-past one nearly all the officers of the battalion had become casualties, and Major W. E. Brown was sent up to reorganize. A strong enemy counter-attack now took place, and this seems to be what one narrator describes as an "obviously impending eventuality," in which Captain J. R. Symes was wounded. After attention he was able to walk to the regimental aid post, "but found solace in his pipe." So severe was the pressure on the left company that it had to give ground and fall back to one of the rides. One company was still cut off near the village, but with the aid of a tank it succeeded in cutting its way back and getting in touch with the rest of the line. Possibly this is the same incident as has been related in the previous paragraph; in the thick undergrowth the battalion had become disintegrated into isolated groups, and it is difficult to reconcile the various narratives consulted. About three o'clock Lieutenant W. M. Evans was sent up to help Major Brown, all the other officers of the battalion having by this time been knocked out. An hour later the enemy counter-attacked heavily. Both flanks of the Borderers were in the air at the time, but the 18th Welch came up just in time to stave off disaster. The attack was beaten off, and the 18th Welch advanced and occupied the high ground in front of the sunken road.

On the right the 19th Royal Welch Fusiliers had been able to make more progress. It had pushed on across the ridge in the wood, meeting "a very gallant defence by the Boche," who, however, gave way and fled when his flanks were turned. The Welshmen then consolidated themselves on the northern side of the ridge, and established posts beyond the northern edge, eastward of the village, having suffered very heavily in the operation. As has been related, the South Wales Borderers had been moving more slowly owing to the severe machine gun fire from the village, and it was while the "dressing" had been thus lost that the 17th Welch came up from its position of support and lined the sunken road running athwart the wood and threw out defensive flanks. In the preceding paragraph a strong enemy counter-attack is described as taking place about four o'clock, and this is almost certainly the attack as described in a narrative dealing with the 19th Royal Welch Fusiliers as being launched at 3.10 p.m. "by first class troops, the Guard Fusiliers." By it the Welch Fusiliers and the Borderers were both affected, and the general line now ran roughly south-west to north-east across the upper part of the wood and half way to the railway, with the right flank sharply refused back to the eastern edge of the wood; this defensive flank being rendered necessary by the fact that Fontaine-Notre-Dame still defied the efforts of the 51st Division. However, the 18th Welch now came up from reserve, launched a vigorous attack, and established posts beyond this line.

The enemy's barrage of 5.9's, 4.2's and 77's was very heavy, and the commander of the 18th Welch, Lieutenant-Colonel Kennedy, was killed by a bullet while leading his men. ("One of the finest commanders a battalion could wish for rode right up to us on horseback, jumped off when he got up to us, and rushing in front of us rallied us and waving his cane urged us on; he had only gone about half a dozen yards when he fell dead, shot by the Bosch.") His

second-in-command was severely wounded, and the
command of the battalion was taken over by the
adjutant, Captain F. H. Mathias. Though himself
wounded, he displayed a thorough grasp of the situation
and continued to carry out his duties in very difficult
circumstances. At this time an act of great gallantry
was performed by acting Company Sergeant-Major
Davies of the same battalion. He led his company in
attack when its commander fell wounded, and, in order
to facilitate the firing of a Lewis gun, rushed forward
in the open and knelt down, allowing his shoulder to
be used as a gun-rest until himself wounded in the
head. For initiative, resource, self-sacrifice and iron
nerve this action stands out even on a day when
self-sacrifice and nerve were freely shown. By five
o'clock the light had begun to fail, and the two
battalions dug in along the north edge of the ridge,
with two lines of posts at intervals of 150 yards along
the line.

About four o'clock Lieutenant-Colonel Plunkett had
been reinforced by some 200 dismounted cavalry. The
Germans made desperate but unavailing attempts to
regain the wood; at one time pushing in the centre of
our line. Shortly before seven o'clock the 119th
Brigade was reinforced by the Brigade Works Company and the Brigade Salvage Section, and a quarter
of an hour later further assistance was brought by the
arrival of the 14th Argyll and Sutherland Highlanders
from the 120th Brigade in reserve. This battalion,
under Lieutenant-Colonel J. Couper, and eight guns of
the 244th Machine Gun Company, were placed under
General Crozier's orders, as well as the dismounted
battalion of the 15th Hussars. Lieutenant-Colonel
Benzie was now put in command of all operations in
the forward area on the brigade front, and to him the
officer commanding the Argyll and Sutherlands
reported with a portion of his battalion; the remaining
troops formed a composite battalion under Lieutenant-
Colonel Plunkett, assisted by Major Brown. The

Highlanders pushed forward strong patrols towards
Bourlon village; the 15th Hussars moved up in
support of the 19th Royal Welch Fusiliers, while
machine gunners reinforced the right flank. Part of
the King's Own also came up from the 120th Brigade.

To go back now to the 121st Brigade. General
Campbell had received the divisional attack orders
shortly after midnight. At 3 a.m. in the Sugar Factory
he met his battalion and machine gun company commanders, when he explained the operation and issued
his instructions verbally. These were to the following
effect : The 20th Middlesex Regiment was to be on the
right, and, for its first objective, was to seize the spur
which has already been mentioned in the description
of Bourlon Wood given on an earlier page. This spur
can be seen protruding from the deep indentation in
the wood near Bourlon village, but it is essential to
bear in mind the " flattening " effect produced in
aeroplane photographs; the spur has lost some of its
prominence in consequence, and this applies to the
terrain in the photograph generally. The crests of the
trees in the middle of the wood are more than 150 feet
above Anneux Chapel, and even the southern edge is
some forty feet above the level of the right-hand block
of buildings. These facts might not be realized by a
casual glance at the photograph, but unless they are
borne in mind it is impossible to form a correct impression of the fighting. The spur projects beyond the
area taken in by the photograph, and the first objective
of the 20th Middlesex was to the left of the point where
the heavily-shaded sunken road leaves the left edge of
the picture, and about a quarter of a mile from it.

To the left of the 20th Middlesex were the 13th
Yorkshires, who were at first to advance in conjunction
with the 107th Brigade of the 36th Division. Later the
Yorkshires were to pivot on the 20th Middlesex Regiment, swing half-right and attack Bourlon village from
the west; while the 20th Middlesex thrust at it from
the south, in conjunction with General Crozier's

brigade, working up through the wood. Of the other
two battalions of the brigade the 21st Middlesex
Regiment was to move in support of the 13th Yorkshires echeloned in rear of the left of that regiment,
and to cover its flank in the event of the 107th Brigade
of the 36th Division being held up. The brigade
reserve was to be found by the 12th Suffolk Regiment
in trenches south of the high road to Cambrai. Detailed
instructions were also given to the commander of the
machine gun company. One section was to follow the
infantry of the front line and assist their advance, while
three sections were to take up a position near the Sugar
Factory and open barrage fire, covering the left flank.
Further instructions were also given for a forward
movement of the machine guns, particularly with
reference to the capture of the village.

From General Campbell's orders and dispositions it
is clear that considerable opposition was expected from
the left front. The expectation was not belied. At
dawn the outpost companies of the 13th Yorkshires
began to suffer heavy casualties from enfilade fire from
guns firing from the south-east corner of Quarry Wood,
the first officer casualty being Second-Lieutenant
Stanford (killed); and, later, fifteen minutes before
Zero, a liaison officer from the 13th Yorkshires reported
enemy machine guns active inside the 121st Brigade
area just west of the spur and from Quarry Wood. A
message was accordingly sent at once to the artillery
asking them to turn on two howitzers on to each spot.
The intense bombardment broke out all along the line
at 10.30 as arranged, and at once the advance began,
tanks leading, followed by the infantry in column of
sections. " The attacking companies followed the
tanks and barrage according to book; in fact, the whole
show looked more like a field day than very much the
real thing." This advance was in full view of
Lieutenant-Colonel Plunkett, commanding the right
battalion of the 119th Brigade, who says : " I saw the
121st Brigade, under cover of tanks, move forward to

attack Bourlon village. It was rather a nice sight
seeing the men moving leisurely along as if they were
having a day out.'' It is typical of the difficulties
encountered by the historian that whereas General
Campbell describes the advance as starting at 10.30 a.m.,
Lieutenant-Colonel Plunkett twice gives 10 a.m. as the
hour; the former is undoubtedly the correct time.

Almost at once there happened one of those things—
foreseen, but hoped against till the last—which so often
in war throw carefully-made plans out of gear. The
resistance opposite the right of the 36th Division was
very severe, and the 107th Brigade was soon held up.
This reacted on the 121st Brigade of the 40th Division,
for although the tanks, followed by infantry, were seen
crossing the spur at eleven o'clock, the 13th Yorkshires,
on the left, had already come under a hot machine gun
fire, and, without support on their left, were forced
gradually inwards. The casualties to this battalion
were now serious; Captain Mason, Lieutenants Walton
and Phillips, and Second-Lieutenant June were killed,
and several other officers wounded. Nevertheless, both
the 20th Middlesex and the 13th Yorkshires were
able to push on, and to report that the attack was progressing favourably, so much so that the leading waves
of the 20th Middlesex crossed the neck of the spur about
11.45 a.m., and, at the same time, the left company of
the 13th Yorkshires passed through the enemy's trench
system on the outer edge of the spur on the left.

So far, everything was satisfactory on the whole, and
news had come in that the 119th Brigade was successfully dealing with the wood; and, as a matter of fact, it
had reached the northern edge, but owing to the fact
that the 51st Division on the right had been checked,
and the advance of the 121st Brigade slowed down, the
119th had now formed defensive flanks. Then, exactly
at 12 noon, advanced detachments of the 20th
Middlesex Regiment were seen entering Bourlon
village at its south-eastern extremity. These were the
battalion scouts; for the battalion itself, as well as the

21st Middlesex Regiment, were stopped by continued machine gun fire from the west. About the same time the leading company of the 13th Yorkshire Regiment captured some 60 prisoners in dug-outs about half-a-mile west of the southern extremity of Bourlon village, but a counter-attack freed the Germans, and but few of the escort survived. Meanwhile the inner company of the 20th Middlesex was held fast on the spur, exposed to heavy machine gun fire from the left flank, rear, and the west edge of the wood. The tanks on the spur were suffering severely from armour-piercing bullets, and the infantry were deprived of much of their support, for three tanks out of six were put out of action. At half-past twelve the left company of the 13th Yorkshires having suffered very heavily was compelled to fall back to the support and reserve companies just south of the village.

It will be remembered that the 21st Middlesex Regiment had been directed to follow to the left rear of the 13th Yorkshires. It had duly complied with the order, but about noon was held up by an enemy strong post south-west of the spur, although every effort was made to overcome the resistance by envelopment and advance under rifle grenade barrage. Here the situation began to be unfavourable, and at 12.25 p.m. General Campbell received a visual signal message from the 21st Middlesex to the effect that the left company had been detached to go to the support of the 107th Brigade of the 36th Division, which was apparently forced to give ground; and that two platoons were being sent up from the reserve company to endeavour to form a defensive flank. Within the next twenty minutes two further messages were received of similar import, and it was abundantly clear that the resistance of the enemy to the left of the 121st Brigade was very determined.

By one o'clock the situation had so far improved that the support company of the 13th Yorkshires, now on the left, had reached the western outskirts of the village, and the reserve company had got up to the southern edge.

Further, the right company had been seen to enter the village, but for the moment no more was seen of them; the company commander had been killed. The resistance of the Germans was now everywhere very marked, and their artillery was active and persistent.

From now onwards until dusk the situation of the 121st Brigade was that, in face of stiffening enemy opposition, continual annoyance from the left front, and a counter-attack, attempts were made, but in vain, to obtain possession of the village. By 2 p.m. some of the left company of the 20th Middlesex entered Bourlon, and the left company of the 13th Yorkshires established itself in a house near the château in the wood, but was soon ejected, and only a few stragglers were able to rejoin the reserve company south of the village. Good news now came in from the division on the left, for at twenty minutes past two General Campbell received a message stating that the 107th Brigade was moving almost abreast of the spur. This advance, if it could but be continued, would materially ease the pressure on the left of General Campbell's brigade, and he at once passed on the news to the 21st Middlesex Regiment. Unfortunately, however, the 107th Brigade, so far from being able to make any progress, was compelled to send the following message: " Our advance completely held up . . . shall probably be reorganizing on old line "; by 3.30 p.m. it was back in its original position. Reinforcements had by this time been asked for, and a company of the 12th Suffolk Regiment was sent forward, but no further advance was made, and about four o'clock one of our aeroplanes was shot down and crashed, the pilot being killed in a gallant attempt to harry the Germans holding the strong point south-west of the spur, from a height of but fifty feet.

It had now become plain that Bourlon village could not be successfully attacked without reinforcements, and, until the necessary arrangements for such accession of strength could be made, there was nothing for

it but to consolidate the ground already won. Orders
to this effect were given about a quarter past four; half
an hour later a small local counter-attack by the
Germans threatened to develop, several parties of the
enemy, each about twenty strong, being seen to move
in a south-westerly direction from a point south of the
outer end of the spur. It appears that they advanced
to within a hundred yards of our line, when they were
dispersed by rifle and Lewis gun fire.

When darkness fell the units of the 121st Brigade
were strung out from Bourlon village almost to the
Sugar Factory on the Bapaume—Cambrai road. The
situation was far from reassuring. A message had
been received by General Campbell at a quarter past
five, stating that "the Yorks and 21st Middlesex are
practically obliterated," and, as a precautionary
measure, he then ordered both brigade headquarter
details to cover Graincourt from the north-west, with
the view of protecting the guns; this party was, however, withdrawn on the receipt, about 6.45, of word
from the commanding officer of the 21st Middlesex that
all was quiet. As for the position of the 121st Brigade,
in Bourlon village itself, but out of communication,
were elements of the 20th Middlesex and the 13th
Yorkshire Regiments. On the southern edge of the
village was an advanced or outpost line; the right of
this line was held by a company of the Suffolks, which
was in touch with the 119th Brigade inside the wood,
while on the left, with the left flank refused, were some
of the 13th Yorkshires. Behind them, on the spur,
were the remainder of the 13th with the two Middlesex
battalions, the whole being considerably intermingled,
and their line stretched back from the spur, mingling
with bits of the 107th Brigade, to the sunken road
about a quarter of a mile north-west of the Sugar
Factory. To the right front of this spot were some
companies in shell-holes and the deeply-marked sunken
road on the left of the photograph. One company of
the Suffolks was still behind the Sugar Factory.

The objective of the 121st Brigade had not been obtained, but this was due to circumstances outside of the control of the battalions of which it was composed or of the general who commanded it. In the official narrative on the day's work subsequently rendered by the Division, high praise is given. " Throughout this arduous day the 121st Brigade fought with extra-ordinary gallantry against very heavy odds, and numerous opportunities for the display of individual bravery were eagerly taken advantage of. Company Sergeant-Major Edward Hall, of the 21st Middlesex Regiment, showed conspicuous courage on this occa-sion. When the officer in command of his half company was killed, he at once took charge, displaying the greatest initiative and resource; and, although three times wounded, remained at his post until relieved by an officer of another company. Two other N.C.Os., Sergeant W. Odam and Lance-Sergeant J. Kerridge, both of the same battalion, set an equally fine example of courage and determination, and suc-ceeded in keeping their men together in very difficult circumstances."

The 120th Brigade had been in reserve, but it had not been entirely at rest during this first day's fighting. It had been the last brigade of the Division to enter the battle area, being a day's march behind the others. It was apparently on the 19th that the first definite orders were received as to participation in the fighting which was going on at Cambrai, and excitement ran high. " As the news of the battle's progress kept coming in the excitement prevailing in the camp became more marked, and speculation was rife as to what part the battalion was destined to play in it. The placing of the brigade under an hour's notice was the signal for a scene of immense bustle and enthusiasm. All super-fluous kit was dumped, and the battalion stood by. It was wonderful to see them during the twenty-four hours preceding the move forward. Everybody was in such high spirits. The men stood round in groups discussing the fight with much zest, or played football with the officers in a field close by." Another chronicler puts the matter a little more acidly : " All day we were on the rack, and what a camp it was to try and get some comfort in. Cold, bleak huts and mud and dirt everywhere; no wood for firing, and raining." But this least little touch of spleen was dissipated next day : " On the morning of the 21st the first prisoners began to pass along the road to Bapaume, and this cheered up the men no end." Still, this pessimist had something up his sleeve : " It was still raining, of course," and although " the thought and anticipation of fighting was enough, little did we know of, or imagine, the weary tramp to the actual fighting."

By midday on the 21st the 120th Brigade was on the road for Lebuquière, and here " we found a green field and tents " (" just dumped, and not even out of their bags," as the matter-of-fact man points out). Next morning at 3 a.m. the brigade pushed on, crossing the Canal du Nord at dawn on that famous November 23rd; " what a struggle to get out of that boggy camp, and what a weary tramp; the roads were a foot deep in mud." (" Have you ever tried to walk in that?" is the sardonic question the matter-of-fact man puts to the historian.) However, General Willoughby now arrived with news of the state of affairs, and there was much excitement watching the tanks collecting for the advance at 10.30 a.m. The brigade now soon reached its position of reserve between Graincourt and Havrincourt, and here Fortune smiled upon it. In an abandoned German dug-out were found " enormous supplies of preserved meat and cases upon cases of aerated water " (" no wines, however," as the matter-of-fact man is careful to point out). Every man was issued with two tins of beef and two bottles of " fizz," and as one narrative remarks : " I had a first-class dinner and watched the battle."

Early in the afternoon urgent orders began to arrive; the first was to the effect that the battle was going

satisfactorily, and that the 120th Brigade must be prepared to move off at short notice. Later came another
message, with nothing about the battle going satisfactorily, but with " very short notice " given as the
time at which the brigade might be required. Reading
between the lines, it was fairly obvious that the situation
had altered—and unfavourably; and it was clear to most
that something to eat and as good a rest as possible was
advisable, in view of a hard task on the morrow. The
matter-of-fact man—who had, in reality, been aching
to get into the fight—consoled himself by entering in
his diary : " Bourlon Wood does not look at all
pleasant—explosions in the wood and puff balls of
shrapnel over it."

So ended the first day's fighting of the battle for ever
known as that of Bourlon Wood. Within a few hours
the 40th Division, which, so far in the war, had been
afforded no outstanding opportunity of showing its
special worth, had leaped to the forefront as one of the
fighting divisions on the Western Front. Its objective
had, indeed, not been fully secured; the wood was not
entirely clear of Germans, and the village still remained
in enemy hands. Nevertheless, it must be remembered
that if the goal had not been reached the progress made
had been farther than that achieved by the divisions on
either flank, and the inability of those divisions to get
forward had had the effect of leaving the 40th Division
in a salient with all the disadvantages and difficulties of
such a position. The divisions right and left had done
all that men could do. Fontaine-Notre-Dame, on the
right, had proved a terrible obstacle, and the resistance
on the left in front of the 36th Division had been most
severe and obstinate. Further, the divisions on the
flanks had been continuously engaged since the 20th,
and had exhausted their strength, whereas the 40th
Division had been flung fresh into the fight and trained
to the hour. But the comparative advantage thus
enjoyed by the 40th Division must not be allowed to
conceal the sterling success which it had achieved. It

was a triumph of staff work and organization that a division which had stumbled late at night into unknown trenches, in relief, should have been able to start, with orders detailed, clear-cut, and complete, into the battle on the morrow. And the regimental officers and men, by their boldness and resolution, rivalled the Roman soldiers of old. " What valour had been in Catiline's people was plainly to be discerned. For what parcel of ground anyone made choice of to stand on in fight, the same, being slain, his slaughtered body covered. Only a few, violently overborne by the first charge of the Pretorian cohort, lay somewhat further removed, yet all with their death wounds on the foreparts of their bodies."

CHAPTER VII.

BOURLON WOOD (continued).

D URING the night of the 23rd/24th part of the
9th Cavalry Battalion, comprising the 19th
Hussars and 1st Bedfordshire Yeomanry, under
Lieutenant-Colonel Parsons, was placed at General
Campbell's disposal, and took over the left of the 121st
Brigade position from the 13th Yorkshire Regiment
and the 21st Middlesex, which were withdrawn into
reserve. In this sector of the battle the night passed
fairly quietly. A counter-attack was expected on the
left, and all preparations were made to meet it, but it
never materialized. During the night a warning order
was received from divisional headquarters to prepare
for a renewal of the attack on Bourlon village. The
original intention had been that this attempt should be
made by fresh troops from the 120th Brigade, namely,
the 14th Argyll and Sutherland Highlanders and the
14th Highland Light Infantry; but the former, as has
been related, had been sucked into the sphere of the
119th Brigade in the wood, and it was therefore decided
that the 14th Highland Light Infantry and the 12th
Suffolks should carry out the operation. 'At 8 p.m. on
the evening of the 23rd, Lieutenant-Colonel Battye,
commanding the 14th Highland Light Infantry, had
reported with his battalion at 121st Brigade headquarters, when it had been decided that his battalion
should go back for rations and water. This was done,
and early on the morning of the 24th the 14th Highland
Light Infantry had moved up to a position of readiness
at the south-western corner of the wood. Lieutenant-
Colonel Battye then proceeded to brigade headquarters,

I

about seven o'clock, to discuss the situation with the brigadier and the commander of the left group of artillery. The attack was discussed, and General Campbell issued verbal orders which were subsequently confirmed in writing.

These orders, which are given below, were based on instructions from the Division, the formal issue of which, however, did not take place till some hours later. These divisional orders were to the effect that the day was to be devoted to the capture of Bourlon village, and to rounding off the capture of the wood, which was almost, but not entirely, in the possession of General Crozier's 119th Brigade. The former task was to be carried out by the 121st Brigade, with one battalion of the 120th (*i.e.*, the 14th Highland Light Infantry), assisted by twelve tanks. It was stated for information that the division on the right (which might be either the 51st or Guards) would consolidate, and that the Guards would arrange to have one brigade in reserve near Bourlon Wood. On the left the 36th Division would endeavour to push forward towards Quarry Wood and Inchy. Further, two dismounted brigades from the 1st Cavalry Division would be at the disposal of the 40th Division.

General Campbell's orders for his brigade were as follows. The 14th Highland Light Infantry were to attack upon the right; the 12th Suffolks on the left; the tanks pushing off at Zero + 20. The attack was to be carried out in three stages, the first objective being the outer edge of the village, the second objective the inner edge, and the third the northern outskirts. At each objective there was to be a halt of twenty minutes to allow of mopping up, a feature upon which General Campbell, realizing the possibility of the Germans lying doggo in houses until the attackers passed—and then shooting them in the back—laid especial stress. When the village should be won, both the 121st and 119th Brigades were to push forward and consolidate, practically speaking, on the line laid down in the orders

for November 23rd and given in the previous chapter.
After the village had been entered it was arranged that
some tanks should remain at the various important road
junctions and cross-roads to form strong points, while
the remainder should push on to assist in consolidation
on the final line. The heavy artillery attached to the
Division would bombard Bourlon from an hour
before Zero till Zero + 20, when it would lift to the
north side of the village. The field guns would also
put down a barrage, and at 3.20 p.m. the barrage would
move forward by bounds, resting for twenty minutes on
each objective and finally forming a defensive barrage
on the line to be consolidated. In addition, the field
artillery were to put down a flank barrage on the
enemy's trenches on the left front of the attack. Two
sections of machine guns were detailed to barrage the
same quarter, and particular attention was called to the
necessity of watching the flanks.

During the morning a section of the 244th Machine
Gun Company came up to relieve the 62nd Divisional
Company, which then withdrew. Reports kept coming
in of losses inflicted by German enfilade fire on the
front line and spur, but otherwise nothing of importance happened, and the battalions concerned were able
to get on with the task of preparing for the attack. This
had been provisionally fixed for three o'clock, and as
the morning wore away General Campbell anxiously
awaited the formal intimation confirming his previous
instructions. As a matter of fact, one of those things
had happened which in war make the best laid plans
"gang aft a-gley." While General Campbell, at his
brigade headquarters, was chafing at the non-receipt of
definite instructions, the corps commander came to divisional headquarters to confer with General Ponsonby.
After some discussion the conclusion was reached that
the number of tanks with the 121st Brigade was not
enough to ensure success, and it was decided to post-
pone the attack until more should be available. The
necessary orders were hastily drafted, but it was found

impossible to get them through to Graincourt, tele-
graphic and telephonic communication having been cut
by the enemy's shell fire.

Left without any definite instructions General
Campbell rightly decided, in the absence of any
instructions to the contrary, to carry out the attack as
arranged. He accordingly issued the necessary orders
and communicated them to the tanks, heavy artillery,
battalions, and machine gun company. Punctually at
3 p.m. the attack began, and, as usually happened in
such operations, there ensued a long period unbroken
by any report or message. It was growing dark before
General Campbell was handed a message from the
officer commanding the Suffolks, timed 4.45 p.m. So
far as it went, it was satisfactory. The left company
had suffered heavily, but it had been replaced by the
company in support; the right company was passing
through the village; and the reserve company was duly
mopping up. Further, a company formed from the
remnants of the 20th Middlesex on the spur had been
pushed forward and taken over from the Suffolks just
south of the village.

Such was the situation about a quarter to five. About
five o'clock, however, it had become obscure.
The commanding officer of the Suffolks at that hour
received the welcome intelligence that his right company
had reached its objective clear of the village on the
northern side, and at once transferred his battalion
headquarters towards the village; but almost immediately afterwards further news came in to the effect that
the situation of the right company was obscure and
that on the left not reassuring. It was now growing
quite dark, and the tanks were withdrawing; there was
no indication of any advance by the 36th Division on
the left; and, apparently, no touch with the battalion
on the right; the orders for the attack, which were
formally issued in writing at 1 p.m., had contained no
reference to either supports or reserves; the village still
contained bodies of Germans familiar with every inch

of it. In these circumstances it seemed only prudent to withdraw the Suffolks to the southern edge of the village, where they could be reformed and reorganized; and there we may leave them while we follow the fortunes of the Highland Light Infantry on the right.

In the archives of the 121st Brigade it is stated that the 14th Highland Light Infantry was in position by Bourlon Wood as early as 6 a.m., but this is inaccurate, for narratives from members of the battalion show clearly that it did not come up from the reserve till several hours later. " The morning of the 24th broke with everyone anxious for the fray, and we fell in and marched to Anneux at midday," says one writer; and the adjutant, in a very detailed account, mentions the battalion passing through Graincourt at 11.45 a.m., where more tools and bombs were picked up. The Highland Light Infantry must have been observed by the Germans on debouching from the village, for shelling instantly started. The second shell was dis-astrous, for it dropped into the middle of No. 7 Platoon, killing or wounding everyone in it except the officer and his batman. " To tried troops this would have been nothing, but to untried like ours very unnerving; the men never flinched, just plodded on."

The order was now passed down to move in artillery formation by sections, and the battalion proceeded in this formation for the remaining distance, its destination being the south-west corner of Bourlon Wood. The enemy shelling was persistent. " I remember looking round once or twice at the battalion coming on. They were splendid. Suddenly a screech, followed by a resounding crash; a cloud of earth and pungent smoke among those little bodies of men. Then out of the débris emerge the few figures and move steadily on. Perhaps one or two had fallen, and, if so, they were left; not one could be spared even to bind their wounds." Within a hundred yards of the main Cambrai road a regular barrage was encountered, and the leading sections were held up by wire; then a quarry; then more wire; then another barrage. The battalion plodded steadily on, and arrived at last at its rendezvous at 12.30 p.m. " We thus had two and a half hours before the probable Zero hour of 3 p.m., and the time was spent in eating and resting." Another writer adds this significant detail : " Captain Stevenson got orders from the C.O. to go and find the position of the Welsh regiments, also our front of attack on Bourlon village. Which we got alright. But we saw nothing of the Welsh regiments except a lot of dead."

At two o'clock came the written brigade orders for the attack. Their substance had been communicated to Lieutenant-Colonel Battye early in the morning, and the gist of them has been given earlier in this chapter. A conference of officers was immediately held, and notes made of the various positions to be occupied. Zero hour was now fast approaching, and the difficulties of a military historian will be realized when it is pointed out that whereas the brigade archives state that the attack started at 3 p.m., the adjutant of the battalion has placed on record : " We moved to the attack at 2.30 p.m.," and a diary of a non-commissioned officer contains the entry : " At 3.15 we formed up for the attack." These discrepancies are part and parcel of military history. It may be said that of any given incident of the war no two separate accounts *ever* agree as regards the exact hour. An error as to the precise day is very common. Sometimes the month is given wrong (a capable narrator places Bourlon Wood fighting in September); and in a most useful account (by a staff officer) the first day's fighting in the wood is placed on November 23rd, 1918, or twelve days after the last shot was fired in the war.

In the front line were " A " and " B " companies, the latter on the right, and the battalion moved along the western edge of the wood, keeping entirely within it. Inasmuch as the 119th Brigade had the previous day cleared the greater portion of the wood and was at present occupying a position within it, no opposition was encountered by the Highland Light Infantry in its advance, with the result that by four o'clock the battalion was well forward, and shortly afterwards it was reported that three companies had safely reached the third objective, namely, the German trenches on the north and north-east side of the village. Prisoners, too, had begun to come in in twos and threes, and battalion headquarters put up a couple in a farmhouse which eventually became the commanding officer's post. By this time it was growing quite dark, and at five minutes past five a message was sent back to brigade headquarters to the effect that the 14th Highland Light Infantry were now north of the village, and that little opposition had been encountered; the casualties were about thirty-five.

During the advance one company had become separated from the battalion, but about 6 p.m. it rejoined and was formed into a local reserve. Shortly after this Lieutenant-Colonel Battye and Major Foster visited the three companies in front, but found some difficulty in reaching battalion headquarters—a house on the east side of the village—owing to the growing activity of bodies of Germans, who were now emerging from cellars after the withdrawal of the Suffolks, which had taken place some time previously. Major Foster, however, managed to bag a couple of Huns who spoke English, and "they were immediately sent down to brigade headquarters, as they were talking freely." The disconcerting feature now was that no touch could be obtained upon the flanks, and this was reported to brigade at 6.35 p.m.: "Have sent patrols to right and left. A considerable distance. Can get touch with no one."

What had happened was that the Highland Light Infantry had pushed on ahead of the positions at the moment being held by the 12th Suffolk Regiment on the left and the 119th Brigade on the right, and was now distinctly in the air. In more than one message sent back by Lieutenant-Colonel Battye he stressed the

importance of a real " mopping up " of Bourlon village
in the morning, and he was undoubtedly under the
impression that the Suffolks had passed through the
village and were on the northern side of it.   The conclusion was not unnatural, for when Lieutenant-Colonel
Battye had crossed one of the streets running east and
west in his (the right) sphere of the village, "the
Suffolks were well up with me." Parties of the
Highland Light Infantry were, therefore, wandering
about Bourlon village in complete ignorance of the
fact that, so far from having been definitely captured,
the village was at best a kind of No Man's Land.   One
private soldier's narrative is worth quoting here : " The
village by this time must have been filled with Germans,
as we could hear the shouts of them ; any of our men
who were sent out never came back again." *Vestigia
nulla retrorsum* conveys a good deal in war.

How far the Highland Light Infantry were in the
air will be understood by an exposition of the situation
of the front of the 40th Division generally about 8.30
p.m. on the evening of November 24th. The 12th
Suffolk Regiment had withdrawn from the village and
was holding some trenches just south of it.   As regards
the Highland Light Infantry, one company was on the
railway ; its exact situation was on the western edge of
the bulge which the railway makes down towards the
north of Bourlon Wood. From there two companies
held a trench running westwards across the north of the
village. In other words, the Highland Light Infantry
were lying north of Bourlon, and the Suffolks lying
south of it ; the village itself being occupied by bodies
of Germans. To the left of the Highland Light
Infantry there was nothing ; nothing, that is, except the
German Army, for the 36th Division had not been able
to get forward. On the right, the 119th Brigade was
still on the forward slope of the ridge in the wood. If
the reader will visualize an equilateral triangle of which
the apex is formed by the 14th Highland Light Infantry,
and the base by the 12th Suffolk Regiment *plus* the

119th Brigade, he will have a sufficiently accurate impression of the position of the Highland Light Infantry on the evening of the 24th.

In their isolation the Highland Light Infantry were fortunate in their transport officer and quartermaster. About midnight rations and rum came up. "They came up just as an ordinary ration party in a quiet sector." Eight pack mules and some horses were in the convoy, and for ten hours, delayed by shell fire and by lack of information, it had a strenuous time. Its route lay along the sunken road west of the wood which the Germans were shelling unmercifully through the night; but although the animals stampeded several times, not a man, nor a horse, nor a mule was hurt. "What a cheering and reassuring effect their arrival had. The unconcern with which the convoy pulled up on a machine gun swept road and offloaded sandbags of rations and rum was grand to see. There was a stiff rum issue that night you may be sure, and welcome it was, and there was not a man who refused." The battalion medical officer claimed a jar for his wounded, and there is a testimony that it saved their lives. Then the transport officer was ordered to go and find a small arms ammunition dump "somewhere near Anneux Chapel"—pitch dark, remember,—and return with full loads. He did it, somehow; "and that ammunition was undoubtedly the factor that enabled us to hold on as long as we did." People who manage to bring up rum, rations and ammunition in darkness, through shell fire, to companies "in the air" deserve naming; and Lieutenant E. J. T. Thompson, the transport officer, and Lieutenant J. Dicks, the quartermaster—as well as the company quartermaster-sergeants—can be put down as having "lined up amongst the red-blooded men."

Before passing to deal with the 119th Brigade, in the wood, we may for a moment transport ourselves back to Havrincourt to divisional headquarters. Divisional order No. 102 had been issued at 11 a.m.; this contained the general plan of attack, and has been referred to on an earlier page. It was cancelled by a message sent during the morning, but this was not received by General Campbell. The attack duly took place, as we have seen, but no inkling of the fact reached Havrincourt. While the Suffolks and Highland Light Infantry were actually traversing the streets of Bourlon, divisional headquarters, five miles away, were drafting orders for an attack upon the village on the morrow, November 25th. " 5.45 p.m. Divisional order No. 103 issued. It was not then known at divisional headquarters that the cancellation of the order No. 102 had not been received by 121st Brigade, or that the attack ordered in No. 102 had actually taken place." Thus the divisional war diary; and the lack of information lasted two hours and a quarter. To quote the war diary again : " 8 p.m. First news received from G.O.C. 120th Infantry Brigade that 121st Brigade had attacked and captured Bourlon village at 3 p.m. in accordance with order No. 102."

The work of communication between Havrincourt and the forward area was not easy. The roads were congested, and the work of the Signals was made exceptionally difficult owing to the continuous shrapnel breaking the different lines ; as fast as one line or break was repaired, the shrapnel would break it again in another place. The signal office and divisional headquarters were situated within the wood, the work there was carried out under great difficulties, everyone seemed to be getting in each other's way; the operators were all squeezed into a small tent, and generally tried to do their best, although pushed about while trying to do their various duties. The cable teams were out nearly all the time the Division was in action.

When divisional headquarters realized that the attack upon Bourlon village had taken place, the remaining two companies of the 11th King's Own (two having been sent to the 119th Brigade) and the 13th East Surrey Regiment were placed at the disposal of General Campbell. The latter battalion had meanwhile moved up to the Hindenburg Support Line, about three quarters of a mile south-west of Graincourt, and at 9.15 p.m. the commanding officer was instructed to report for orders to 121st Brigade headquarters. The general situation having been explained, Lieutenant-Colonel Warden was ordered to clear the western portion of Bourlon village of any parties of the enemy holding out there, for which task his battalion would have the assistance of tanks, if these were available. This done, the East Surreys were, if possible, to prolong to the westward the line held by the 14th Highland Light Infantry north of the village.

Lieutenant-Colonel Warden at once started from Graincourt to carry out his personal reconnaissance, and, if possible, to make his way to the headquarters of the Highland Light Infantry, there to concert a plan of action with Lieutenant-Colonel Battye; sending back at the same time a message to his own battalion to meet him at Anneux Chapel at 3.30 a.m. On arriving at the quarry half a mile west of Anneux Chapel (the one on the left of the photograph) Lieutenant-Colonel Warden was greeted with the disconcerting intelligence that " there were no British troops north of the crossroads just ahead of the quarry, and that the Highland Light Infantry must have been wiped out." Undeterred by this information, Lieutenant-Colonel Warden pushed on and made himself as acquainted with affairs in the wood as was possible in the darkness. As the Germans were shelling the south-western portion of the wood, Lieutenant-Colonel Warden interpreted this as an attempt to prevent reinforcements reaching the Highland Light Infantry, and he decided accordingly to bring up the East Surreys under cover of darkness, reinforcing the Highland Light Infantry with one portion and mopping up the village with the remainder. He was in time to intercept his battalion about half a mile north of Graincourt, and he led it thence across country to the sunken road at the south-west corner of the wood.

To turn now to the 119th Brigade, which was left in the previous chapter clinging to the hard-won ridge within the wood. When night set in, machine and Lewis guns "made an awful din, and the Boche artillery shelled the wood continuously with gas shells." About 1 a.m. on the morning of the 24th, after a particularly heavy bombardment, the shelling suddenly ceased. The men of the 119th Brigade were, however, not deceived by this cessation of frightfulness, and when the German infantry pressed forward to attack it was driven back with considerable loss. This was sufficient for the enemy for one night, and although heavy firing continued till daybreak no further attack was made.

On the morning of the 25th, between half past eight and nine, the enemy attacked in considerable force, both from Fontaine on the right and Bourlon on the left, "coming on in droves, without any particular formation." They were allowed to approach in most cases to about 150 yards, when rapid fire from rifles and Lewis guns checked them with such effect that "they melted away completely, and not a single German reached the line." A few of our advanced posts had been driven in, but with the failure of the German attack these were quickly reoccupied. A temporary retirement had also been necessitated on the left about nine o'clock, when, in response to a request for assistance from our artillery, the barrage proved a trifle too short and the South Wales Borderers fell back about 300 yards to a sunken road, where they were reinforced by two companies of the 14th Argyll and Sutherland Highlanders. About a quarter to ten the barrage lifted and the line moved forward again, the Highlanders taking over the front position, with the South Wales Borderers in close support.

By eleven o'clock things had eased a bit, and Lieutenant-Colonel Benzie was able to report that the situation in the wood was "quiet." This euphemism does not mean, however, a cessation of noise. The German guns were very busy indeed putting down a heavy barrage on all the sunken roads leading up from Graincourt and Anneux, a circumstance which led Lieutenant-Colonel Benzie to conclude that another German attack was pending, and to notify brigade headquarters accordingly. His forecast proved correct, for about one o'clock a heavy attack was made against the right from the direction of Fontaine. Our artillery did great execution against the waves of advancing Germans; nevertheless, the attackers pressed on and drove in the right of the 119th Brigade; while the machine gunners forming the belt of fire on this flank, remaining gallantly at their posts, were cut off or killed. A counter-attack, composed of elements of the 19th Royal Welch Fusiliers, 14th Argyll and Sutherland Highlanders, and 15th Hussars succeeded in stemming the enemy's advance and in reoccupying the original line.

All through the afternoon sporadic attack and counter-attack more and more turned the fighting inside Bourlon Wood into a veritable "soldiers' battle." In this fighting the battalions of the 119th Brigade well held their own, but they had begun to reach the limits of physical endurance. Unlike the Germans, who were able to throw fresh troops into the fight, the Welsh soldiers had received but little reinforcement. As the afternoon wore on the reserves available in Bourlon Wood were very small indeed; the fact that the attack on Bourlon village had not started till 3 p.m. had enabled the Germans to concentrate their attention on the 119th Brigade in the wood; the approaches to the wood were being heavily shelled; the wood itself reeked with gas; and, to add to these difficulties, telephone communication with divisional headquarters had been, and still was, interrupted. The situation, indeed, looked far from promising, and about half past five an urgent request for assistance came from the wood, and the brigade intelligence officer returned with the information that the situation, owing to the exhaustion and fewness of the troops, was so serious that a determined

German counter-attack was all that was required to throw the 119th Brigade out of the wood.

Reader—whether of to-day, or of a century hence, when of all those who fought within the wood it may be said, "their swords are dust, their souls are with their God, I trust "—wouldst thou form some opinion of the scramble and skirmishes in the tangled under-wood of Bourlon Wood on that 24th November, 1917? If so, let us follow the fortunes of a simple Highland private, who went through the perils of that day unscathed and has left a vivid tale of his doings. He belonged to the 14th Argyll and Sutherland High-landers, a battalion from the 120th Brigade in reserve, which was sent up to reinforce during the night of the 23rd/24th, but of which some elements apparently were delayed in the darkness and passed the night on the hither side of the wood. The day of the 24th opened full of incident for the Highlander. " As soon as day-light broke and stand-to was over, another fellow and I started to explore a few of Jerry's dug-outs, and so far we were very successful; we found a good frying pan and a lovely side of smoked bacon which to all appear-ance seemed quite wholesome, so we did not waste much time in making a small fire and cutting up a few rashers. However, we had not the pleasure of eating them, as Fritz opened up with his heavies and our frying pan was obliterated beyond recognition," " Probably for the best," as this philosopher adds. Shortly afterwards this detachment was led by its officer into the wood, and deployed " not individually, but by platoons, to the right of the road in the wood, that is, the road which runs south to north." So far all seemed quiet enough, and there was compensation for the ruined breakfast in the issue " of a very good food ration and also a ration of tobacco." An enjoy-able meal was taken, but about midday the silence was broken by heavy enemy shelling on the north-east of the wood, also by " a very marked activity by enemy aeroplanes flying at a very low altitude, in some instances skimming the tops of the trees and firing their machine guns at intervals, but very much at random." About two o'clock orders came to advance and clear the wood of any of the enemy still left in it. After a short move forward the order was passed along to halt and lie down, " and it being a beautiful day for the month of November, as the sun shone brightly and fairly dry underneath, we would have been here about twenty minutes, and I thought it was one of the best fall outs we had that day." When the advance was resumed a check was soon caused by enemy machine gun and rifle fire, but " we got down to it " and " returned as much fire as we received, which silenced him for a little while." Eventually, on reaching a position some hundred and fifty yards from the north edge of the wood, the resistance became very severe indeed, and about this time the Highlander was sent out to the right flank to scout.

Scouting in the undergrowth of Bourlon Wood at a time when it was still uncleared of Germans was an occupation not without thrills. Soon a figure was seen for an instant, but it slipped behind a tree. " Having confidence I was unobserved I made for the tree as noiselessly as I possibly could, and to my surprise I seen no one." But almost simultaneously there was a hissed-out " Halt!" and a rifle muzzle protruded from the brake. A moment of considerable tension followed, broken by a cheery " Hullo, Jock, old boy. I thought you were a damned Jerry, but I noticed the kilt below your coat." The voice came from a 15th Hussar who had become separated from his regiment, but who now formally attached himself to the Highlander. " I'll attach myself to you, Jock; wherever you go I'm with you." It is like Ruth and Naomi in the Bible.

This happy woodland reunion was too much for a German sniper in the vicinity, who proceeded to pump out hate as fast as his weapon would permit. " A near thing, that, Jock " remarked the Hussar, to which his companion " answered in the affirmative." " In front

of us two Jerrys could be seen crawling to a thicket.
Without further counsel we both fired." One German
dropped his rifle and fled. The little scrap soon blazed
out again for a bit, but died away in that inconclusive
fashion characteristic of such encounters. The two now
decided to try to get back to the main body, and
started crawling through the underwood, but soon the
cavalryman grew impatient and suggested a tree-to-tree
series of rushes. "I did not approve of this sugges-
tion" says the man from across the Tweed, "but he
was headstrong and intended to carry it out. So I said,
'All right. Do as you like, but I will carry on the way
I have been doing.'" His native caution was quickly
justified. The Hussar reached one tree in safety:
before he could make the second a rifle cracked and he
"fell without a quiver." "A gallant little soldier" is
how the Highlander describes him; and so the unknown
Hussar passed out of the war. Not in a fierce cavalry
melée; just "shot like a rabbit in a ride," but doing his
simple duty no less than his forbears had done it in the
glories of Sahagun.

The Highlander managed to get back safely and
reported to his platoon commander, Second-Lieutenant
Allison, who decided to clear up the situation on the
right flank by sending out five men under the command
of the former. Before the little party had gone fifty
yards through scrub and bramble one man was fatally
shot through the head, and in little more than two
minutes three more were knocked out—two killed outright and one fatally wounded. After the loss of four
men the commander of the party made up his mind
"to get into a dip of ground where there was at least
nine inches of cover." However, the German snipers
soon discovered this little retreat, and the usual duel
ensued. "Still they didn't get me, and I done a bit
of twisting and riggling, and the dip being full of
thorns my knees were badly scratched, but I did not
feel this at the time. Still, if the end might appear to
be near I decided to die game, so I got into position

and fired several times." Just at this moment the
narrator's chum, Private C. Mackay, was killed outright, and immediately the Highlander saw red.
Jumping up, he waved his rifle in a fury of rage, and
was amazed to see, standing under a large oak, a group
of four Huns. "They looked at me in amazement,
more like startled deer than men." The Highlander
shook his clenched fist at them, shouting out, "Come
on, you dirty German bastards," but the amazed Huns
could only gape, until a few shots shook them from
their lethargy and laid two of them out. A German
machine gun now got going, and the survivors of the
scouting party made their way back to the road where
their platoon was at the moment.

The mention of a machine gun made the platoon
commander all agog to capture it. A sergeant, Rossi (?)
by name, volunteered to crawl up and snipe the Germans
from a flank while the remainder of the platoon kept up
a rapid fire. "Poor fellow; he only fired once, when
he fell dead." "Our officer was not discouraged with
this blow," and it was proposed to carry on with the
attack when the gathering darkness would favour
an attempt at a surprise. But now, "about two
hundred yards away, German Very lights were
being sent up, it appeared in the form of a
semi-circle; they were fired four at once. The officer
said, 'What are they up to now?' so I formed the conclusion that we were being surrounded, as any sane
man would have thought likewise; our party was only
seven men and officer, the latter a gallant soldier and
gentleman. So, after a discussion as to our procedure,
we decided to retire and form a line of resistance."
But—and, reader of 2025 A.D., from this judge the high
discipline of the 14th Argyll and Sutherland Highlanders a century ago—"before any man retired we was
to have the sanction of the captain, which happened to
be Captain Cooper."

Our Highlander was selected to find the captain
and explain the situation to him. The messenger soon

discovered that the thrills of the day were not yet over.
Starting down the road to the chalet " as fast as my legs
would carry me," he was soon confronted by fixed
bayonets and a peremptory order to halt. " Which I
did. ' Who are you'? they asked; and I told them
' an Argyll.' So they said, ' My God, Jock, you are
lucky that you are not riddled with bullets, as we have
been playing up this road the last half hour.' " Thus
the machine gunners. Captain Cooper was now found,
and at once gave his consent to the proposed short
retirement. The Highlander made his way back and
found his party hotly engaged with the enemy, but the
retirement was carried out safely in the dark to a position about two hundred yards away. And so, after a
strenuous day, the narrator took his turn of sentry-go,
and " The officer sent another fellow and I out from
time to time to listen, for our ears were better than our
eyes." That is how William Falconer spent November
24th, 1917.

Shortly before six o'clock the commander of the
119th Brigade sent a message to the 120th Brigade,
asking for two companies to be sent up to assist, and
a letter was also sent to the G.O.C. 3rd Guards Brigade,
asking for help. At this time the situation in the wood
was becoming precarious; news concerning the 121st
Brigade on the left was obscure, and from such information as came in it seemed that there was a large gap
between that brigade and the 36th Division; further,
with Fontaine still in German hands, the right flank
was by no means secure. In these circumstances the
brigadier decided to rush ammunition and water up to
the wood and to make doubly sure that visual communication with Graincourt was maintained (here it may
be said that it had been extraordinarily good since the
battle started, and there are eulogies upon the brigade
signalling officer—" one in a thousand " and " the best
signalling officer in France.") Advanced brigade headquarters would then be pushed up into the wood, and
every effort made to hold the ridge within it, pending

a further attack upon Fontaine. The brigade transport officer had orders to establish his dumps within the wood at all costs, a task which was duly carried out.

At eight o'clock the 119th Brigade was still holding the northern slope of the ridge within the wood, together with part of the southern outskirts of Bourlon village, and with patrols pushed out north of it. Half an hour later a welcome reinforcement arrived in the shape of two companies of the 11th King's Own from the 120th Brigade. Meanwhile, the commanding officer of the 3rd Coldstream Guards had opened one of the letters addressed to the Guards Brigade, and had begun to co-operate on the right with machine gun and rifle fire. The brigade major of the 119th Brigade now reported that he had been reconnoitring Bourlon village and found the situation "most obscure"; and about half past nine the 2nd Scots Guards arrived at the sunken road leading north-west from Anneux Chapel. Lieutenant-Colonel Benzie was told not to use this battalion in driblets, but to use the King's Own first; and, if possible, to employ the Scots Guards on the right flank, which, however, the situation did not permit.

In order to make up for the heavy losses experienced, and to provide a reserve, the 1st and 2nd Cavalry Battalions were placed under the G.O.C. 120th Brigade as a divisional reserve, and not to be employed without reference to the Division; about 11 p.m. the former of these units was directed to move up to the sunken road running westwards from the cross-roads which had originally formed the boundary between the 121st and 119th Brigades, and to come under the orders of the former. During the night the IV Corps promised twelve tanks to assist in further operations to be carried out upon the morrow.

The story of the day cannot close without an account of the good work of the engineers. The 229th Field Company was detailed for co-operation with the 119th Brigade during the attack on Bourlon Wood. On this November 24th, after the infantry had gone forward

K 2

and brigade headquarters had moved into the vaults
of Graincourt church, the 229th Field Company, which
had improvised tracks and crossings over the old No
Man's Land and front line system, moved up early
from Doignies via Havrincourt, and stood by in the
sunken road near Graincourt cemetery overlooking the
plain between that village and Anneux. By this time
the enemy artillery had fully reasserted itself, and
Graincourt and vicinity were shelled continuously.
The field company took cover under the bank of the
cemetery road without serious loss, pending orders to
move forward to the wood.

At 11.30 a.m., following a consultation at brigade
headquarters, Major Clark and Lieutenants Voce and
Borrie went forward across the open plain to reconnoitre the possibilities of getting up the wiring
material for the consolidation of the forward line. The
enemy shelling was very heavy, and there were many
casualties amongst the infantry who were moving up by
platoons in extended formation. On reaching the outskirts of the wood, the Royal Engineers officers at once
observed that there were ample supplies of barbed wire
and pickets available which could be used for the
consolidation, being material stacked by the enemy for
work on the rear Hindenburg Line, which ran at the
base of the wood parallel with the Cambrai road.

The position in the wood itself seemed to be somewhat obscure, and it was soon evident that owing to
the enormous thickness of the undergrowth, and the
absence of any paths or tracks outside the rides, that
the wiring in the dark of an outpost line would be a
difficult proposition. Furthermore, it was quite clear
that it was no use moving up until dusk. A move was
made from the cemetery at about 4.30 p.m., after a
meal of emergency rations, and the wood was reached
shortly before six o'clock. Major Clark and Lieutenant
Voce took a party of six sappers forward to act as
guides, while the remainder, under the direction of their
section officers, collected the wire and pickets. About

nine o'clock it was found possible to move the material up the rides, and three infantry posts were wired in front for a distance of about fifty yards, each with a double apron fence in two rows, making 16ft. deep in all.   The Royal Engineers withdrew at about 2.30 a.m., and returned to Havrincourt.

To anticipate somewhat, the following morning Major Clark and Lieutenant Borrie visited the wood again, and joined forces with the 224th Field Company, who had wired the left flank on the previous night.   There was intermittent fighting along the whole front, but, as the line seemed fairly stable, it was decided to continue the wiring at dusk.   Three sections of sappers again went to the wood and strengthened and extended the wiring of the posts; the programme was repeated on the night of November 26th.

And so ended the second day's fighting of the Battle of Bourlon Wood.   The 24th had been a day with some remarkable features, the chief of which was the attack by the 121st Brigade on Bourlon village without the knowledge, and, as a matter of fact, contrary to the orders, of Division.   This state of affairs had been brought about by the breakdown of cable communication; and, left without definite orders, General Campbell had decided to act upon the latest instructions given him, a decision which the divisional archives have recorded as the right and proper one.   Another curious feature was the state of affairs in Bourlon village.   At the close of the day the village was somewhat in the position of a nut within the jaws of a pair of nut-crackers, the levers of which were not tightly pressed; that is to say, there were troops of the 40th Division north, south and east of the village—and the village had been traversed—but the " nut " was still uncracked. The official despatches of Sir Douglas Haig, speaking of the operations of this day, record : " On this afternoon our infantry again attacked Bourlon village and captured the whole of it," but this statement does not accurately represent the condition of affairs.

By the evening of the 24th one thing had become
clear. The 40th Division was distinctly in the air,
and unless some progress could be made by the
divisions right and left its position might become
untenable. Further, the casualties had been severe;
there were no reserves left from the Division itself; the
fighting had been very strenuous for over forty-eight
hours; no division could keep up this kind of thing
indefinitely.

CHAPTER VIII.

BOURLON WOOD (*continued*).

WHEN during the night of November 24th/25th the firing had died down, and the troops of the 40th Division " had sunk on the ground overpowered, the weary to sleep and the wounded to die," the outstanding feature was that a gap in the German line had been almost, but not quite, effected. It was to secure such a gap that the operations had been undertaken; and the intention had been to pour a mass of cavalry through the fissure when once it had been created. But until Bourlon village had been unmistakably " made good " such a movement was impossible. Of all the divisions engaged since November 23rd the 40th Division alone had made any sensible advance, and it was unfortunate that the village of Bourlon happened to be located just at the spot, where otherwise a fine gap would have existed. There was, however, no intention of giving up the struggle, and at two o'clock on the morning of November 25th orders were issued from divisional headquarters for an attack upon the village, to be carried out by the 121st Brigade, assisted by twelve tanks. Inevitably such a bare statement will convey to the reader the idea of a brigade stretched out in line with the objective, to be attacked, in front of it. Such a presentation would, however, be quite inaccurate. Rather the disposition of the 121st Brigade resembled a ladder, and between two of the rungs was Bourlon village. A brief résumé of the dislocation of the brigade is essential before the narrative of the day's fighting is begun.

The topmost rung was formed by three companies of the 14th Highland Light Infantry holding the railway

north of Bourlon, headquarters and one company being
in rear in a house on the south-east of the village.
Inside the village were still many of the enemy, and at
1.10 a.m. Lieutenant-Colonel Battye had reported that
the Germans there were becoming more active, and that
his runners had to be accompanied by escorts of a dozen
men. The great difficulty experienced by the Highland
Light Infantry was to get rations forward to the three
companies in front; some success was at first achieved
by parties under Lieutenant Black, but a second attempt
was defeated by very heavy machine gun fire in the
village, and the effort had to be given up.

The next rung of the ladder was composed of three
companies—two from the 12th Suffolks and one from
the 20th Middlesex—" garrison of the front line," a
statement which appears to indicate the trenches just
south of Bourlon village. Behind these again, on the
Spur, was a company of the King's Own, with another
in support in a sunken road. These companies had
relieved five companies of the 12th Suffolks and 20th
Middlesex, which had been withdrawn beyond the
Sugar Factory. In the same area was the 120th
Machine Gun Company. As regards the dismounted
cavalry, placed at the disposal of the 121st Brigade,
accounts are at variance; brigade archives mention " a
dismounted cavalry battalion " and " two dismounted
cavalry brigades," while divisional records mention
" two cavalry battalions " in all. Of these, the 1st
Battalion, made up from the 2nd and 5th Dragoon
Guards and 11th Hussars, under Major Rome, was,
during the night moved up to reinforce the 121st Brigade. Then there was the 13th East Surrey Regiment
assembling, or assembled, at the south-western corner
of Bourlon Wood. It will be noticed that the 121st
Brigade had now become greatly changed in composition, for of the units above mentioned the Highland
Light Infantry, the King's Own, the East Surreys, and,
of course, the cavalry, were from other formations.

The fighting of the 121st Brigade on this November

25th was necessarily somewhat confused owing to the
task of attacking a village which was only nominally in
our hands—even three months later General Headquarters were under the delusion that " the whole of it
had been captured on the 24th "—and was wedged
inside the area occupied by the brigade. Possibly the
best method will be to follow, for the moment, the
fortunes of the 13th East Surrey Regiment, which was
the only complete and collected battalion in the day's
fighting.

In the previous chapter it has been related that
Lieutenant-Colonel Warden had received orders to mop
up Bourlon village and to assist the Highland Light
Infantry. We left him leading his battalion towards
the south-west corner of Bourlon Wood. He assembled
his battalion in the small hours of the morning of the
25th in the sunken road, which can be seen in the photograph skirting the trees on the left hand corner of the
wood. Here he explained his scheme to his company
commanders while German shells kept bursting all
around, and then led it to the position of assembly just
south of the village, which was reached and occupied
just before six o'clock. The 13th East Surreys had now
three companies in line, and to each was allotted a
definite sector of the village and a definite frontage.
The leading platoon of each company was to go straight
through the village under cover of darkness and join
the three companies of the Highland Light Infantry
on the railway, and to prolong the line westward. The
remaining three platoons of these three companies were
to mop up such portions of the village as lay within
their company sectors. The fourth company was posted
as battalion reserve at the north-west corner of the wood.
Zero hour was fixed for 6.15 a.m.

A dozen tanks were expected to arrive at 6 a.m.,
but by Zero none had put in an appearance.
Lieutenant-Colonel Warden, however, gave the order
for the advance to begin, and within a few minutes he
himself reached the headquarters of the 14th Highland

Light Infantry at a house on the south-east side of the village. The exact situation of this house, now occupied by Lieutenant-Colonels Warden and Battye, was E.12.d.5.6, for the information of those who wish to locate it on a "squared" map. Lieutenant-Colonel Warden was the bearer of a written message to Lieutenant-Colonel Battye from the General Officer Commanding 121st Brigade, timed 10.25 p.m. November 24th, and now delivered it, and at the same time he explained the scheme by which he had sent the 13th East Surreys forward. Lieutenant-Colonel Battye, who was the senior officer, expressed his approval of the plan.

Hardly was this conversation over when intense fire was directed against the house from the north, south and east, and it was now obvious that strong parties of the Germans were still in the northern part of the wood. The reserve company of the East Surreys was at once sent southward and eastward to round up the Germans attacking from the south. Just at this time the right "mopping up" company in the village was forced to withdraw and was brought into the wood, and the two East Surrey companies, reinforced by the reserve Highland Light Infantry company and Highland Light Infantry headquarters personnel, repelled the German attack, but so far no information was available as to the position of the 119th Brigade. As regards the remaining two companies, "A" and "B," of the East Surreys, which were engaged in mopping up the village or in sending a platoon each forward to the Highland Light Infantry on the railway, they were all involved in heavy fighting in the village, but the leading platoon of "A" Company managed to get through and to occupy a trench recently captured by the Highland Light Infantry.

Exactly at a quarter past seven, Lieutenant-Colonel Battye left the headquarters house to cross the road behind to see a Lewis gun in position, when a burst of machine gun fire swept down the road. A bullet

went through Lieutenant-Colonel Battye's heart; he was
just able to stagger back to headquarters and to tell
Lieutenant-Colonel Warden that he had been hit, when
he collapsed; although attended at once by the medical
officer of the Highland Light Infantry, he died within
a few minutes. The command now devolved upon
Lieutenant-Colonel Warden, who shortly afterwards
received a message—addressed to Lieutenant-Colonel
Battye—from the brigadier. This was timed 5.20 a.m.,
and was to the effect that, pursuant to divisional orders,
the Highland Light Infantry were to capture the re-
entrant of the railway north of Bourlon (as a matter of
fact, three companies had been there since the previous
afternoon) " in order to allow the cavalry to get forward
to-day," and there was also included information about
tanks and barrage and that the probable hour of attack,
apparently of the cavalry, would be 9 a.m.

These orders, however, did little to help matters.
The section of railway line was already held by the
Highland Light Infantry, but they were almost as
remote from their headquarters as if they had been on
the Rhine. There was a mention of tanks, but twelve
of these new engines of war had been expected at six
o'clock and had not, as yet, been seen. And the letting
loose a flood of cavalry would only be possible if
Bourlon village was cleared of Germans, which so far
had not been possible. Further, at the moment when
Lieutenant-Colonel Warden was reading these instructions his headquarters had just been heavily attacked,
and the enemy was massing for a fresh attempt. The
messenger bearing the above instructions from General
Campbell had, indeed, been passed by a messenger
from Lieutenant-Colonel Warden, giving the tidings of
the death of Lieutenant-Colonel Battye; stating that
the East Surreys were still engaged in " mopping up ";
informing the brigadier that the enemy had opened
heavy machine gun fire from the interior of the wood
and *from the village;* and reporting the non-arrival of
the tanks. This was received by General Campbell at

9 a.m., *i.e.*, the hour at which it was hoped that the deluge of cavalry would be set free. But the reader will probably have begun to realize that such scheme had definitely gone west, and that the East Surreys and the Highland Light Infantry would have their work cut out to hold their own.

It was impossible for Lieutenant-Colonel Warden to comply with the letter of the orders he had opened; the most he could do was to endeavour to carry out their spirit. One handicap under which he was now labouring was that touch had not been gained with the 119th Brigade in the wood, for, with the exception of the officer of the 18th Welch, who had appealed for assistance very early in the morning, no one of the 119th Brigade had been seen. At first sight it may seem strange that no touch had been gained, but what had happened was that Lieutenant-Colonel Warden's headquarters were not abreast of the line of the 119th Brigade; they were in front of it, or, rather, echeloned to the left front, and this fact, coupled with the thick undergrowth of the wood, and the presence of numerous small parties of Germans still in the wood, rendered patrolling difficult. Further, it must not be forgotten that at this hour (7.45 a.m.) on a morning in late November visibility under the dripping fir trees and in the thickets was exceedingly poor.

Lieutenant-Colonel Warden quickly made up his mind that the enemy was clearly in great strength in Bourlon village, and that any attempt to utilize the three companies under his hand in the dog fight which was going on there, or to try to push them forward to the railway line, was impossible until touch with, and support by, the 119th Brigade had been definitely obtained. He accordingly decided to try to join up with that brigade, but his intentions were forestalled by an advance in force of Germans from the east. An attack quickly developed against the house in which were Lieutenant-Colonel Warden's headquarters. The building was really north of the outpost line he had decided to hold—for these German attacks coming from the eastward were sure evidence that he must be in front of the line of the 119th Brigade—but he decided to maintain it and make of it a strong point. The east front of the house was at once loopholed and manned ; shortly afterwards the southern face was similarly treated, and snipers were posted in the upper parts of the house to fire through gaps in the tiles. The Germans used machine guns with telling effect, but the attack was met by rifle and Lewis gun fire both from the house and from the three companies in the wood, and was beaten off before nine o'clock with considerable loss to the enemy.

All this time the " dog-fight " was proceeding in the village, and the three companies of the Highland Light Infantry on the railway were still completely isolated. Several attempts were made to push through the village, two platoons being sent at 10.40 a.m. to support the " moppers up," but they were unable to make any progress, and were withdrawn, and now, along with small parties of the companies originally sent into the village, who had been driven back, were utilized for establishing a line within the wood. The Germans were still active, and many parties were observed reconnoitring the ridge in the wood, but were dispersed by fire. Thus the morning wore away, and early in the afternoon Lieutenant-Colonel Warden obtained touch with a representative of the commanding officer of the 12th South Wales Borderers of the 119th Brigade, from whom he gained a knowledge of the line held by that brigade. This was all to the good, and Lieutenant-Colonel Warden now joined up with it by continuing the outpost line just south of the house where he had been, to the west edge of the wood, but the house was still retained as a strong point. A refused flank was also made upon the left, and the position generally organized in depth, the digging being done with entrenching tools, which were the only ones available. About this time Lieutenant-Colonel Warden endea-

voured, by written message sent by runners, to ascertain
from the 12th Suffolks, 20th Middlesex, and 11th King's
Own their detailed positions, but no reply was received,
the runners probably having become casualties. Late
in the afternoon an officer of the 121st Trench Mortar
Battery arrived with two mortars, which were used with
appreciable effect in subduing the enemy's fire.

Shortly before dusk the enemy began to use *minen-
werfer*, but, as it was too dark for him to range on
the headquarters house, Lieutenant-Colonel Warden
resolved to remain there for the night. Enemy snipers
had all day been busy from houses and trees, and from
reports from the village it was clearly inadvisable to
employ any further strength to reduce it. During the
evening a message was received from the brigadier to
the effect that the Division would be relieved by the
62nd Division that night, although this good news was
qualified by the statement that the relief was not to
begin until some tanks should arrive, and, pushing
through Bourlon, relieve the three companies on the
railway line. These companies were now obviously in
a precarious situation. When darkness fell, several
attempts were made to get into touch with them, but
the messengers were never able to get through; every
road through the village was carefully watched by the
Germans and covered with machine gun fire on the
slightest provocation. 'Apparently, about six o'clock,
some units of the relieving brigade began to arrive.
The order had been that the relief was not to begin
until the tanks arrived, but these did not put in an
appearance either then or throughout the night. In
these circumstances it was realized that no good purpose
would be served by having two lots of troops congested
in one spot, and accordingly one company of the East
Surreys was relieved and withdrawn. The night was
therefore one of expectation; a constant looking out
for tanks which did not appear.

It was about this time, too, that Captain Gaffikin
arrived from the field ambulance, bringing with him some

stretcher bearers. The assistance was badly needed, as
the battalion stretcher bearers were quite worn out,
having to carry for six miles over shell-strewn wood and
open country; in this way the most they could achieve
was two trips in the twelve hours. Captain Gaffikin had
come up against orders, but he "felt it his duty," and
the arrival of his party relieved the congestion at the
headquarters house to a great extent. Wounded were
removed as quickly as possible, and "the dead
were got out of the way; it was impossible to bury
them." A grave was, however, dug for Lieutenant-
Colonel Battye, who was laid to rest in the garden of
the house, and a rough cross erected over it by the
pioneers. Lieutenant-Colonel Battye was a Regular
officer, who possibly may not at all times have realized
the difficulties experienced by those whose soldiering
was numbered but in months. But in more than one
diary or narrative there is a tribute to him as a man.
"With all his faults he was a good soldier: a braver
man never walked; and he could handle troops."
Could there be a nobler epitaph?

Save for a series of false alarms the night was without serious incident. "Altogether, one might say the
night was calm, except for sniping, machine guns, and
Very lights," which shows that calmness is a relative
term. Although the withdrawal was to be contingent on
the arrival of the tanks, none of these put in an
appearance during the night.

To turn now to the 119th Brigade in the wood.
Early in the morning of the 25th Lieutenant-Colonel
Plunkett was counter-attacked, and two companies of
Scots Guards, followed later by the remaining two,
were thrown in on the right to stem the tide. "Needless to say, the Guards did all that could be expected
of them." Heavy, if desultory, fighting continued,
and about noon the officer commanding the 4th
Grenadier Guards reported for orders, and was
requested to lead his battalion to the sunken road
leading north-west from Anneux Chapel, his probable

rôle being to reinforce the right flank in case of a counter-attack. Shortly after this the brigade major went up to the front line, "as a whisper had come through that something had happened on the left, but this was not authenticated." About four o'clock he returned with reassuring news. The situation was better than he had expected. With the extra troops available, commanding officers were confident that they could not only hold their own, but were in a position to inflict losses on the enemy.

Orders had, however, been received that the brigade was to be relieved by units of the 62nd Division, and about half-past two Brigadier-General Bradford, of the 186th Infantry Brigade, had come up to arrange the relief. This began at 5.30 p.m., and the brigade records, with a fine gesture of precision, say that " it was completed at 11.16 p.m." All through the operation the enemy was active, and a really serious counter-attack took place about eleven o'clock. However, the wearied 119th Brigade disentangled itself from the wood, and was met by guides from brigade headquarters, who led the battalions to Anneux Chapel. The shelling was severe; the casualties to men and animals were numerous; and the evacuation of the wounded was a matter of very great difficulty. But the medical officers at regimental aid posts in the wood and the medical personnel throughout as usual " behaved with extraordinary gallantry."

Meanwhile the 121st Brigade, or, at any rate, the 13th East Surreys and the 14th Highland Light Infantry, was held up by the non-arrival of the expected tanks. At 8.30 a.m., on the 26th, a search party was sent out, but failed to find them. Two hours later Lieutenant-Colonel Warden reported to brigade headquarters that the relief had not yet been effected, and asked for orders. Owing to a chain system of runners which had been arranged, this message was carried quickly and without casualty to Graincourt. The enemy, on his part, repeatedly showed signs of attacking, and in the afternoon began to register on Lieutenant-Colonel Warden's headquarters.   As the house was being gradually demolished it became necessary to leave it.   But this could not be done until dusk on account of the machine gun and rifle fire on all sides.   Towards five o'clock the headquarters personnel of the 13th East Surreys and the 14th Highland Light Infantry were withdrawn in parties of three from the house, and headquarters were established in a dug-out in the wood.   In anticipation of an attack upon the ridge at night two more lines of trenches had been dug facing north and extending through the wood.   Repeated efforts to obtain communication with, and to send food and ammunition to the Highland Light Infantry companies on the railway line had failed.   All that could now be hoped was that a further forward movement by the 62nd Division might effect their relief.   Unfortunately, the hope was not fulfilled, and the majority of those three gallant companies were captured by the enemy.

In order to clear the front for this projected attack by the 62nd Division, it was decided to withdraw the troops under Lieutenant-Colonel Warden's command. Accordingly, before dawn, on November 27th, so soon as the leading troops of the 62nd Division had passed through, Lieut.-Colonel Warden's advanced troops were collected under cover near his headquarters dug-out. Beginning at noon, all were withdrawn in parties of ten each, under an officer and a non-commissioned officer, to the farewell of heavy artillery, aeroplane and machine gun fire.   And a junction of the brigade with the 40th Division was then effected in the Hindenburg Support Line north of Havrincourt, except the artillery, the engineers, and the 120th and 244th Machine Gun Companies, which remained at the disposal of the 62nd Division.   Divisional headquarters had meanwhile been shifted to Neuville, and the troops were moved partly by road and partly by train to the Basseux area.   Refitting was at once put in hand, but before the month closed the Division had been transferred to the VI Corps and a warning order had been received concerning the relief of the 16th Division.

Thus ended the share of the 40th Division in the Bourlon fighting, an operation which will for ever stand out in the records even of a war distinguished by incidents of endurance, fortitude and resolution. " In years to come," wrote the army commander, " I shall remember with unqualified satisfaction that the capture of Bourlon Wood was performed by the splendid division with which I have been associated for some time." The Commander-in-Chief himself personally informed the divisional commander " that he wished all ranks of the 40th Division to be congratulated on their success." Forty-two machine guns were captured from the enemy, and the prisoners numbered over 700. Seven officers were awarded the Distinguished Service Order. Forty-four Military Crosses were conferred. Two bars were also given, and Captain Redding, of the Suffolks, received a second bar. Twenty-seven Distinguished Conduct Medals proved the worth of the non-commissioned officers and men. Such a record was not achieved without sacrifice. The casualties during the operations amounted to 172 officers and 3,191 other ranks.

It was an infantry battle. That arm bore the brunt of the casualties, and upon that arm practically all the decorations were conferred. But the infantry was enabled to carry out its strenuous task only by the assistance of the other arms to which the divisional records pay tribute in the following terms :—

" No account of these operations could be complete without some mention of the excellent work done by the divisional artillery, under Brigadier-General G. Nicholson, C.M.G., whose co-operation with the infantry was everywhere successful. Among the Royal Artillery personnel many instances of individual gallantry may be cited. For example, on November 30th Sergeant (A./B.S.M.) C. Jolly, D/181st Brigade, Royal Field Artillery, kept his battery in action from

9.30 a.m. until dusk—during which time eighteen wagon-loads of ammunition were brought up and unloaded—and showed a complete disregard of personal danger throughout. Again, when the left group headquarters, 40th Divisional Artillery, were established at Graincourt, during the operations of November 23rd to 25th, telephone lines connected to the group were being continually broken. That communication with the various brigades was successfully maintained is largely due to the splendid work done by Lieutenant J. C. Lloyd, Royal Field Artillery, to Sergeant W. A. Walker, and to the non-commissioned officers and men of the Royal Engineer sub-section of the 178th Brigade, Royal Field Artillery. In this connection may also be mentioned the work of Sapper (A./Lce.-Corpl.) R. Evans, 40th Divisional Signal Company, Royal Engineers, who laid and repaired telephone wires under heavy and continuous fire for three days, regardless of personal risk.

" Great credit must be given to the divisional machine and Stokes mortar gunners, whose conduct throughout the operations was deserving of the highest praise. One example of each may be considered typical. On November 24th, when his section officer was killed, Sergeant H. McCarthy, 121st Machine Gun Company, crawled up to him under heavy fire, took his maps and orders, and carried on in charge of the section. He was himself shortly afterwards severely wounded in the thigh, but despite the fact that he was bleeding freely and scarcely able to walk, remained in charge and handled his section with great ability, refusing to have his wound dressed until ordered to return. Again, on November 26th, Second-Lieutenant G. Henderson, 21st Middlesex Regiment (attached 121st Trench Mortar Battery) kept two Stokes mortars continuously in action until all available ammunition was expended, afterwards withdrawing his guns and teams under very heavy fire.

" Mention must also be made of the invaluable

assistance rendered by the Royal Engineers under
Lieutenant-Colonel A. Baylay, D.S.O. Their early
pioneer work upon the roads greatly facilitated the
passage of transport, and they afterwards succeeded in
digging and wiring a trench through the centre of
Bourlon Wood, which was converted into a strong
position and proved of great value to the 62nd Division.

" That the ceaseless and plentiful supply of ammunition and rations never failed was due not only to the
excellence of the divisional arrangements, but also to
the industry and zeal of the divisional train (Major
Lake) and ammunition column (Lieutenant-Colonel
Stewart), and to the indefatigable efforts of individual
Army Service Corps drivers, who performed their
duties with admirable coolness under the most trying
conditions.

" Last, but not least, must a tribute of praise be paid
to the splendid work of the field ambulances. Two
N.C.Os., Sergeant A. McDougall and Sergeant-Major
F. Hulbert, both of the 137th Field Ambulance, Royal
Army Medical Corps, worked without ceasing to
evacuate the wounded from the advanced dressing
station at Graincourt, under heavy shell fire, and
exposed themselves fearlessly throughout. Here, too,
it may be added, the Rev. Frank Stone, C.F., set a fine
example of heroism to all ranks by working incessantly
under fire, tending the wounded and vying with the
Rev. C. Close, C.F., in unremitting devotion to duty
in the face of considerable danger."

The opening days of the Battle of Cambrai had set the
joybells ringing in London, and, coming as it did not
many weeks after Londoners had experienced a really
bad doing from air raids, the jubilation over what promised to be a break through was immense. But the
success was short lived. After the great initial advance
the battle began to " barnacle," and, although the
splendid action of the 40th Division in capturing
Bourlon Wood caused hope to rise anew, ultimate
victory was not achieved. The German commander,

von Marwitz, gathered sixteen fresh divisions and started to win back what had been lost. Taking a leaf from the British book the Germans dispensed with a preliminary bombardment, and although without any tanks brought off an undoubted surprise on November 30th. The British right was quickly pushed in, with the result that Bourlon Wood became absolutely untenable, and a retirement was essential. Out of sixty square miles and fourteen villages the British retained but sixteen and three respectively, while the Germans had secured seven square miles and two villages held by us before the battle began.

In this great German counter-attack the infantry came on in thick masses, and with such disregard of danger that several accounts available to the historian suggest that the enemy had been doped. At any rate, they gave a target almost unbelievable, and one which had probably not been presented since the great onrush at Mons. It is the proud boast of " D " 178 Battery that it was the first to spot the advance, and it lost no time in taking advantage of an opportunity so rare. " We fired two rounds of smoke shell per gun into the brown. Then the battery proceeded to fire ' gun fire,' using H.E. shell with 106 instantaneous fuze. The Boche was in full view, and our gunners were aiming over open sights, the only occasion I know of for 4.5 howitzers to do so. Every gun in the neighbourhood, I should imagine, slewed round on to this target. The Boche was stopped. How they were ever driven on I can't imagine, unless they were doped, as was rumoured."

After the relief of the 40th Division by the 62nd, the 40th Divisional Royal Engineers and the pioneers also remained in the line, and, as conditions gradually became more defined, it was decided that a combined wiring operation on a large scale should be carried out : for this purpose the 231st Field Company was detailed to co-operate with the 229th, along with two companies of the 12th Yorkshire Pioneers.

The operation was fixed for the night of November 27th, and on the morning of that day Major Clarke (officer commanding 229th Field Company), Major Johnson, V.C. (officer commanding 231st Field Company), and Captain Harris (commanding the two companies of pioneers), proceeded to make a daylight reconnaissance of the wood. It was a fine day, with good visibility. The officers reached the Cambrai road shortly before ten o'clock, and proceeded up the main centre ride on foot, after calling at battalion head-quarters in the quarry. A halt was made about half way up the ride at the kiosk, this being a shooting box, a relic of the days of peace. The company head-quarters were situated in the basement, and information was obtained regarding the approximate position of the posts and the present whereabouts of the enemy.

On reaching the main cross-road which led through the wood from Bourlon village to Fontaine-Notre-Dame, the party turned to the left, and followed the road in the direction of Bourlon, keeping well down in the drain. According to the map, they were then about 100 yards behind the line of the forward posts. The three climbed out of the drain, over the bank, and turned at right angles in a northerly direction to where an outpost was believed to be. After traversing a distance of about twenty-five yards, a party of eight to twelve Germans sprang up at a distance of about forty yards and fired a volley, killing Captain Harris on the spot. Major Johnson and Major Clark sank in the scrub and worked their way back to the road, and under cover of the bank pushed on towards Bourlon village, with the idea of doubling back by a side path shown on the map, which would bring them approximately to the position where Captain Harris must be. In the meantime, however, the Germans moved their position and suddenly appeared again, firing a further volley, one fatal shot catching Major Johnson through a vital spot in the neck. Major Clark regained the road in safety by wriggling backwards through the scrub, pursued the whole time by a constant stream of bullets. He returned to company headquarters at the kiosk, and they, though unable to furnish a Lewis-gun detachment at the moment, undertook to send out a search party at dusk to bring in Major Johnson and Captain Harris.

This unfortunate occurrence considerably delayed the reconnaissance for the wiring, but enough information was obtained to enable the approaches and line to be mapped out. The supply of wire and pickets from the rear Hindenburg Line at the foot of the wood was exhausted, and a large party of infantry and pioneers was organized to carry up material which was brought on G.S. wagons from Havrincourt to the west side of Graincourt. Unfortunately, two of the wagons were knocked out by a shell at the Graincourt dump. The wiring carrying-party commenced their journey at 4 p.m. from the supply dump formed at the Anneux cross-roads, the 229th Field Company officers and non-commissioned officers acting as guides for the combined forces, consisting of the 229th and 231st Field Companies, with " A " and " C " Companies of the 12th Yorkshire Pioneers, in charge of Lieutenant Crosby.

The weather deteriorated considerably before night-fall, and the going in the wood was very heavy. Shrapnel continually burst overhead, causing numerous casualties to the party. The coils of barbed wire, each containing 56lb., were slung on poles, two men carrying one coil, and it says much for the spirit of the men, already tired out with four days' fighting and shortage of sleep, that an unusually large proportion of the material was delivered on to the site. The actual wiring began shortly before nine o'clock, and after about four and a half hours' strenuous work a complete double-apron fence, in duplicate, extended from the junction with the left division on the outskirts of Bourlon village, to the junction with the Guards Division on the Bourlon—Fontaine-Notre-Dame road. The total length of the line was just over 1,150 yards, this including the wire put up on the previous nights.

It was for this exploit that the following message was transmitted to the C.R.E., 40th Division :—

" The G.O.C. 62nd Division wishes to convey his appreciation of the fine work of the 40th Divisional Engineers and 12th Yorkshire Regiment (Pioneers) in Bourlon Wood, 29-11-17."

As a division, the 40th shared neither in the swift opening phase nor in the swift *débâcle* of all the high hopes founded upon it. It was put in at a critical time and given a stiff task. It did what it was asked, and handed over Bourlon Wood intact to its relief. As a remembrance of its heroism and success the acorn and oak leaves were added to the divisional badge and, displayed upon the diamond, typifying Bourlon Wood and conveying to heralds yet unborn the achievements of November, 1917. The success had been achieved against a resolute and enterprising enemy. There had come into fashion amongst armchair critics and politicians by 1917 a tendency to depreciate the fighting worth of the enemy. Those who were in the front line knew better. The Hun had many objectionable qualities, but lack of " guts " was not one of them.

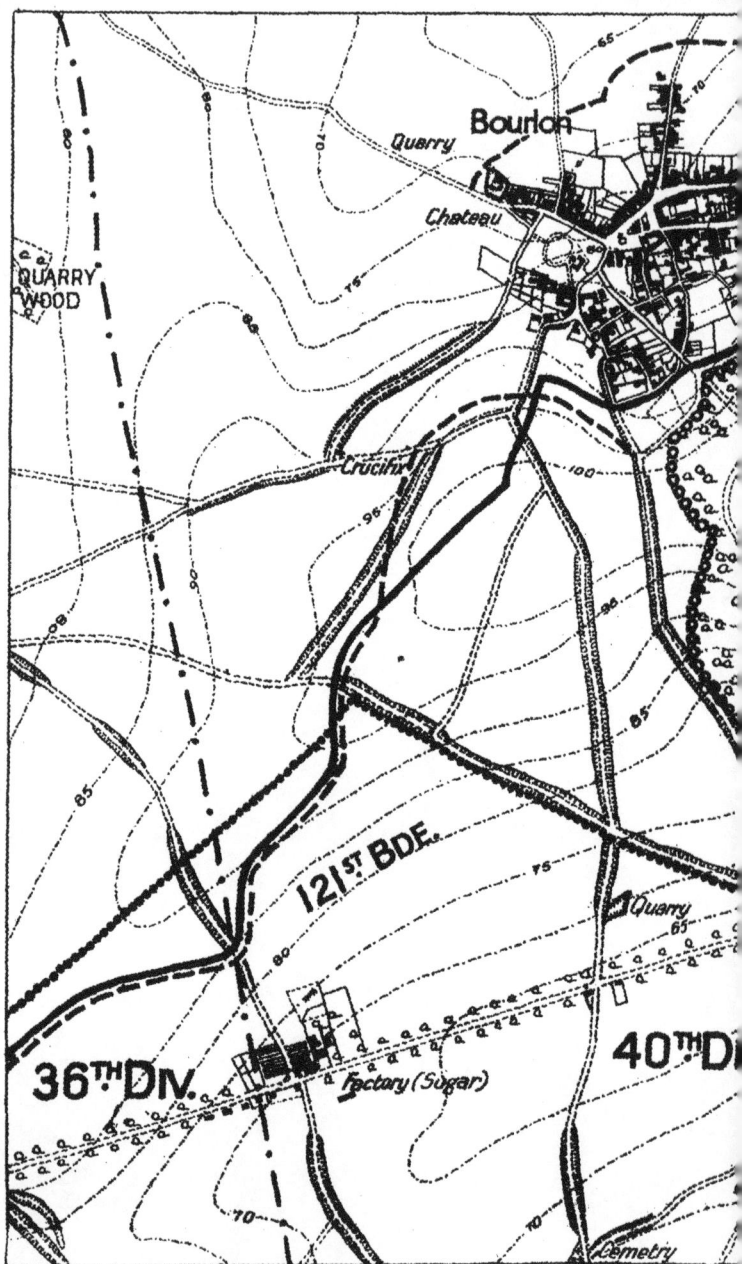

BOURLO[N]

REFERENCES

Original line as taken over from
62ⁿᵈ Div. on night of 22ⁿᵈ 23ʳᵈ Nov.

Most advanced line as held on
evening of 24ᵗʰ November.

Final line as handed over t[o]
62ⁿᵈ Div. on night of 25 26 [...]

Boundaries between Divisi[ons]

Inter Brigade Boundary.

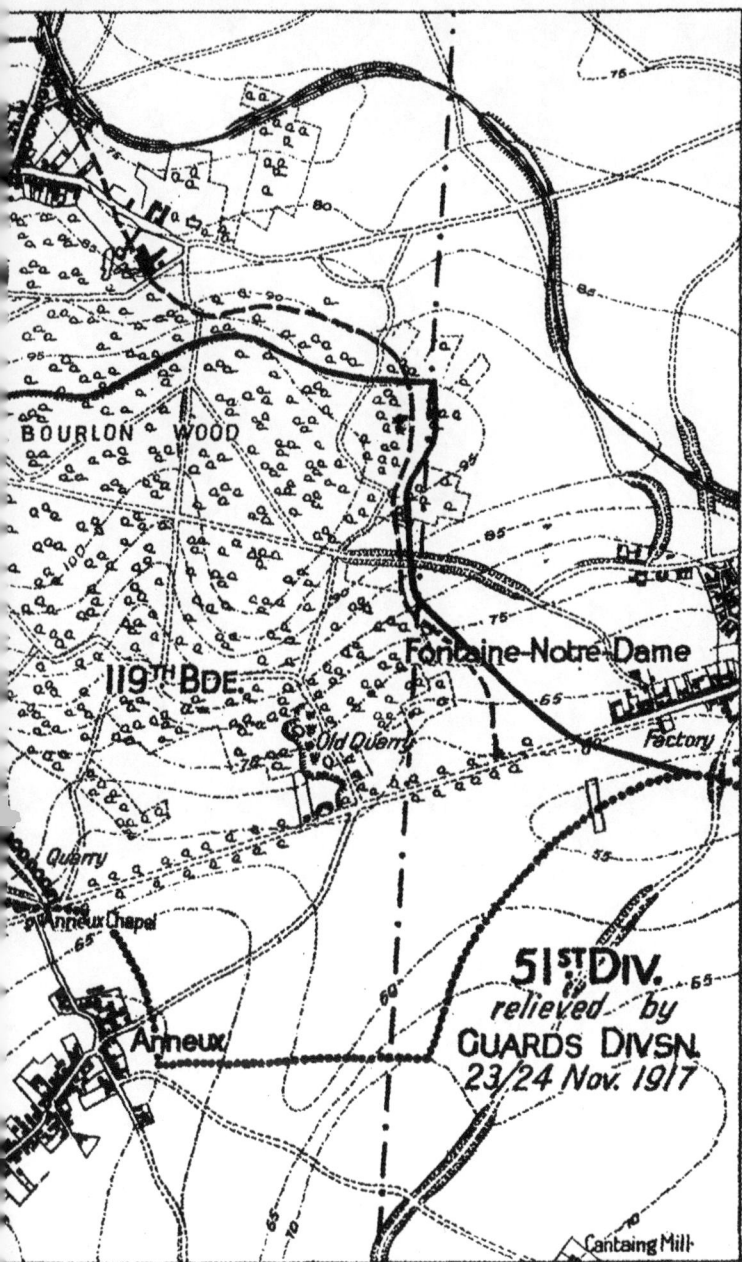

WOOD

BOURLON WOOD

119TH BDE.

Fontaine-Notre-Dame

Old Quarry

Factory

Quarry

Anneux Chapel

Anneux

51ST DIV.
relieved by
GUARDS DIVSN.
23/24 Nov. 1917

Cantaing Mill

To face page 152.

Scale 1:20,000, 1inch to ·3156 mile.

yds. 1000   500   0   1000 yds.

CHAPTER IX.

THE WINTER OF 1917—18.

AFTER the Battle of Cambrai the 40th Division became part of the VI Corps, one of the series of changes which within a month had made the Division successively part of the III, V, IV and VI. For a few days there was the possibility that the 40th would be sucked back into the vortex caused by the great—and successful—German counter-attack; but after a succession of orders and counter-orders it was rumoured that the 40th Division would relieve the 16th in the trenches at Bullecourt. This turned out to be true, and the relief was carried out on December 3rd, the divisional headquarters being at Behagnies, whence they were transferred on the 14th of the month to Gomiecourt. A captured document brought to light about this time mentioned that the 40th Division had been "annihilated" at Bourlon, and doubtless the Germans were later surprised to find that it had again come up smiling.

In the neighbourhood of La Fontaine the Division found itself in possession of a slice of the Hindenburg Line which had been bitten out of that colossal defensive system, and here was a portion of the famous shaft tunnel. This tunnel was hewn out of the solid chalk to a depth of some thirty feet or more, and when the Germans were driven from it a support to our front line was provided ready made. The trench—or tunnel, as it is indifferently called—was said to extend for some seventeen miles, and was fitted throughout with electricity for lighting. Only a portion had actually been captured, and the ends had been blocked, so that the Germans were able to deny the use of the electric light. Nevertheless, part of the Division had a very dry and comfortable support line, the only objection being the necessity of ensuring means of rapid exit in case of a gas attack. The line was on high ground, which favoured observation, and, what was no less important, rendered the approaches dead, so that movement in rear could be carried out safely, or comparatively so, in broad daylight.

The weather during December was especially inclement, the fine summer being succeeded by a particularly cold winter. Heavy snow fell, and this, freezing on the duck-boards, rendered progress difficult in the trenches, and later, when a thaw came, the sides of the trenches invariably collapsed, and in places it was difficult to keep the water down even with constant pumping. " Trench feet " were the natural result. It was considered that a hot drink, available at any hour of the day or night, would keep up the circulation of the men in the trenches and thus minimize the casualties—and they were numerous—of trench feet. An ingenious method was evolved by the commanding officer and the pioneer-sergeant of the 21st Middlesex. Empty petrol tins were inserted in wooden cases of slightly larger dimensions, the intervening space being packed with asbestos, cotton waste, or any other available non-conductor. These improvised Thermos flasks were fitted with D's to admit of them being carried on a man's back, attached to the ordinary webbing equipment. It was found that tea remained hot within the tins for ten to twelve hours, and each post in the front line of the battalion was furnished with its great Thermos, replaced constantly by a fresh one. When the divisional commander visited the battalion headquarters of the 21st Middlesex he was so impressed by the excellence of a cup of tea thus provided, that he urged all commanding officers of the Division to adopt the system.

The successful German counter-attack which had robbed the British of the fruits of their great initial

success in the Battle of Cambrai had produced a
general feeling of uneasiness. More than one diary
consulted for this period of December, 1917, contains
expressions such as " much wind," " windy," and " a
certain amount of wind last night." It was not, however, until the 12th that the Germans made any serious
effort near Bullecourt. They attacked at 6 a.m., just
before dawn, the bulk of their effort being directed
against the 3rd Division, on the 40th's right. " We
all nipped out of bed, and hung about waiting for
news." About seven o'clock the S.O.S. went everywhere, and every available gun was busy. 'Apparently
the Germans had attacked the 3rd Division in force
and succeeded in occupying a trench. The attack
against the 40th was confined to artillery and smoke
barrages, which turned out to be merely feints; but
they were successful to the extent that they kept the
40th Division guessing as to whether a real attack was
to take place or not.

During the afternoon of the 14th the divisional
headquarters were moved two miles to Gomiecourt,
being located in the village château, which, strange to
say, was the only house standing. It was not particularly healthy to occupy any house which stood up in
ostentatious solidity amid neighbouring ruin—for such
houses had a knack of suddenly going sky-high even
six months after the gentle Hun had left. The divisional commander was rather too old a bird to be taken
in by such a confidence trick, and said so frankly, but
on being assured that the sappers of the last division
had removed *several tons* of dynamite, gun-cotton,
etc., from the cellars, it was considered that the château
might be regarded as having a clean bill of health, and
headquarters were duly installed.

On the next day there took place the chief piece of
offensive work carried out by the Division during the
month. It was a raid by a party from the 19th Royal
Welch Fusiliers, with the object of clearing the enemy
out of portions of their support line opposite

Bullecourt and of destroying dug-outs. The raiders
were divided into two parties of 2 officers and 44 other
ranks and 2 officers and 38 respectively, each party
being supported by a platoon, and 24 sappers
under an officer to do the demolition work.   There also
co-operated the 119th and 244th Machine Gun
Companies and the 119th and 121st Trench Mortar
Batteries.   The raiders attacked the German trench
just north of Bullecourt, from both sides, at 3 p.m.,
after a heavy bombardment, chiefly from trench
mortars.   The enemy were late in putting down their
barrage, which fell chiefly on the left front of the
Division.   The Huns fought very stubbornly and
refused to surrender, consequently some very hot
scrapping took place.   They were eventually overpowered, and a good number disappeared into the dug-
outs, which were blown up by the sappers.   A couple
of prisoners were taken, while the casualties in the
Fusiliers were 4 killed and 16 wounded.   Two " pill
boxes " were blown up, and the 40th Division was
enabled to consolidate a trench behind the German line
for the time being.   The corps commander sent his
congratulations to Brigadier-General Crozier on the
success of this smart little operation by the 119th
Brigade.

Although there were not the mud and slime and
general ruin of the Somme battlefield which the
Division had experienced the previous December, the
conditions at the end of 1917 were uncomfortable
enough.   There were constant alarms and a tenseness
which had not been experienced on the Somme, where
the Germans had had their bellyful of fighting and
were thinking chiefly of retirement.   The weather, too,
in December, 1917, was very trying; " snowing and
very cold " is a typical entry.   By Christmas, however,
there was a respite to the continuous policy of attack
and advance which had lasted for nine months.   It
was officially announced that a defensive policy was to
be the key-note for some time to come, and that steps

were to be taken to devise a system which would give the best results in case of strong attacks by the enemy. As a general principle three zones were arranged, a " forward," " battle " and " rear " zone, and for these defensive preparations were made in the following order of priority—wire : shell-proof accommodation : communications : and earthworks. Of these wire was the most important : " Wire, wire and more wire is to be put in front of our lines."

Thus closed 1917, and thus passed the second Christmas of the 40th Division in France. No longer a new division, or the " Forgotten Fortieth " as the men had once called it, but the Division which will ever be remembered as the victors of Bourlon Wood.

The New Year was ushered in with war and peace. As for war, the 1st of January was marked by a rather heavy *strafe* by the British artillery; and, as for peace, on the same day some sixteen misguided Germans started a trek across No Man's Land, apparently with the object of fraternizing. Fired on heavily and continuously, these doves returned to their ark in double time. A day or two afterwards the enemy became active with his artillery—the prelude to an attack made upon the 5th. This was carried out by some 200 to 250 Germans against the centre sector, which was at that time held by the 121st Brigade. In one spot the Germans got through and penetrated to the support line, but a counter-attack was carefully organized by Major Lloyd, temporarily in command of the 12th Suffolks, and the enemy were driven out, the front line re-established, and 18 Germans taken prisoner. All this, however, was not the work of a day. The Germans came on again on the three succeeding days, but were repulsed each time.

The expected thaw set in on January 10th, and at once the conditions in the front line trenches became very bad. A German prisoner had stated that a strong attack was about to be launched almost at once, but the ground over which it would have to be made had become so bad that nothing on a large scale was likely. Rain had now begun to fall heavily, and the trouble was that if it continued with the frost still in the ground the trenches would feel it, as is indeed borne out by the record : " January 15.—Trenches falling in owing to thaw." The weariness and discomfort of a winter in France were now pronounced, although there is nothing important to record beyond " the usual daily bombardment on both sides and an occasional raid organized by the commander of the 119th Brigade." The snipers of the Division were particularly active and successful, having recently been supplied with a fresh lot of snipers' rifles to replace others which had become somewhat inaccurate through wear and tear. Thus the winter of 1917-18 wore on ; four days in the front line, four in support and four in reserve ; baths for the men, when available ; change of clothing ; musketry ; an occasional battalion parade, and gaffs.

February, 1918, is memorable in the annals of the Division for the reorganization of the infantry brigades which came into effect officially upon the 16th. Owing to the severe drain on the man-power of the country the Army Council had decided to reduce the number of battalions in a brigade from four to three, or, in other words, to have a division on a nine instead of a twelve-battalion basis. Consequently, in the 40th, as in all other divisions, it was necessary that some battalions should be disbanded—or, rather, broken up. The battalions selected for destruction were to be those recruited from districts whence it was impossible to comb out more men, and the lot fell on the 19th Royal Welch Fusiliers, the 12th South Wales Borderers, the 17th Welch Regiment, and the 11th King's Own Royal Lancaster Regiment. Thus these fine battalions, whose record has been but too imperfectly recorded in these pages, vanish from them henceforth. In a touching letter of farewell to them General Ponsonby declared : " Although the battalions in which you have served so long in this country are to be broken up, the

memory of their splendid achievements will never fade.
The record of your past services, the fine fighting spirit
you have invariably displayed, and your constant
determination to maintain the high traditions of your
battalions, not only redound to your credit and to that
of the 40th Division, but will add still further to the
glorious reputation of your regiments."

The loss of these units necessitated the regrouping
of those that were left; *plus* the 10th/11th Highland
Light Infantry, which had recently joined the Division.
The reorganization took the following form :—

    119th Brigade.—13th East Surrey Regiment,
18th Welch Regiment, and 21st Middlesex
Regiment.

    120th Brigade.—10th/11th Highland Light
Infantry, 14th Highland Light Infantry, and 14th
Argyll and Sutherland Highlanders.

    121st Brigade.—12th Suffolk Regiment, 13th
Yorkshire Regiment, and 20th Middlesex
Regiment.

The 120th, from its composition, received the title
of the 120th (Highland) Brigade, in spite of the fact
that the war diarist—apparently from south of the
Tweed—refers to it merely as " a Scotch brigade." The
surplus of commanding officers now " gave rise to all
sorts of problems . . . X——and Y—— are now
both at a loose end, both extraordinarily good officers
. . . it is a case of *embarras de richesse.*"

An erroneous impression is often gathered from war
histories, namely, the idea that every unit which
crossed overseas was engaged in more or less desperate
hand-to-hand fighting from that moment till the
armistice. Within the limits of a history it is so difficult—if not impossible—to do justice to the actual
narratives of battle that the less strenuous periods in
the line are sometimes dismissed with a mere reference
to " quiet period," " usual routine," and so forth. But
the reader who has had no actual experience of
conditions in France, and in much less than a hundred

years every reader of this volume will be in that
category, will certainly find a difficulty in visualizing
those " off " days which were, of course, necessarily
in the majority. A survey of the Intelligence Summary of the Division for a typical " quiet " day will,
perhaps, be of assistance. The summary was an
unemotional *précis*, issued daily, of the chief occur-
rences of the previous twenty-four hours, ending with
8 a.m. of the day of issue. It came very soon to have
a " sealed pattern " form of style and matter. It began
always with Operations, *i.e.*, the operations of our side,
and dealt with the infantry of the front line first. Thus
we learn that the right brigade had managed to put a
belt of wire twenty yards long at a place where a devas-
tating Hun shell had opened a nasty gap a few days
earlier, and we are told that the left brigade has
improved the communication trench from Dead Dog
Corner to Bunny Hug Trench. A patrol of this
brigade had also stumbled across a dead Hun in No
Man's Land during the night, and had carted him in :
we shall learn all about him when we come to Identifications, but we must finish Operations first. From
the infantry we pass to the machine guns : they have
had a very quiet twenty-four hours, but just to keep
their hands in they performed for five minutes—from
3.33 p.m. to 3.38 p.m.—on the enemy's defences in the
neighbourhood of R.16.d.5.3, which has interest of
its own but may leave the reader of 2025 rather cold.
The light trench mortars had almost an entire holiday :
a call was made upon them, but their services were
rung off before things got going. The artillery just
kept up a gentlemanly pin-pricking which never
degenerated into a vulgar *strafe*, but for five minutes
there was a burst of demoniac activity from one battery,
the reason for which we shall see later.

Section II tells us all that is to be told of Hostile
Attitude and Activity. It begins with Artillery;
and, this typical day being a " quiet " one, the
Summary merely states coldly that " there was a certain

amount of activity from 0021 to 0023 hours," with a reference to the particular projectile used; or there may be a little more detail, which may mean that divisional headquarters were tickled up. From hostile artillery the Summary switches over easily to Movement, and here there will be traced a co-ordination with the sudden burst of our guns referred to in the preceding paragraph.

The Summary says, perhaps, that " enemy movement was observed during the forenoon at ———," and mentions a conglomeration of letters and figures which pans out as a piece of ground visible about two miles from the front line. Possibly a lynx-eyed company officer has spotted through his glasses a bevy of Germans moving suspiciously and crouching under walls and hedges. The forward observing officer of the artillery is in the vicinity : the company officer calls his attention to it : the forward observing officer is young, bloodthirsty, and enthusiastic : he makes rapid and scientific calculations : he telephones back certain technical information to his battery : shells are as plentiful almost as grains of sand : and immediately that speck of terrain two miles away is an inferno of bursting shells. This intensive fire is gravely logged in the Summary, and the suspicious movements of the enemy similarly chronicled. And, perhaps, all that really happened was that Otto and Fritz and Hans and Heinrich, being out of the line, had captured a stray mongrel. There were some rats in an old barn. A morning's ratting was a welcome diversion, as also thought all the Ottos and Fritzes within a radius of a mile. " Considerable movement " naturally took place. Of course the Summary does not say all this; but then, summarists have very little imagination.

After a line or two about the enemy's aerial activity, the summarist passes on to Hostile Defences, and every new strand of wire, each fresh loophole and every additional sandbag are noted. If two Huns were actually burying a dead mule the summarist is

M

inclined to suspect the construction of a new and improved Hindenburg Line; at least there is something ominous in the reference to "work was proceeding uninterruptedly at so-and-so from 1 p.m. to 4 p.m." The next section, entitled Miscellaneous, was generally rather hard to fill, but "visibility bad" was often a refuge when in doubt. Finally, there was the paragraph marked "Identifications," and the dead German referred to earlier is logged as having belonged to the 477th Bavarian Infantry Regiment of the 129th Bavarian Division. The information in the summaries during a quiet period was, of course, invaluable at the time, but forty or fifty of them on end, nearly ten years later, make tough reading.

On February 8th the S.O.S. went up early in the morning. The Germans attacked the 3rd Division, on the left, and put down a strong barrage on the front and support lines of the 40th. The attack failed, and the operation was probably merely a raid. In the afternoon Sir Douglas Haig paid a surprise visit and went round all the staff offices. Then on February 11th the 119th and 120th Brigades went out of the line for a month's rest, the former to D'Airville and the latter to Mercatel. They were followed the next day by the 121st, which went to Ervillers and Hamelincourt.

The headquarters of the Division, which had been for about a fortnight at Behagnies, moved back again to Gomiecourt on the 13th. A new moon came into being at this time, with the result that "bombing has started again, and night is made hideous with the noise from Archies and the crashing of bombs." The weather was ideal for this kind of business, cold frosty nights and brilliant sunny days; and the moon getting bigger and brighter every night. In view of the narrative of the great offensive by the Germans, to be described in the following chapter, it should be stated here that such action, when it came, was not unexpected. "February 22nd.—Conference at corps headquarters. . . . The coming offensive by the Germans, and how to meet it, was the principal subject for discussion." This is one entry from a diary, and another reads : " February 25th.—Everybody in high circles thinks a German offensive is imminent." At the end of the month the Division moved to Basseux to be in General Headquarters reserve.

Training, inspections and field days were soon in full swing. Sometimes the make-believe so characteristic of training at home was to be met with here just behind the fighting line. In one scheme there was a supposed advance of tanks which were to break down at different points, but as no tanks were available they were represented by men with flags. The divisional commander, meeting a solitary man walking down a road wearing his box respirator, was somewhat disconcerted to hear, in reply to a question, a sepulchral voice reply " I am a tank." The weather now took a turn for the better—ideal days of spring sunshine and warmth succeeding the cold of February. The suspected German attack was everywhere the topic of discussion, and March 13th was regarded as a sure tip, but although there was a slight increase of shelling nothing more serious happened. All three brigades were, however, moved up to the Boisleux area to be in readiness, though the headquarters remained for the moment at Basseux. On the 14th " the betting had gone up to evens on a Boche attack to-morrow," but the next entry reads : " March 15th.—Nothing doing, only a great *tintamarre* all night from our own guns." On the 17th a Polish deserter came over during the night and said that the Germans were to attack in the morning under cover of a great gas bombardment. But the morning passed most peaceably. Then on the morning of the 19th : " a Hun was captured early to-day. He states the Boche is daily expecting an attack from us ; so far as he knows no attack is meditated on us—and so the game goes on." It poured with rain all day, but the Army was cheered by the news of the

M 2

birth of a son and heir to the commander-in-chief. The Division sent Sir Douglas Haig a telegram to say that " all ranks offered their congratulations on the arrival of your latest reinforcement."

As the Germans were apparently delaying their offensive, it was obviously a good opportunity for working off rounds in various football competitions, and this was done. Thus the days of waiting passed pleasantly enough. The 120th Brigade had suffered a severe loss on the 15th, when the brigade commander was invalided home. General Willoughby had been in very poor health for some time, but had struggled to remain at his duty in order to see the big offensive, though the delay in the opening of the attack rendered this impossible, and to the great regret of the divisional commander—who recorded in his diary, " very capable, and everybody has confidence in him : he will be most difficult to replace "—Brigadier-General Willoughby returned to England.

Under date March 20th, an entry in a diary concludes as follows : " T. S. M. and J. S. came to dinner tonight. B. bought a turbot in Amiens for the occasion." Then the diary passes immediately to the words " March 21. The battle has begun ; heavy firing from big guns started about 5 a.m. All back areas are also being shelled."

This was " March 1918 " ; " The Big Push " " The Great German Offensive," or whatever you like to call it. Incidentally, it was the most mighty attack ever made since arms were first borne by men.

CHAPTER X.

MARCH, 1918.

HISTORIANS will probably agree in maintaining that never in the course of the world's history has there existed a period so fateful as that which began on March 21st and ended on November 11th of the year 1918. In that space of just eight months the whole future not only of Europe but of the world hung in the balance, and there took place an ebb and flow of military success of an unprecedented kind. Within the space of just 235 days England sustained the greatest defeat which had ever attended her arms, while Germany, on her part, experienced an overthrow so stupendous that its significance could scarcely be grasped at the time. Future generations will stand bewildered at the survey of the events of that *annus mirabilis,* and will speculate upon what must have been the experience of their forefathers whose life embraced that eight-month span of the history of the world.

Properly to understand the conditions which prevailed at the opening of the great epoch, it will be necessary to regard the picture of that time from the Allied and German standpoints. The situation towards the end of 1917 has been reviewed in the opening sentences of Chapter VI; and although in some respects things had altered to the advantage of the Allies, particularly in the influx of American troops, this was offset by the definite defection of Russia. As for the Allied armies, the Belgians were still quiescent; the French Army had been profoundly depressed after their failure on the Aisne—so much so that there had been open mutiny, and it was partly on this account that the British had been committed to the bloody struggle in Flanders in 1917. As for the British Army, the strenuous efforts of that year had left it at a low ebb as regards training and numbers, and this was accentuated by the fact that the British in January, 1918, took over, by extending its right, a sector of twenty-eight miles from the French. At the same time a change took place in the organization of the forces. Under instructions from home a reorganization of divisions from a twelve to a nine-battalion basis was completed in February. Apart from the reduction in fighting strength, the fighting efficiency of the units was to some extent affected. The general situation, therefore, was that Germany was now in a position of being able to force a decisive battle on French soil with her own resources, and in this theatre of war she had three enemies to reckon with—France, England and America. It was on this great battle royal that the fortunes, even the fate, of all the contestants in the tremendous struggle which had lasted for over three years would obviously depend. The decisive theatre was now clearly France. Other fronts sank to a subordination as marked as that of Russia. The war that counted in the eyes of the civilized world was that being waged between the North Sea and the Alps.

From the German point of view the situation was such as to warrant Ludendorff in believing that there now existed a definite prospect of winning the war, and under the influence of this hopeful outlook the German Supreme Command decided in favour of a decisive battle in the western theatre of war in the spring of 1918. By the end of March forty-four divisions had been transferred to the west, and others had been detailed to follow. The question which then remained to be solved was on which of the two allies, England or France, the blow should fall. The British had borne the brunt of the fighting of 1917, when the Battle of Ypres towered over all other events in significance, whereas the French had made but minor efforts after the fighting on the Aisne, and their cautious strategy gave ground for the belief that the loss of *moral* which had set in after that battle had not been overcome. Nevertheless, the general opinion on the German side appears to have been that a success over the British would be more easily and certainly obtainable. One voice, indeed, was raised in opposition, for the chief of staff of the Army Group of the German Crown Prince considered that an attack against the French forces would be better policy. "England," he said, "with her dogged self-confidence, is not likely to end the war on account of a partial defeat of her army. She will be more inclined for peace when the power of the French is broken by a heavy defeat." Ludendorff, however, held fast to the plan of directing the blow against the British, and on January 24th the German Supreme Command definitely adopted this view. In view of the growing strength of the American forces, it was imperative that the offensive decided upon should be undertaken at the first possible moment, and preparations were pushed forward including an intensive system of training. On March 10th Hindenburg sent out an order fixing the morning of March 21st for the attack.

Although the claim has been made by the Germans that their great offensive took the British by surprise, this is not borne out by facts, and in the records of the 40th Division there are constant references to a state of continual anticipation of an attack. Further, on March 19th Sir Douglas Haig's Intelligence Department reported that the final stages of the enemy's preparations on the Arras—St. Quentin front were approaching completion, and that from information obtained it was clear that the actual attack would be launched on either the 20th or 21st. The British armies against which the great thrust was to be made were the Fifth and Third, of which the former was on the extreme right, extending from the junction with the French forces northward to the neighbourhood of

Gouzeaucourt. Next came the Third Army, under the command of General the Hon. Sir Julian Byng, which held a front of some twenty-seven miles from the north of Gouzeaucourt to Gavrelle, which is some six miles north-east of Arras. This army was composed of the V, IV, VI and XVII Corps, and our interest is focussed on the VI Corps, which was made up of the Guards, 3rd, 31st, 34th, 40th, 42nd and 59th Divisions. As for the 40th Division, the three brigades which had been brought out of the line about a fortnight earlier into G.H.Q. reserve were moved on March 20th into positions of readiness at Mercatel (119th Brigade), Hamelincourt (120th), and Blaireville (121st), the divisional headquarters remaining at Basseux. The period immediately preceding the battle had been utilized by the units of the 40th Division in making reconnaissances of the front into which they were certain to be called when the big push came, and in this way " we knew every hole and corner of the front and for five miles back," a knowledge which was to prove of immense assistance when the flag fell.

The fateful March 21st, 1918, was ushered in with a thick, white fog, and at dawn a bombardment of great intensity was opened against practically the whole front of the Fifth and Third Armies. The front of the VI Corps stretched approximately from Guemappes in the north to Noreuil in the south, and was held by the 3rd, 34th and 59th Divisions. About a quarter to nine a strong German force raided the trenches of the 3rd Division on the extreme left, but was immediately afterwards ejected by a counter-attack. An hour later, however, the main German offensive in this sector of the great battle was launched against the 59th Division and southwards, with the result that by 11.30 a.m. the enemy had broken through south-east of Bullecourt and was holding the Noreuil—Bullecourt road. It was now that the 40th Division was called upon to take its part in the fight. Orders were immediately sent to Major-General Ponsonby to move the 120th Brigade

into the Third Defensive System astride the Bapaume
—Ecoust road north-west of Vaulx Vraucourt, while the
121st Brigade was transferred from Blaireville to
Hamelincourt. As for the 119th Brigade, orders were
sent to it from divisional headquarters to be ready to
move at half an hour's notice.

To turn now to the movements and action of individual brigades. At twelve noon Brigadier-General
John Campbell was visited by the divisional commander
at Blaireville and received verbal orders to move the
121st Brigade forthwith to Hamelincourt, as the enemy
had attacked along the whole front. The divisional
commander then took the staff captain with him in his
car to Hamelincourt, in order that the latter might
arrange the necessary accommodation for the brigade.
At two o'clock brigade headquarters reached Hamelincourt, and found the headquarters of the 120th just
moving out. An hour and a half later the battalions
of the 121st Brigade began to march in, and orders
were now received for them to move at once and occupy
the Third System from the left of the 120th Brigade to
the right of the 34th Division—in other words, from the
Mory—Ecoust road to St. Léger exclusive. Brigade
headquarters proceeded to a sunken road south of
Mory; here were the headquarters of the 120th Brigade,
and also of the 178th Brigade of the 59th Division,
which had been holding the right sector of the VI
Corps front.

The front of the 121st Brigade was formed by the
12th Suffolks and the 13th Yorkshires, the former
being on the right. During the period of waiting
which took place before March 21st the 13th Yorkshires
had received large reinforcements of trained men, and
the day of the opening of the battle found the battalion
at full fighting strength and in a very effective state.
Careful reconnaissance had been made of nearly the
whole front of the Third Army, and so " we awaited
the attack with a good deal of confidence and full of
fight." At dawn the battalion, then in huts at

Hendecourt-les-Ransart, had been awakened by the intense bombardment by the German artillery and at once stood to arms. Shortly after nine o'clock the commanding officer was directed to move his battalion to Hamelincourt, and there the brigadier informed him that the position was very obscure, but that it was believed that Ecoust and Croisilles had fallen. Some discrepancy in exact hours exists between various sources consulted, for in the preceding paragraph, while it would appear that the 121st Brigade did not receive orders to move to Hamelincourt till after twelve noon, an account supplied by the 13th Yorkshire Regiment speaks of such order having been received three hours earlier. The discrepancy, however, is not material, and it is clear that on arrival at Hamelincourt the 13th Yorkshires received orders to move forward to St. Léger and to occupy an existing defensive line from the south-east corner of that village towards L'Homme Mort, and to get in touch with the 12th Suffolks in that direction.

It was apparently about three o'clock when the battalion deployed from the north-east corner of Hamelincourt and advanced, the leading companies being preceded by officers' patrols. Battalion head-quarters were established half a mile south of Judas Farm, and about five o'clock a report came in from the left company to say that St. Léger was occupied by the enemy patrols, who had been driven back into it, but that railway engines were still in the village trying to get away two heavy howitzers, apparently covered by some odd units of the 34th Division who were holding the cemetery. The commanding officer then ordered this company to hold the east of the village so as to cover the withdrawal of the guns, an operation which was successfully carried out. Shortly afterwards a report came in from the right company to the effect that the Blue line was found to be held by enemy machine gun posts. Late in the evening battalion headquarters were moved to a sunken road just west of St. Léger, and efforts were made, but without complete success, to close the gap that existed between the battalion and the 12th Suffolk Regiment. By dawn on the 22nd the position of the 121st Brigade was one of extreme difficulty.

When the big push started the 119th Brigade was in the Mercatel area, at three hours' notice to move by day and at one and a half hours by night. During the forenoon orders were received from the Division to be ready to move thirty minutes after warning, but as a matter of fact the forenoon passed away peaceably. So peaceably, in fact, that "we played off the finals in the battalion football competitions," and in the afternoon the brigadier inspected the battalions in fighting order. Battalion orders of the 20th had stated that "the Gamecocks will perform in the theatre near Northumberland Camp to-morrow evening, the 21st, commencing at 6 p.m." But the Gamecocks had another engagement when that time came. In response to telephonic orders direct from VI Corps, about one o'clock the brigade started off for Hamelincourt, but while *en route* this order was cancelled, and the brigade returned to Mercatel. It was not long, however, before the brigade was genuinely called upon, for at 5.30 verbal orders were received from a staff officer of the VI Corps directing the brigade to occupy Henin Hill forthwith and to hold it at all costs. It so happened that when this order arrived the brigadier was inspecting a guard from each battalion, the best of which was to be detailed as a guard for divisional headquarters. The selected guard, however, marched off in a noticeably dejected manner, and on inquiry it was discovered that "they objected to being penalized for their smartness on guard mounting parade." It turned out that the penalization was missing the fight which was the obvious sequel to the move to Henin Hill. The matter was amicably adjusted by reversing the usual procedure and detailing the least smart of the three guards for divisional headquarters.

It was dark when the brigade moved off, and

it was not known even who held the hill, the leading battalion being the 21st Middlesex, under Lieutenant-Colonel H. C. Metcalfe. " We got here before the Boche," writes Colonel Metcalfe, " and held on all through the night, and, as an old musketry staff officer, never had I dreamed of firing into such grand targets as were fired into that night! The gunners with their field guns were alongside us in the line and firing over open sights. The Boche casualties were extremely heavy." From another narrative, by an officer of the 13th East Surrey Regiment, we have a little vignette of the night on Henin Hill. " As the battalion moved along the Arras road the commanding officer called the company commanders to the head of the column and detailed orders. ' A ' Company was to form a line on the left of the road leading over Henin Hill at right angles to the road, ' B ' Company was to extend this line on ' A ' Company's left; both companies were to dig in. ' C ' Company was to form a line on the right of the road at right angles to the road, while ' D ' Company was to be in close support to the rear of ' A ' and ' B ' Companies. The 21st Middlesex were believed to be forming a line in front of the battalion. There was a meeting of officers in a dug-out towards the top of Henin Hill; as there was a big crowd present, including officers from the K.R.R. (where they had come from I do not know—I suppose they belonged to the 34th Division) it was rather an uncomfortable affair. After much exertion, and in pitch darkness, the companies managed to get into position, but about 12.30 a.m. on the 22nd March orders were received for the battalion to concentrate and march to Judas Farm. " On Henin Hill the most extraordinary row was going on—the transport of two battalions seemed to have got thoroughly mixed, our companies were streaming into the road, the Lewis gun sections were shouting for their respective limbers, and, when they found their limbers, had lost their companies and so started again to find them; to add to the confusion, a couple of six-inch guns

came through with eight horses apiece. This was the
first moment I realized things might be going badly,
when I saw them pulling out the heavy guns. The
enemy must have got precious near these guns.
Eventually the battalion was concentrated, and moved
off at about 200 yards interval between companies, but
as it was very dark it was rather difficult to keep in
touch. Later the battalion practically closed up. It
was a most gruelling night march to the Army line
near Judas Farm, and everybody appeared to have the
greatest difficulty in keeping awake. Eventually the
battalion arrived at the Army line at Judas Farm about
5.30 on the 22nd March. We got some rations about
7, for which everyone was duly thankful." " A "
Company of the 40th Machine Gun Battalion, which
had been acting with the 119th Brigade, remained,
however, in position on the hill.

What had happened was that at 10 p.m. the 40th
Division, reinforced by the 177th Infantry Brigade and
the surviving elements of the 59th Divisional Artillery
(fifteen guns) and machine gun battalion, had been
ordered to take over the defence of a line extending from
a point about a mile north of Vaulx Vraucourt to the
south-east corner of St. Léger Wood. This necessitated
the recall of the 119th Brigade, which in the preceding
paragraph had been detached to Henin Hill. Its
mission there had been to assist the 34th Division
around Boiry Becquerelle, but the fresh disposition of
the 40th Division required that the 119th Brigade should
revert to it. Accordingly, the 119th Brigade was sent
to hold a line running across the Sensée River, roughly
due south from a point west of Hill Copse, and covering
Ervillers. Its headquarters were now at Hamelincourt;
those of the other two brigades in the sunken road south-
east of Mory. Divisional headquarters had in the
meantime moved up from Basseux to Hamelincourt.

So ended the first day of the great German offensive
of March 21st, 1918. At the end of it the enemy had
made very considerable progress, but was still firmly

held in the battle zone in which it had been anticipated that the real struggle would take place. The greatest success to the enemy had been against the Fifth Army, to the south, where a withdrawal of part of the line had been rendered necessary in the afternoon. Less progress had been made against the Third Army, but the Germans had reached St. Léger in their efforts to thrust a wedge between Arras and Cambrai, and several villages had been captured. Speaking of the fighting in this sector on this day, a leading German historian states that here the British defended themselves with great stubbornness, and speaks with appreciation of the strong British counter-attacks, which required the bringing up of several German divisions from the second line. For the 40th Division the day had been one mainly of marching into the battle area and of relieving troops which had borne the first onslaught.

The night passed quietly enough, and even when the morning of the 22nd dawned—again with a white mist—the lull still continued for a while. Small bodies of the enemy were successfully ejected from the vicinity of Vaulx Vraucourt and St. Léger Wood. In the 121st Brigade touch had not yet been established between the 13th Yorkshires on the left and the 12th Suffolks on the right, but a report, timed 7.5 a.m., came from the former battalion to say that an attack on the enemy in front line had been successful, six machine guns having been captured and 20 of the enemy killed. Touch with the Suffolks had, however, not yet been secured, as another nest of machine guns intervened, and an enemy counter-attack succeeded in reoccupying the front line. Then, shortly before noon, an organized attack with artillery support was launched by the 13th Yorkshire Regiment, which was completely successful.

In this attack there were heroic deeds. The attack was led by Captain de Quetteville, who, for his skill and gallantry, was awarded the Distinguished Service Order. Captain Simpkin, with his company, destroyed the nest of eight enemy machine guns, and by this operation touch was at length gained with the 12th Suffolks. It was this officer also who had dealt with the other nest of machine guns, the destruction of which was reported in the message to brigade headquarters timed 7.5 a.m. Unfortunately, Captain Simpkin was killed in an enemy counter-attack which temporarily regained part of the front line. On this occasion, too, Second-Lieutenant E. F. Beal, of the 13th Yorkshires, with two men, was proceeding up a section of trench when he was challenged by a German machine gunner. He sprang forward, shot down the whole of the enemy team, and captured the gun. Continuing his advance up the trench, Second-Lieutenant Beal repeated this performance three times, bringing back four captured guns and one wounded prisoner. Later in the morning this dauntless officer went out under heavy machine gun fire and brought in one of his men who had been wounded. Shortly afterwards, however, he was himself hit by a shell and killed. For his noble conduct in this action he was posthumously awarded the Victoria Cross.

The narrative above given is the result of careful collation of divisional, 121st Brigade, and 13th Yorkshire Regiment narratives, but it is necessary to point out that there is a considerable disagreement between these accounts, and all that the historian has been able to do is to compare the three versions, to eliminate the impossible, to bring together the probable, and then to endeavour to construct a coherent narrative. Thus, as regards the gallant action of Second-Lieutenant Beal, this is fully described in the divisional and battalion narratives, but with some discrepancy of detail and with a difference of twelve hours as regards time. The account of the operations submitted by the brigade contains no mention of it, but, on the other hand, describes the feat of Captain Simpkin in duplicate, i.e., it credits him not only with the eight machine guns taken in the attack, but with the four machine guns taken earlier as well. In the preceding paragraph, therefore, there is some doubt as to whether the

four guns reported in the 7.5 a.m. message fell to
Captain Simpkin, and it is possible that these are the
four so gallantly captured by Second-Lieutenant Beal.
Even in the total number of guns captured in the two
operations the three accounts are at variance. The
divisional report gives six and eight; the report of the
brigade says four and eight; and the battalion narrative
mentions four and six. This particular discrepancy is
immaterial, except as illustrating the difficulties which
every moment confront the historian, and nothing can
dim the outstanding fact that two heroic officers
of the 13th Yorkshire Regiment performed actions of
outstanding gallantry on this 22nd March.

To resume. When the Germans were being pushed
back by this organized attack of the Yorkshires, the
divisional artillery, under Brigadier-General Palmer,
got on to the enemy with 18-pounders and 4·5 howitzers,
inflicting heavy casualties. The Germans, however,
came again in a strong, renewed attack. " The Boche
attack was one of the prettiest sights I have ever seen."
Thus a fire-eating brigadier, who adds, " Our machine
guns got into them beautifully." The enemy, however,
meant business, and both the 13th Yorkshires and the
12th Suffolks (whose commanding officer, Lieutenant-
Colonel Eardley-Wilmot, had been killed in the
morning, the command then passing to Captain Cross)
had to form defensive flanks in order to maintain touch.
And already for two hours " A " Company of the 40th
Battalion Machine Gun Corps—which, it will be
remembered, had been left on Henin Hill—had been
hotly engaged against a mass attack of the enemy.

The battle had now reached a stage when reports began
to come in with increasing frequency and vagueness.
At half-past twelve information was received that the
Germans were on Henin Hill, and patrols from the 20th
Middlesex were at once sent out to clear up the situation.
Hardly had they left when from the other flank came a
rumour that the enemy had broken through at Vaulx
Vraucourt, and part of the 20th Middlesex were sent off

at once to that flank.   An hour or two later word was sent from the Division that the brigade headquarters were to fall back to Behagnies.   Farther to the rear alarmist reports had begun to spread, and apparently about this time in the back areas there was talk of the Germans having burst through with tanks and armoured cars.   It seems indisputable that Hun emissaries, dressed in British uniforms, were moving about endeavouring to infuse alarm and despondency behind. In front, however, "the fighting troops were making a magnificent stand against heavy odds," and although at the close of the day the situation was obscure and the Germans were putting down a vicious bombardment, the troops of the 121st Brigade were in high fettle.

The 120th Brigade, on the right, seems to have had a comparatively quiet time until half-past twelve, when "very heavy attacks were launched by the enemy."   Two battalions were in the front line, the 14th Argyll and Sutherland Highlanders on the right, with the 10/11th Highland Light Infantry on the left. The weight of the enemy's attacks made a dent in the centre of the brigade line, but by one o'clock it was straightened out again.   Half an hour later information was received that the enemy had forced back the left of the 6th Division, which was immediately to the south of the 120th Brigade.   This left the flank of the Highlanders in the air, but as the commanding officer was informed that the IV Corps was preparing a counter-attack he decided, in spite of his perilous position, to hold on in front of Vaulx Vraucourt, while brigade headquarters returned to Behagnies. During these continuous German attacks the enemy endeavoured to bring forward and establish machine guns in front of their infantry, but this game was spoilt by Major Nesham.   He was forward observing for D.181 Battery, which knocked out the enemy machine guns one after the other before they could come into action.

N

At six o'clock the promised counter-attack had not matured, and, accordingly, the 14th Argyll and Sutherland Highlanders were forced to retire to a defensive position along the Beaugnatre road, where they were so heavily attacked and enfiladed by rifle and machine gun fire that they had to fall back still farther. Eventually, at 7 p.m., the position of the 120th Brigade was as follows : The Highlanders were on the right; the 10/11th Highland Light Infantry, who had suffered severe losses, were in the centre; and the 14th Battalion of that regiment was on the left. Touch had now been re-established with the 6th Division on the right. Owing to its heavy losses, the 10/11th Highland Light Infantry was withdrawn into reserve during the night.

It is a truism to say that outsiders see most of the game. Certainly a bird's-eye view of a battle is obtained more easily by one who has had a roving commission over the field, rather than by an actual occupant of the front line. In the narrative of Bourlon Wood we were enabled to get a vivid picture of the minor incidents of the fighting from the story of a private soldier, and we shall now follow the fortunes of the same historian as regards March 22nd, 1918. It happened to be his luck to be detailed to remain with battalion headquarters, "for what motive at the time I did not know," but it soon turned out that he was to act as runner, to carry messages up to the front line, "which is not so cushy in open warfare as one may imagine." At 8 a.m. his first journey began. The morning had been very foggy, with a thick haze, so that the sole indication of the progress of the battle was the incessant sound of artillery, rifle and machine gun fire, and it appeared that the enemy was using field artillery to a great extent, "according to the holes they made." The runner's goal was to be "D" Company of his regiment, the 14th Argyll and Sutherland Highlanders, who at the time were, generally speaking, holding a position between Vaulx Vraucourt and Ecoust. In the haze it was difficult to see more than a few hundred yards ahead, but the proximity of the front line was at length indicated by "a few of our fellows lying dead." Stooping down to examine one who had been shot on the left side of the head and "was not yet stiff," it was seen from his arm band that he had also been a runner. This sight very naturally came as a reminder of what might be expected, and so "I reduced my height a little by stooping and putting on a smarter pace."

However, the front trench was safely reached, the runner being greeted with the shout, "Damn ye, man, come doon into the trench, de ye want yer heid blawn aff?" The message was duly delivered, a receipt obtained, and a safe return was made to headquarters. Shortly afterwards, the colonel desired the runner to accompany him to the front line. A brief general view of the left of the front position was soon obtained, the mist having cleared off, and then the colonel, "after thinking for a few minutes near a light railway line," desired the narrator to push up a road and collect any stragglers he could find. Five Argylls were picked up, and soon a Highland Light Infantry officer and about thirty men came running up. The officer called out " Come on the H.L.I., we'll show them how to drive them back." This was rather a challenge to the Argylls, especially as the officer added, as if in after-thought, " and the Argylls can come too, if they like." A remark like this from one Highland regiment to another admitted of but one reply. " Needless to say they did, that gallant little band both H.L.I. and Argylls, and the last that I saw of them was crossing a ridge in a glorious style, whether to death or victory I cannot tell, but I looked long after they had disappeared, with great admiration."

The runner seems now to have had some spare time on his hands, so he decided to try to reach the top of the ridge himself and see what was happening on the far side. Passing through a trench, he met " nine

bodies huddled up closely, the effect of a shell," but
he "did not examine them closely." On drawing
near the ridge, it was seen that to top it was inadvisable,
as "bullets were actually lifting the turf from it." The
runner frankly admits that he "hesitated for a moment
or two," and just then he observed a fellow soldier
sitting quite unconcerned at his side, "a fine-looking
young man, and his eyes red as if he were crying."
Inquiries elicited the fact that the fellow soldier had
lost his officer, "and a finer man never drew breath,"
and that he was going to look for him "over there,"
pointing to the extremely unhealthy edge of the ridge.
The runner deprecated the foolhardy attempt, "and
ended up by telling him that he was insane," but the
other soldier was not to be dissuaded. "He crossed
the ridge, and I could see his body all but his legs,
and to my surprise he raised his rifle and fired twice
before he fell. I have no doubt he fired at a Hun, but
I will say what a Frenchman said years ago, 'It was
magnificent, but it was not war.'"

This put an end to any idea of trying to cross the
ridge, and the runner made his way back to battalion
headquarters, whence he was despatched up to "D"
Company with ammunition. He was assisted in his
task by "another soldier nicknamed Skipper, I cannot
remember his real name, but he was well known in
11th Platoon, 'C' Company." After passing through
"B" Company beyond Vaulx Vraucourt the excitement began. Two enemy aeroplanes were lurking
about, and the sight of two soldiers carrying a box of
ammunition in the open was a thing not to be missed.
"Like birds of prey they swooped down upon us and
opened up their machine guns we were their targets
for at least two or three minutes we were of course
lying down flat and every time they turned we fired at
them to tell the truth if they had a hook they could
have lifted us from the earth they were so close to us
and thanks to their poor shooting we arose unharmed,
but it is I think very terrifying to have the propellers

of an aeroplane humming over one's head and the
firing of a machine gun." There is certainly a good
deal of truth in the statement that the life of a runner
in open warfare is not exactly "a cushy one." To be
a good runner, however, you must take things just
as they come. This one merely "said to Skipper that
I thought this would be the advance party and so
it was."

As snipers were becoming busy, and as "there
were two or three runners lying dead about 50 yards
away," it seemed advisable to cease carrying the box
of ammunition between them, and, accordingly, the
bandoliers were taken out and carried by each man
separately. Having accomplished this task, which
"was a hurried one," the pair started crawling towards
the ridge, on the other side of which they expected to
find "D" Company. What was their surprise to see,
instead of "D" Company, a German battalion coming
on as if they were on parade, with an officer in front—
"and I will give the devil his due they were in
splendid order extended I should say to two yards
between each man and all in line." It is not surprising
to read that "our decision was flight," but before
retiring, the couple gave four rounds apiece and then
"ran for our lives the ammunition we had on our
backs were like so many feathers." It was not long
before they got back to "B" Company and gave the
warning of the enemy's advance. "The stand-to went
and the men responded to the order." In a few
moments "we could see the enemy were advancing about
seven hundred yards away sharpshooters in front they
would run probably fifty yards then drop in this
manner of advancing they were very hard to hit."

However, our special correspondent, who was a good
shot, got off a few rounds, apparently with effect, for,
as the firer sagely remarks, "I don't think they
were acting to amuse me." Meanwhile, about two
thousand yards away, enemy artillery could be seen
galloping into action and unlimbering in the open.

" I don't know when ' B ' Company retired but I do know that they and their gallant commander put up a stubborn defence against unequal odds." Skipper and his friend had by this been sent back to battalion headquarters to give information about the attack, and on their way they met bodies of men retiring, apparently from another division. Battalion headquarters, which were in a sunken road apparently west of Vaulx Vraucourt, were found to be empty, and the enemy with machine guns was streaming through the village. However, by making their way past the battered sugar refinery the pair reached a main road, and about two hundred yards to the left " was our gallant colonel as large as life with about a dozen men holding a good position."

" The colonel said the Argylls would stand firm or words to that effect which would mean the same." And soon the fight began. " And by God they did stand firm our gallant little party and we were not idle true we had not any machine guns but we had rifles." At this time Germans could be seen in the south (west?) part of the village, with their machine guns projecting from the shattered walls of the houses. The fighting which ensued has made the narrator grow enthusiastic, and although we are aware that eulogy of a superior is supposed to be contrary to regulation, not all the orders ever penned will lead us to omit this tribute from a private soldier to his commanding officer : " I would like to say a word or two regarding our colonel as to his exemplary courage with his men ; his unselfishness ; a gentleman, and last but not least a very brave soldier and I think any soldier who fought under Colonel Benzie will vouch for the statement I have written."

This little isolated engagement apparently lasted for about an hour, when the increasing pressure by the enemy necessitated a retirement. This was carried out in small parties of two or three at a time, the runner and his comrade being about the last to leave. They engaged a machine gun on one of the shattered walls

of the village, but had at last to go, " not that we were
scared but owing to force of numbers." It is distinctly stated that the whole of the party disputed the
ground yard by yard, and the engagement is typical
of many that must have occurred during the day—a
small and isolated party doing what it could against
vastly superior numbers of the enemy, who still
preserved the impetus of a surprise attack. Eventually, after more fighting and further enforced
retirement, the narrator and his comrades found
themselves back on the line, well to the west of Vaulx
Vraucourt, which some, if not all of what was left
of the battalion had reached. A battalion of the
Highland Light Infantry was now upon the left, and
the situation had apparently reached that phase
described in a preceding paragraph, where it is
related that the 120th Brigade had fallen back to a
position along the Beugnatre road, from which, however, it was soon dislodged. These excerpts from
Private Falconer's narrative will probably convey to
the reader the feature which characterized the fighting
by the Division on March 22nd, 1918, namely, a
gallant attempt by the units composing it to dam the
flood of the attack, whose waters swirled everywhere
along the front of the Third and Fifth Armies.

As for the 119th Brigade, it had been heavily shelled
during the forenoon, and it was found necessary to
shift advanced headquarters from time to time on this
account. About two o'clock two companies—one from
both the 20th Middlesex and the 13th East Surrey
Regiments—were hastily ordered to proceed towards
Croisilles to the assistance of the 34th Division, and
during the day the 18th Welch Regiment thoroughly
reconnoitred the Sensée Valley and the road leading
to St. Léger. At 6 p.m. it was noticed that a withdrawal was taking place from that village in a north-
westerly direction. Orders were now sent to the
officer commanding the 13th East Surrey Regiment
to attack St. Léger, in order to facilitate the retirement

of the 120th Brigade as mentioned in the preceding paragraph. Two tanks were to co-operate, and these were to rendezvous at Judas Farm, where the officer commanding the East Surreys was to get in touch with them. Meanwhile, however, the Germans made a determined attack on the 18th Welch Regiment, which was holding the Sensée switch, and the commanding officer of that regiment "very rightly commandeered the services of the two tanks above mentioned, and by a brilliant counterstroke put a stop to the German advance and captured five enemy machine guns." This rendered the attack by the 13th East Surrey Regiment unnecessary, and it did not take place. The action of the 18th Welch, under Lieutenant-Colonel W. E. Brown, M.C., received high praise, and is reported to have reached "the Bourlon standard." It was apparently on this day that the VI Corps club was gutted. The liquor was destroyed, but cigarettes and cigars were issued out to the men, and the commander of the 119th Brigade reports that "on going up to the line I found the little Welshmen doing rapid fire, each with a big cigar in his mouth."

The attack referred to by the 18th Welch Regiment is such an admirable example of opportunism, tactical insight—with just the least little touch of bluff—and promptness of decision that it merits rather a fuller account than that given above. The 18th Welch had taken up a line in the switch in front of Judas Farm in the early hours of the morning. The night had been quiet enough, but before dawn a party of German machine gunners made a reconnaissance towards the trench. Lieutenant-Colonel Brown ordered the officer commanding the company flanking the road to allow the Germans to come on unmolested. Then, just as the Huns were searching for the trench, "we quietly surrounded them and captured the party without fuss." This was a good beginning, but later in the morning the Germans heavily shelled Judas Farm, and the battalion headquarters were forced to retire a short distance. From this new position the enemy could be seen advancing in mass formation down a slope, and such a target called for prompt measures. An 18-pounder battery was communicated with, and the gunners, firing over open sights, had the time of their lives for nearly an hour. " We could actually see the enemy dropping in scores and their ammunition animals galloping all over the place."

By four o'clock in the afternoon, however, the Germans had managed to make their way forward under cover, and were merely some 500 yards away from the position of the 18th Welch. The men of that regiment were strung out in a thin line about twenty paces apart, and were keeping up a steady fire with machine guns and rifles, but the Germans were still creeping forward in a most disconcerting fashion, so that it seemed as if a hand-to-hand struggle must ensue. Just then a *homo ex machina* appeared in the guise of the tank officer asking his way to St. Léger, whither he was bound with two tanks. It was pointed out to him that St. Léger was now in the hands of the Germans, and it was suggested that he should now co-operate with the 18th Welch. The officer at first naturally demurred at departing from his original instructions, but after some persuasion, backed up by a show of authority on the part of Lieutenant-Colonel Brown, he agreed to advance with his two tanks on the Welch flank, turn at right angles, and make a demonstration between the lines. The operation met with unexpected but well-deserved success, and the Germans fell back over 400 yards. In this action a German pigeon was captured bearing a message to a German headquarters to the effect that the British had received strong reinforcements and had *brought up a battalion of tanks*. That is the kind of thing that promptitude, decision, and a little bluff will often make the enemy think in war. And it is certainly worth adding that while the Germans were temporarily disorganized, an officer and three men of the 18th Welch went out and captured " a very surprised nest of German

machine gunners." The tanks kept up their good work
until dusk, when their officer was compelled to withdraw them. So unnerved were the Germans by this
smart little offensive, that they made no serious effort
in that quarter during the night that followed. Be it
remembered that the men of the 18th Welch were so
strung out as to be almost out of sight one from
another, and there was no reserve except battalion headquarters, and the full worth of this brilliant little
counter-stroke will be grasped.

What with the constant pressure by the Germans
for the past forty-eight hours; the hurried counter-
attacks; the constant ebb and flow of troops thus necessitated; the relief, in darkness, of divisions right and left;
the inevitable number of stragglers and " lost " detachments, a certain amount of confusion and intermingling
had necessarily set in, and it is difficult, if not impossible, to show clearly the dislocation of the 40th Division
on the morning of March 23rd. Piecing together,
however, a number of separate reports and narratives,
it is possible to present a picture more or less as follows :
To take the 119th Brigade first, the 13th East Surrey
Regiment had finished up the 22nd in the Sensée
Valley immediately west of St. Léger. During the
night the 4th Guards Brigade was busy relieving troops
in the Sensée switch, and before dawn the East Surreys
were ordered to withdraw; to work down the valley and
round to the east of Ervillers; to defend that place, and
eventually to counter-attack and drive the Germans out
of Mory, for a telephonic message had just come in
from divisional headquarters to say that troops on the
right of the 119th Brigade had been driven out of that
place. The East Surreys accordingly complied, their
precise movements being given in full detail below.
The movements of the 21st Middlesex are not easy to
follow, but there was to be " a side slip to the right," and
to be a co-operation by one company—subsequently by
the whole battalion, apparently—with the East Surreys
in the attack on Mory. The 18th Welch were ordered

to retire from the Sensée switch and to become brigade
reserve, which movement was completed by 6.30 a.m.
on this 23rd March.

Next to the 119th Brigade came the 121st. Its left
unit was the 13th Yorkshire Regiment, with the 12th
Suffolks on the right, and the 20th Middlesex apparently in second line. During the night of the
22nd/23rd the left of the 13th Yorkshires was on the
St. Léger—Ervillers road, in touch with the 34th
Division and—later in the night—with the Irish Guards
of the relieving division; but although the 13th East
Surreys were in the neighbourhood until between 3 and
4 a.m. there is no record of any touch between the two
battalions, and it is possible that the left company of
the 13th Yorkshires was a short distance in front of the
East Surreys, but that the fact was known to neither
unit. Early on the 23rd the right of the 13th
Yorkshires was in the air. At 6 p.m. on the previous
evening it had been known that the 12th Suffolk
Regiment had been obliged to fall back on Mory.
About 11 p.m. heavy machine gun firing and confused
shouting in that direction showed that things were
happening. As a matter of fact the 12th Suffolk
Regiment was forced to retire, and it dug itself in on
the high ground east of Ervillers, with its right on the
Ervillers—Mory road. This, however, was not known
to the commanding officer of the 13th Yorkshires, who
could only wonder what was happening, but whose
anxiety was relieved when the 21st Middlesex Regiment,
of the 119th Brigade, came up, as already related, on
his right.

At the risk of anticipating slightly the story which
is to follow, it may be said, generally speaking, that
about 11.30 a.m. on the 23rd the situation was
developing as follows : The 119th Brigade was in the
second line covering Ervillers, and with it were the
12th Suffolk Regiment and two companies of the 20th
Middlesex Regiment, the two latter units belonging to
the 121st Brigade. The remaining battalion of the

121st Brigade, *i.e.*, the 13th Yorkshires, had its left on the Ervillers—St. Léger road, in touch with the Guards, and its right in touch with the 21st Middlesex, of the 119th Brigade. As for the 120th Brigade, it was occupying a line running westwards from the Vaulx Vraucourt—Beugnatre road, the front consisting of the 14th Highland Light Infantry on the right; two companies of the 20th Middlesex in the centre (south of Mory), and a battalion of the Hampshire Regiment (really belonging to the 6th Division) on the left. From one account it seems that a floating unit or two of the 41st Division had also been washed ashore in this sector, but this is not clear. At any rate, it is obvious that the 40th Division had necessarily lost some of its cohesion, and the situation, if occurring on peace manœuvres of the old Army, would have been summarized by a morbid-minded adjutant or sergeant-major as "a rare old box-up." Confused though the formation and alignments were, they possessed, nevertheless, the precision of trooping the colour as compared with the result of the greater pressure against the Fifth Army farther south, and such confusion as did exist seems merely to throw up in stronger relief the tenacity and *moral* of the 40th and other divisions. That they were able to triumph over the handicap imposed is a tribute to their discipline and training.

March 23rd was distinguished chiefly by a noteworthy attack carried out by the 13th East Surrey and 21st Middlesex Regiments of the 119th Brigade. The curtain went up shortly after midnight of the 22nd. "About 1.30 a.m. on the 23rd March there was a terrific firing to our right rear. I thought at the time, from the amount of ginger that was being put into it, that it must be one of our attacks, but I came to the conclusion some weeks after that it must have been an attack by the enemy on Mory or somewhere near it. At this time Very lights seemed to be going up all round to our right rear. There were also rumours of enemy patrols to our rear, and a lot of people were inclined to get nervy, which, perhaps, under the circumstances, was not surprising."

Thus an East Surrey narrative. What had actually happened was wrapt in mystery for the moment, but there were strong grounds for believing that Mory, and possibly Ervillers, were in enemy hands, and it was certain that the brigade on the right of the 40th Division had been forced to withdraw. The East Surreys, just west of St. Léger, were now in the air, and orders were sent to them to fall back, and to look in, as it were, at Ervillers and Mory and restore the situation. Lieutenant-Colonel Warden at once detailed "A" Company (Captain R. W. H. King) to reconnoitre and occupy Ervillers, and "B" Company (Captain J. E. M. Crowther) to reconnoitre towards Mory, but not to become seriously engaged, and to prolong "A" Company's line of defence in front of Ervillers. The two remaining companies and battalion headquarters were sent to Behagnies, to protect that place and the road to it from Ervillers.

"A" and "B" Companies reached Ervillers about 8.30 a.m. and found British troops still holding the spur of the east of that village. Captain Crowther proceeded to reconnoitre the road to Mory, and reached a point well to the east of the bridge over the Sensée River, his party being fired on from the high ground north of the road. The Sensée Valley runs north from Sapignies to Mory, where it bends abruptly westwards towards Ervillers, but passes north-east of that village to St. Léger. Thus, Mory lies in the valley between a spur, running north-east from Sapignies, and the high ground extending towards St. Léger. The front line now "consisted of a most extraordinary collection of troops—Machine Gun Corps, Highland Light Infantry and Leicesters, the latter predominating." On returning to Ervillers, Captain Crowther was informed that Mory was strongly held by the enemy and that to attack it with his company was impracticable. Later in the morning the 21st Middlesex Regiment advanced from the Sensée Valley some distance north of Ervillers against the enemy on the high ground between Mory and St. Léger, and it was decided that " B " Company of the 13th East Surreys should attack in support of the Middlesex men. At 11 a.m., accordingly, " B " Company attacked that portion of the high ground which overlooks the Ervillers—Mory road. It did not succeed in carrying the crest-line, though some of No. 5 Platoon were killed within twenty yards of it, but managed to reach a line some eighty yards from the enemy, where it held on. In this attack, Second-Lieutenants Tarry and Bailey were wounded. While in this position, Private Bark distinguished himself by going forward and retrieving one of the company's Lewis guns, the crew of which had been killed twenty yards from the enemy's line.

Meanwhile it had been reported to Lieutenant-Colonel Warden at Behagnies that Mory village was held by German snipers and machine guns, but not with infantry in strength. He therefore reported the situation, suggesting a counter-attack, and was ordered to move his headquarters and " C " and " D " Companies to Ervillers and attack Mory village in accordance with the scheme which he had proposed. This was, briefly, to make his main attack on the west of the village with " B " Company supported by " C " Company, while " A " Company was to seize the high ground north of the village and so protect the left flank of the attack. " D " Company, in reserve, was to be prepared to co-operate by an attack on the village from the south, and afterwards to mop it up. The headquarters Lewis gunners and all battalion snipers were to cover the attack from the spur south of Mory, to which Lieutenant-Colonel Warden transferred his headquarters.

The advance of the battalion against Mory commenced at 2.30 p.m. (nominally, but as a matter of fact Captain Crowther's watch had stopped, and it was not until " C " Company came up that he was able to ascertain

the exact time, which was then 2.35 p.m.), " B "
Company moving forward by sectional rushes, supported by " C " Company (Captain C. G. Norman);
while the battalion snipers, led by Lieutenant H. W.
Allason, worked their way forward in pairs and kept
down the machine gun and snipers' fire from the
village. The enemy at once commenced to reinforce
the garrison from behind the ridge of Mory, and his
infantry suffered severely while advancing down the
main road from Ecoust into the village. Although
" B " and " C " Companies were gaining ground, they
were exposed to enfilade fire from hostile machine guns
on the high ground to their left and suffered many
casualties, which included both company commanders
wounded. Shortly afterwards the only remaining
officer of " B " Company, Second-Lieutenant F. A.
Simmonds, was also wounded, and the command of the
company devolved on Sergeant Dooley. To assist the
two companies, the reserve company (" D ") was
ordered to attack along the western slope of the spur
south of Mory, and eventually all three companies
gained the western edge of the village. Here they
were reorganized under the few remaining officers
(" C " Company being under Company Sergeant-
Major Reed, as no officers remained), and about
5 p.m. a renewed attack was made which won a
complete success. The village was captured with great
loss to the enemy, and the battalion established itself in
the Army line beyond, whilst the 21st Middlesex
Regiment occupied the high ground north-west of the
village.

In this attack the transport of the battalions concerned did sterling work. A considerable quantity
of ammunition, bombs and the like were required by
the East Surreys, and the battalion transport kept these
needs well supplied, although the whole of the way up
was under shell fire and much of it under direct
machine gun fire as well. The commanding officer
particularly noted Sergeant Holmes, Corporal Bull, and

Private Burrell for their gallantry in action, and Captain F. S. Beecroft was awarded the Military Cross for his services. Fighting continued until dark, and many prisoners were taken and sent back; but as the enemy kept up a very heavy machine gun fire on the village, and his troops were seen to be in great strength, a gradual withdrawal from Mory to a line west of the village was ordered. This was duly carried out in the darkness, and the retirement was not detected by the enemy, who attacked Mory in great strength, a heavy Lewis gun and rifle fire being maintained upon it by the battalion. Soon after reaching its new position in the valley between Mory and Ervillers the 13th East Surrey was for a short time in touch with the 12th East Surrey on its right. Before, however, the trenches of the 13th Battalion were completed it was attacked, and the valley became the scene of confused fighting which lasted for about two hours. When the enemy had been driven off, Lieutenant-Colonel Warden collected and, in accordance with orders received on the previous afternoon, assumed command of the remnants of the three battalions of the 119th Brigade, viz., 13th East Surrey, 21st Middlesex and 18th Welch Regiments. Touch was established with the 4th Guards Brigade on the left, but communication with the 12th East Surreys on the right could not be reopened.

At daybreak on the 24th it was seen that our advanced troops had been forced to withdraw and that the enemy had broken through on the right, and concentrated a large number of troops in the Mory valley with the intention of attacking Ervillers. The artillery was at once informed and very quickly found targets in the valley, firing also on the probable enemy concentration area behind Mory ridge. To meet the attack the eastern outskirts of the village were held by eight Vickers guns while the 4th Guards and 119th Brigades took up a position facing south between Ervillers and Mory, with their left thrown back and their right at the road junction nearest the bridge on the Ervillers

road, the 119th being extended from that point towards
Ervillers. It was arranged that the Guards Brigade
should not fire, unless attacked in flank, until the 119th
Brigade opened heavy fire. Shortly after dawn the
enemy advance began. His scouts were allowed to
proceed towards Ervillers, but when his main body
was well up the valley it was caught in a cross fire from
the two brigades, assisted by the Guards' Vickers guns
and our artillery, and was practically wiped out.
Several prisoners were taken, one of whom stated that
three enemy divisions had been detailed to attack Mory,
but that two of them had suffered very heavy casualties
in the two days' fighting.

The weakness, however, of the Ervillers position soon
became apparent. The formation of a defensive flank
was a temporary measure, and the position of the 119th
and Guards Brigades would be absolutely untenable if
the Sensée switch and the Army line there should
break. It was accordingly arranged with the Guards
Brigade that if the Sensée switch should fall, the two
brigades should withdraw—the Guards in that case
digging in behind the St. Léger valley, while the 119th
should continue their line on the right and protect
Ervillers. In the afternoon the enemy again attacked
Ervillers, under cover of two or three brigades of
field artillery which had been brought up to the ridge
and had been firing at close range though our two
brigades continued to inflict very heavy loss by enfilade
fire. By four o'clock it was reported that the Sensée
switch had fallen and that the enemy was advancing
up the St. Léger valley, a movement that would take
the Guards and 119th Brigades in reverse. In accordance with orders, therefore, the withdrawal was begun.
The 21st Middlesex were the first to be withdrawn,
followed by the 18th Welch. Lastly came the 13th
East Surrey Regiment. But as the enemy was at this
time pressing large forces into Ervillers the 119th
Brigade had no time to dig in in front of that village,
but prolonged the Guards' line behind it, so as to
protect Hamelincourt and Moyenneville.

During the two days' fighting around Mory, that village had been the scene of many instances of individual gallantry. Sergeant D. P. O'Sullivan, M.M., 18th Welch Regiment, when his company commander was wounded, took charge of two platoons and held a position for forty-eight hours without food or water, until his ammunition was exhausted. Finally, when completely surrounded by the enemy, he fought his way back to his battalion with the remnant of his command. Lieutenant-Colonel Warden had displayed his typical *sang-froid*. When the attack on Mory had not been progressing as satisfactorily as he had hoped, he went forward and led it himself, setting a fine example to all ranks. One of the Lewis gunners of the 13th East Surreys also distinguished himself on that occasion. This was Private J. Geary, who worked his gun forward with great bravery to a position from which he could deliver effective fire against some enemy strong points, and, when the order to retire was given, he maintained his position and covered the withdrawal by bursts of Lewis gun fire. After the withdrawal had been carried out he pushed forward to a small trench lately occupied by the enemy, silenced several snipers, and by his gallant conduct materially affected the course of the operations. The battalions which fought at Mory may well be proud of their achievement. Very favourable comment was expressed by those who witnessed the action. Amongst other remarks was that of a senior officer of a Guards' brigade, who, on ascertaining that the battalion which had been observed by him was the 21st Middlesex, observed to its commanding officer, " You ought to be proud of them. The action was carried out with the steadiness of a parade movement."

Inevitably March 24th was a day of some confusion, and amid the swirling current of events only here and there stand out solid rocks of fact. Brigadier-General C. Hobkirk was now in command of the 120th Brigade. That brigade had held up the Germans after they had

forced their way into Mory, having taken over and
reorganized the line from which the remnants of the
59th Division had been withdrawn during the night.
Communication was established with the 121st Brigade
on the left, but no touch could be gained to the east,
where " at about 7.15 that evening the troops belonging
to the division on the right of the Argyll and
Sutherland Highlanders retired to Favreuil, thereby
exposing General Hobkirk's flank and leaving
dangerous gaps which the 12th East Surrey Regiment
from the 41st Division was at once ordered to fill."
The headquarters of all three brigades were during this
day either in or just outside Gomiecourt, and the
neighbourhood was heavily shelled during the afternoon, so much so that the headquarters of the
121st Brigade became untenable, " and we spent most
of the afternoon in a deep trench in the middle of
the camp," and about 7 p.m., telephonic communication having been established with Achiet-le-Grand,
the headquarters were transferred there. Divisional
headquarters and those of the artillery had already
withdrawn to Bocquoy.

During the day orders had been received for the
relief of the 40th Division by the 42nd, and preliminary
arrangements were put in hand. Those who have tried
to follow the story of the confusion of three days'
fighting as described in these pages will appreciate the
feelings of the brigadier who was asked by a representative of the incoming division to point out on the map
" the exact defensive line of the 40th." The reply was
to the effect that so far as his brigade was concerned there
was a sketchy strip of terrain to be handed over, but
whether to the 42nd Division or the Germans depended
on whether Huns or British got there first. The relief,
however, had to be temporarily suspended, for shortly
before ten o'clock that night it was reported that the
Germans had broken through the division on the right
of the 40th, and were advancing from Sapignies to
Gomiecourt. Messengers were sent off hot foot to the

42nd Division to divert the relieving brigades to deal with this new menace, and accordingly the proposed relief was postponed. The 40th Division was, as a matter of fact, withdrawn during the night and ordered to dig in upon a line running practically due north and south, parallel to and slightly to the west of the Mory—Favreuil road, forming a junction with the 31st Division a mile north-west of Mory Copse.

At dawn on the following day, March 25th, the Germans once more launched heavy attacks, which were continued with unabated violence all day. Two of the Division's machine guns had been captured by the enemy near Ervillers, and Lance-Corporal A. H. Cross volunteered to recover them. Advancing single-handed to the German trench, he forced seven of the enemy to surrender to him at the point of the revolver, and made them carry the guns, tripods and ammunition over to our lines. In order to relieve the pressure on the right of the Division a strong counter-attack was ordered and pushed home; nevertheless, by three o'clock the situation was such that a further withdrawal to the high ground south-east of Gomiecourt was imperative. Meanwhile, the command of the 40th Divisional sector had passed to the commander of the relieving 42nd Division at 10.30 a.m., and, accordingly, during the afternoon Major-General Ponsonby moved his divisional headquarters back to Monchy-au-Bois. The three brigadiers subsequently transferred their headquarters from Gomiecourt and Achiet-le-Grand to the neighbourhood of Courcelles, Ablainsville and Douchy-les-Ayette, the troops being withdrawn during the night and concentrating at the last-named place and at Bienvillers.

A feature of the fighting of March, 1918, was that in the back areas there existed an anxiety and alarm exceeding anything of that nature felt by the fighting troops who were bearing the brunt of things up in front. It is now an established fact that German agents dressed as British officers were busy everywhere, and, speaking of March 26th, a brigadier of the Division reports that an officer of his staff, returning from leave, saw "officers dressed in British uniforms" cutting the traces of horses in draught and stampeding the animals. The particular shave that caused alarm on this morning was the news that the Germans had broken through at Hebuterne, but when a brigade was hurriedly despatched to deal with the supposed state of affairs it was discovered that no Germans were, nor had been, in the place. The "armoured cars" which imagination—or German agents—had depicted as careering about full of fiery Huns proved to be "nothing more alarming than French tractors." Orders were accordingly issued at 9.30 p.m. for all the infantry of the 40th Division to withdraw, the three brigades eventually assembling at Sombrin, Warluzel and Sus St. Léger, while divisional headquarters moved to Habarcq, and finally, on the following day, to Lucheux. After a night's rest the Division moved into the Monchy Breton sector, and on March 30th and 31st was sent northwards to take over the right sector of the XV Corps from the 57th Division, whose headquarters were then at Croix du Bac.

The artillery of the Division was not relieved, but remained in action, the brigades being allotted on the 27th inst. as follows: 178th to Guards Division and 181st to 3rd Division. This arrangement was followed by a series of orders and counter-orders, and later the 181st Brigade went to a Canadian division.

The great battle, or series of battles, was still in progress, and when it closed, early in April, the Germans were left in possession of a narrow salient projecting out towards Amiens. But although a great gain of terrain had been made, and although both British and French had suffered enormous casualties, the strategic object of the Germans had not been attained, and although the offensive had gained more than any other operation of the war the Allied line was unbroken at the end. By April 4th the Germans claimed 90,000 prisoners and 1,300 guns, and the British Fifth Army was practically out of action. It has been claimed that this offensive of the Germans was the most formidable in the history of the world, and it is probable that the verdict will be long unchallenged. But it did not exhaust the German effort, and the 40th Division—sent, nominally, to a quiet sector to recuperate—was to be called upon for a further great effort.

Officially the series of battles of which a portion has been touched upon in this chapter is known as The First Battles of the Somme, 1918, and the individual battles in which the Division took part were the Battle of St. Quentin, which is the name of the action which took place along the front of both the Third and Fifth Armies; and the First Battle of Bapaume on the 24th and 25th, the movement of the Division taking it into the area assigned later to that battle. The casualties endured by the Division were severe, amounting to about 2,800 of all ranks, of which number 133 were officers.

The words in which the divisional commander testified to his appreciation of all ranks speak for themselves, and are now reproduced.

" *To all ranks of the 40th Division.*

" I wish to thank the Division, one and all, for their splendid courage and behaviour. You know what the Commander-in-Chief and your Corps Commander think of you, and I can only say you have done your duty like British soldiers always do.

" We shall, no doubt, be called upon again to fight for all we are worth.

" We in the 40th Division, I know, will be ready again, and I feel very proud to be the Divisional Commander of such a splendid body of men as you have proved to be. I thank you all from the bottom of my heart, and whatever may happen I feel complete confidence in the ultimate result with soldiers of your spirit and bravery under my command.

> " JOHN PONSONBY, *Major-General,*
> " *Commanding* 40th *Division.*
> " 28/3/18."

In the official narrative prepared by the Division after the operations, special praise is given to the personnel of the medical units, in the following terms :—

" Owing to the constant shelling the difficulties of the R.A.M.C. were considerably increased, but in spite of this the front line was cleared and the wounded were got away most successfully. Field ambulances of the 40th Division dealt with a total number of 98 officers and 2,082 other ranks, of whom 41 officers and 978 other ranks belonged to the Division. In addition, it is estimated that about 200 other wounded of the 40th Division were loaded into the hospital trains at Grevillers and evacuated on March 22nd. Captain (Acting Lieutenant-Colonel) W. McCullagh, D.S.O., M.C., R.A.M.C., showed conspicuous devotion to duty, working under fire for five days, during which he received able support from Captains J. Linnell, D. Crellin, and P. Gaffikin. It would seem almost invidious to single out any instances of individual bravery shown by R.A.M.C. officers and men, by stretcher bearers and others, when all ranks worked so devotedly and tirelessly; a few typical instances may, nevertheless be cited. T./Capt. F. B. McCarter, M.C., R.A.M.C., attached to the 14th Bn. Highland Light Infantry, established an advanced dressing station at Mory on March 22nd, within 200 yards of the front line, and for forty-eight hours maintained the position under heavy fire and evacuated all casualties. T./Lieut. Daniel Berney, M.O., R.C., U.S.A., Medical Officer to the 13th Bn. East Surrey Regiment, established a similar station close behind the leading waves of our infantry during the counter-attack upon Mory on March 23rd, and subsequently established an aid post

on the Mory—Ervillers road, where he remained under
fire until he was himself twice wounded. On this day,
too, No. 11316 Pte. W. Wannan, a stretcher bearer in
the 13th Bn. East Surrey Regiment, brought in thirty
wounded men under a heavy enemy fire, and, at the
end of the day's work, carried Lce./Cpl. Castle, a
badly-wounded comrade, several miles back to the
dressing station. No. 37559 Pte. F. P. McIntosh,
14th Bn. Highland Light Infantry, who was attacked
by a German while dressing a wounded man, knocked
his assaliant down and bayoneted him with his own
weapon. Last of all one may mention the case of
No. 14231 Lce./Sgt. J. Robertson, 14th Bn. Argyll and
Sutherland Highlanders, who, when all the officers and
sergeants of his company had become casualties, took
command, held out between the Sugar Factory and
Vaulx until surrounded, and then fought his way out,
and later on, at Béhagnies, brought in two wounded
comrades in full view of the enemy and under heavy
machine gun fire."

On March 30th, H.M. the King visited the Division,
showed himself fully cognisant of the work done,
and was pleased to express his high appreciation
of the gallant behaviour and bearing of the 40th
Division. The Third Army Commander, General the
Hon. Sir J. H. B. Byng, K.C.B., K.C.M.G., M.V.O.,
also congratulated the Division on their conduct during
the operations. " By their devotion and courage," he
said, " they have broken up overwhelming attacks and
prevented the enemy from gaining his object, viz.,
a decisive victory." The VI Corps Commander, too, in
a letter to Major-General Ponsonby, said that he could
not speak too highly of the Division. " They have
made a magnificent defence and, tired as they must be
with so prolonged a struggle, have stood like a stone
wall between my right and the Germans. All I can
say is that I am deeply grateful, and feel that they have
nobly upheld the great fighting traditions of the British
Army."

MAP TO ILLUSTRATE THE OPERATIONS OF THE 40ᵀᴴ DIVISION IN THE GREAT GERMAN OFFENSIVE, MARCH 1918.

40ᵀᴴ DIV.

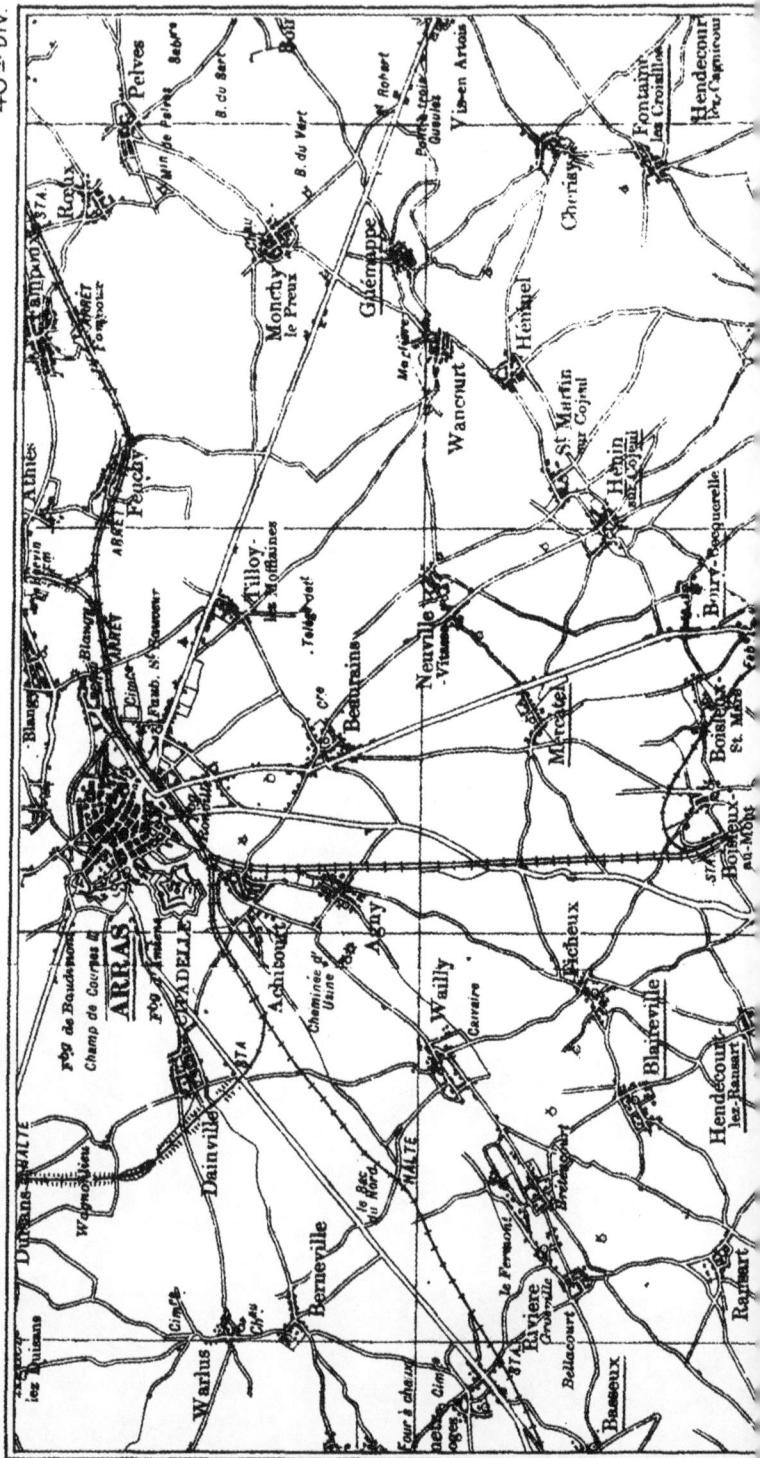

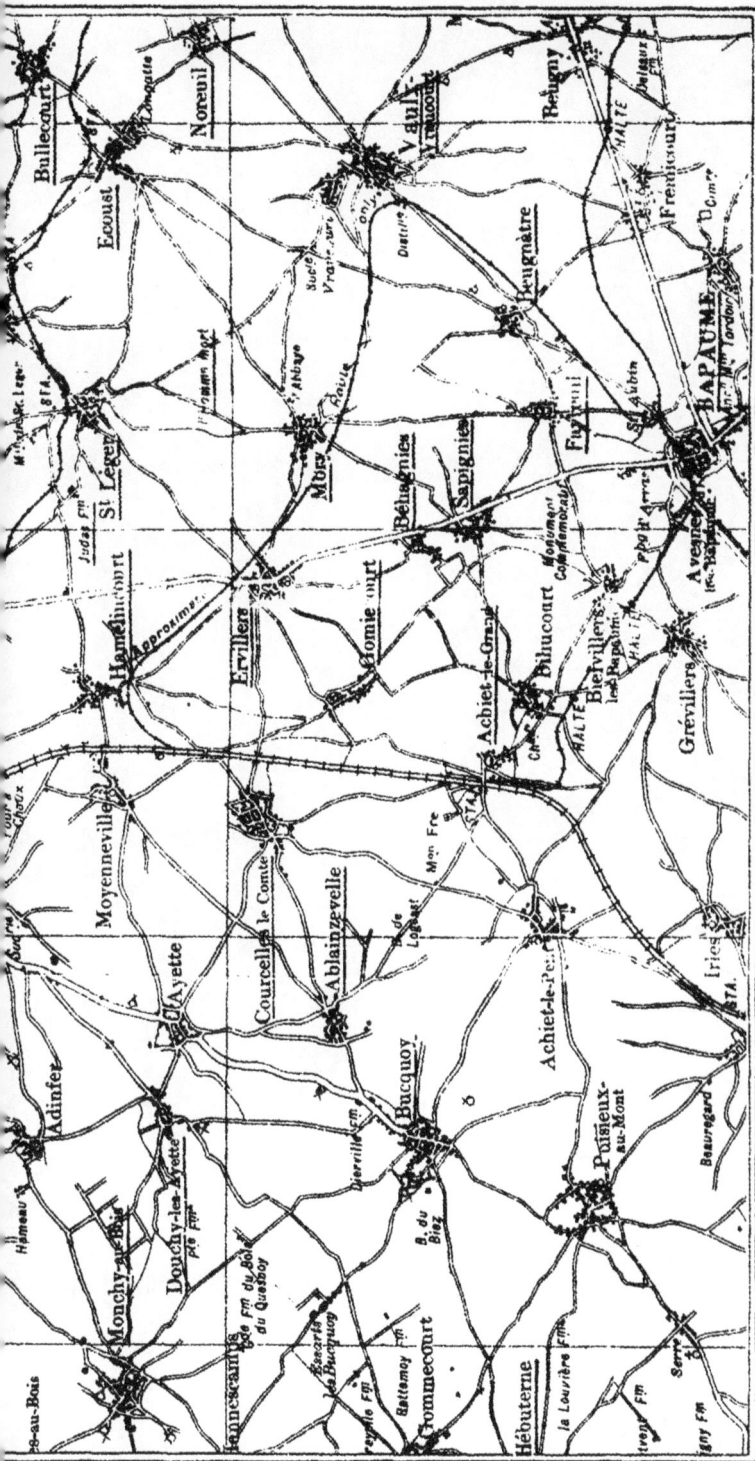

Reproduced by permission of H.M. Stationery Office.

To Face page 200

Mile 1   0   1   2   3   4   5   6   7   8   9   10 Miles

CHAPTER XI.

April, 1918. The Battles of the Lys.

IT is a far cry from London or Glasgow or Cardiff to Portugal, and doubtless few of the English, Scots and Welsh who made up the 40th Division knew much of the entry of our oldest ally into the war. Yet Portugal had come into the struggle before the 40th Division was born. As far back as August 7th, 1914, Portugal had proclaimed her loyalty to the British Alliance, and on November 23rd of that year had formally committed herself to participation in military operations. For two years such action was confined mainly to the defence of her African possessions, and indeed, the British Government had deprecated any very extensive participation by Portugal at all. In February, 1916, however, England agreed to the requisition of German ships lying in Portuguese harbours. Germany retaliated by formally declaring war on Portugal on March 9th. French and British military missions immediately proceeded to Portugal, where war training was put in hand. An expeditionary force was gradually got together, and by July, 1917, there were over 40,000 Portuguese troops on the Western Front.

The contingent was naturally "green," and it was clear to all who had to do with them that the Portuguese troops would have to go far before they could emulate the doings of their forbears in the Peninsula. It was considered advisable that they should be allotted a quiet sector in which to learn the game. The sector chosen was a portion of the line of the River Lys, south-west of Armentières; and at the

end of March, 1918, when the 40th Division was withdrawn from the line to rest and refit after the hammering
it had experienced, it was sent northwards to this
more restful sector, where it found itself with the
2nd Portuguese Division as its immediate neighbours.

Whether any given sector is restful and quiet or not
depends entirely upon the enemy. As a matter of fact
the Lys had been earmarked for trouble. At the end
of March General Ludendorff had prepared an offensive
there. At first it was to be merely a diversion, but
when it became clear that the Big Push on the Somme
would not lead to complete victory the Lys offensive
was extended in scope, with the aim of forcing a final
decision. A break-through was projected in the direction of Hazebrouck and St. Omer, and, since the
Germans had sized up the Portuguese pretty well, the
sector held by the latter was obviously the most
favourable spot for the first sharp thrust. Thus when
the 40th Division was sent to be neighbours of the
Portuguese the move, instead of bringing rest and
ease, was to involve it in fighting even severer than that
from which it had just escaped.

From this brief sketch of the general condition of
things we can now return to the 40th Division, which
was gratefully making its way to the imaginary Peace-
haven. On March 29th it moved to Chelers—" poured
with rain all day "—and here orders were received that
the Division was to move at once by bus and lorry to
join the XV Corps of the First Army at Merville.
The following day the King arrived in his car, and it
was here that he expressed his great appreciation of the
gallant behaviour of the Division in the recent fighting,
and his sincere sympathy for the heavy losses incurred.
The following day divisional headquarters opened at
Merville, and orders were received that the 40th was to
relieve the 57th Division in the line on April 2nd.

On that date the relief duly took place. The XV
Corps, under General du Cane, now consisted of but
two divisions, the 40th and the 34th, the latter old

neighbours of the Bullecourt sector. The line was here rather thin, for the corps was holding some eight miles of front, with no division in support or reserve. Although the sector was nominally a quiet one there was a general feeling in high quarters that the Portuguese might not stand up against a really punishing bombardment, and that the Germans might possibly attack in force down the La Bassée road. However, for the moment the Portuguese had their tails up. They sang nightly in their trenches, to the disgust of their neighbours, the 14th Argyll and Sutherland Highlanders, who much regretted the absence of retaliatory pipes, and during the night of the 2nd/3rd the Portuguese raided the German trenches. The raid was a great success. It is true that these particular trenches were found unoccupied, but so elated were the victors that it was with much difficulty they were persuaded to return to their own lines.

Alas! the Portuguese music was the funeral dirge —the Dead March—the coronach—the Flowers of the Forest—of the Highlanders. On April 3rd the corps commander came with sad news to General Ponsonby. The 14th Argyll and Sutherland Highlanders were to be disbanded and the personnel sent off as reinforcements to their other battalions. The divisional commander sent in a strong protest instancing in his letter that " this battalion has done particularly well," and commenting on the fact that it was deplorable that such a fine unit should be broken up after the Division had been so highly praised by the commander-in-chief. The appeal was, however, unsuccessful. The difficulties of man-power were overwhelming at the time, and the 14th Argyll and Sutherland Highlanders had to surrender their identity and traditions for the common good. The battalion was withdrawn from the line during the night of the 4th/5th, and the personnel was distributed between the 15th, 30th and 51st Divisions. It left the Division on April 7th, and the diary of the divisional commander bears eloquent

testimony to his appreciation of the past services of the
battalion and his deep regret at its departure.   Its place
was taken by the 2nd Battalion Royal Scots Fusiliers.
As some consolation the divisional commander received
during those few days a personal letter from General
Byng, commanding the Third Army.   In it the
general stated that he could not allow the 40th Division
to leave the Third Army without an expression of the
appreciation he felt for the splendid conduct of the
40th in the great battle which had just been completed.
He recalled how the devotion and courage of the
Division had broken the overwhelming attacks of the
enemy, and concluded by wishing all ranks of the 40th
all possible good fortune.

We may omit any description of the initial reliefs
which took place in the Division, and come at once
to its situation on the eve of the mighty attack which
was about to be launched against it.   During the night
of April 8th/9th, 1918, the 40th Division was in the
line in what is known as the Fleurbaix—Bois Grenier
sector; the title is somewhat misleading, for although
Bois Grenier marked one flank, the other was not
coincident with Fleurbaix, but was well to the south-
west of that village, or beyond Rouge de Bout to be
exact.   The area, strip, sector or zone between this line
Rouge de Bout—Bois Grenier and the River Lys in
rear was marked off into three subsidiary strips, the
Forward Zone, the Battle Zone, and Rear Zone respectively.   Of these the first consisted of a line of posts
behind continuous breastworks which ran the whole
length of the Division : the supports were also behind
breastworks, but these were not continuous, although
they were more or less so in the Fleurbaix, or right,
sector.

About a thousand yards behind the support line was a
tributary of the Lys, held chiefly by machine guns.
Immediately behind it came what was, in the right sector,
the forward edge of the Battle Zone, but was, in the
left or Bois Grenier sector, a subsidiary line.   The

rear edge of the Battle Zone was the bridge-head line, *i.e.*, a number of small posts at distances varying from 200 to 2,000 yards from the Lys. Many of these were very small earthworks, some recent, but others old and in poor repair. North of the River Lys was still another defensive line, mostly of recently-dug isolated posts. This line, however, had nothing to do with the division actually holding the sector, whose responsibility was normally confined to the defence of the Forward Zone and the forward edge of the Battle Zone. Briefly, the area allotted to the 40th Division was sub-divided into three longitudinal strips or zones, the general direction of which ran from south-west to north-east, and the intention underlying this sub-division was that, in case of attack, battle should be delivered on the intermediate strip, or Battle Zone, the defenders generally facing south-east. This idea was based on the hypothesis that the general pressure of the attack should be more or less equal along the front assailed. As a matter of fact, what was actually destined to happen was this. The Germans broke through the Portuguese. The pressure on the right of the 40th Division was instant and terrific. This flank was forced back and, so far from battle being joined on the prescribed zone, by noon on the first day the line of the Division lay athwart all strips and faced south instead of south-east. This is to anticipate the story which follows, but it will serve as a useful key to the narrative.

To the left of the 40th the 34th Division held the Armentières sector, with divisional headquarters in Steenwerck. On the right was the 2nd Portuguese Division, with headquarters at Lestrem. The headquarters of the 40th Division were now in Croix du Bac, north of the Lys. As for the internal distribution of the 40th, the front line was held by the 119th Brigade on the right, with the 121st on the left and the 120th in divisional reserve. The guns of the 40th Machine Gun Battalion were disposed so as to cover the whole front, and the artillery protection was given by the batteries of the 57th Division, *vice* those of the 40th, which had been left detached in the VI Corps area.

In greater detail, the 119th Brigade had the 18th Welch and the 13th East Surreys in front line. The former were on the right, and, as it turned out, in the hottest position of all. The 21st Middlesex were in brigade reserve. Of the 121st Brigade the right was held by the 20th Middlesex Regiment, the left by the 13th Yorkshires, while the reserve was formed by the 12th Suffolk Regiment. Both brigades had their Lewis guns and light trench mortars disposed so as to bring the maximum fire along the front. Twenty-four of the machine guns of the 40th Machine Gun Battalion were arranged so as to support the two infantry brigades in the front line; twelve guns were in divisional and four more in corps reserve. It will be remembered that the artillery of the 57th Division was now supporting the 40th, and of that artillery two brigades were south of the Lys and one on the left—or northern—bank. The 120th (Highland) Brigade was the divisional reserve, but only nominally so, for, so far from it being at the disposal of the divisional commander in emergency, it had been found necessary to map out for it a definite programme in case of an attack on the front line posts. The real reserve at the disposal of the divisional commander consisted of two companies of pioneers from the 12th Yorkshire Regiment, in Sailly; such portions of three field companies of Royal Engineers as were not actively employed at the moment; and No. 3 Special Company Royal Engineers, which at this time was at Erquinghem.

It is as well to mention the fact here that the Division was not up to strength when the fighting began in March on the Somme. The casualties there had been some 2,800, and many units were in a reduced and somewhat disorganized condition when they took over the new sector on the Lys. Drafts had been picked up in the trek north, and continued to arrive during the taking over of the new front, so that many infantry units of the Division had a high proportion of unknown officers and men. Further, the Division had left its own artillery behind and was working with that of another division. These features, the inseparable corollary to a big action, would have been merely an inconvenience in a quiet sector, but would naturally be a handicap in case of another serious attack.

Such was the state of the 40th Division and the position now held by it; and such, in outline, but it is hoped in sufficient detail, was the way the position was occupied. As a defensive position that now occupied was not ideal, for the troops of the front line had their backs to the Lys, a sluggish but unfordable river. A more obvious solution doubtless would have been to hold the northern bank of the river and to utilize the river itself as a defensive line, but this was quite impossible in view of the siting of the remainder of the great Western Front, which ran continuously from the North Sea to the frontier of Switzerland. As for the terrain, it was generally flat, for the valley of the Lys was not sharply defined, but it was overlooked by the long, low Aubers Ridge, which died away between Armentières and Lille. A feature of the country was the immense number of deep ditches, both in the zone of the 40th Division and on the enemy's side of it. These ran very generally from south-east to north-west, and, while favouring communication in the Division's sector, served also as covered ways for an enemy attack. On the other hand, the marshy nature of the land, with its numerous pools and swamps, seems to have led to the conclusion in many quarters that a hostile attack could only be made in small force. The country had been fought over before, and in 1914 had been traversed by the 6th Division of the " Old Contemptibles," which in October of that year had driven in the great cavalry screen; had forced the passage of the Lys at Bac St. Maur; and had then fought its way forward to Premesques, almost, but not quite, looking down into Lille. To one who then took part many of the place names of the battle now to be described strike a reminiscent note; and the farm north-west of Fleurbaix which served General Campbell for his headquarters on the night of April 8th, 1918, was the selfsame building which sheltered the headquarters of the writer's company when it was on outpost on the night of October 16th, 1914.

This farm was the scene of a curious incident a few days before the great battle of 1918. During April 5th the Germans had become more active, shelling a good deal and putting gas into Bois Grenier, and between 8 and 9 p.m. they were searching the headquarters of the 121st Brigade with unpleasant accuracy. The staff of brigade headquarters were foregathered for an evening meal, and the general's orderly officer was pouring himself a glass of port wine when a shrapnel bullet cut the stem of the wine glass and spilt the contents. Seldom can Providence have given a broader hint.

To come now to the Battle of Estaires, as the fighting which took place in this sector between April 9th and 11th is officially called, it may be said at once that it is a matter of great difficulty to present it in a coherent and consecutive narrative. Just as was the case with the fighting on the Somme described in the previous chapter, the sudden pressure of the enemy caused a disintegration of the defence, with the result that what could have been described fairly clearly had it been one connected battle becomes much more difficult of presentation when it develops into a series of more or less isolated and desperate engagements. The difficulty may, however, to some extent be eliminated if the fighting be arbitrarily sub-divided into divisions of time or space, or both, and here it will be convenient to bring the story of the battle up to noon upon the first day, with brief and intermediate halts for minor surveys.

Save for the shelling of approaches, the night of April 8th/9th was quiet on the whole line. 'At midnight a thick mist settled down upon the valley, and at 4.15 a.m. on this fateful 9th April a great roar of guns and rifle fire burst forth. The whole front of the Division was plastered with high-explosive and gas shells, and everywhere the bombardment fell not only on the front line but on the supports, battalion headquarters, and headquarters of the two front line brigades as well. For a moment it was thought that the roar was due to a raid which was being made from the left of the Division. But this was no mere affair of a raid; no raid ever launched could have stung the Germans to such activity, and the terrific din must betoken nothing less than an attack in force. At divisional headquarters all doubt was ere long removed. Soon after five o'clock word came in that the Portuguese on the right were retiring from their trenches, and, further south, the XI Corps reported that the Germans were heavily shelling the British front as far down as the La Bassée Canal. The divisional commander immediately ordered the 120th (Highland) Brigade, which was in reserve under Brigadier-General Hobkirk, to move forward to Laventie railway station, where it could strengthen the now exposed right flank of the Division; and next despatched Captain Harry Graham, of the divisional staff, by car to the headquarters of the 2nd Portuguese Division to ascertain the situation there. Meanwhile, orders had been sent to the corps reserve to stand-to, and the engineers of the 40th Division were directed to place in position all the emergency bridges—of which there were twenty-one—over the Lys. Soon after this word came in that the Germans were actually in the front trenches on the right of the Division, and that Brigadier-General Crozier was organizing a counter-attack to drive them out. It was now six o'clock; the mist added to the difficulty of finding out what was

P

going on; but it was clear that a great battle had begun. Captain Graham experienced great difficulty in getting to Lestrem. The roads were being very heavily shelled and he could not get through Estaires at all as the streets were blocked with the *débris* of fallen houses. Finally, however, he reached his destination, and found that Lestrem was entirely deserted and in " rapid process of demolition." It was being shelled and gassed, and much of it was in ruins. The Portuguese headquarters were found in a half-shattered château, in the cellar of which were a few British officers attached as liaison officers to the Portuguese. In a room on the upper floor—wrecked a few minutes earlier by a shell—was the Portuguese commander, General da Costa, " an exceptionally tall and melancholy man, sitting by himself in the attitude of a captain refusing to leave his sinking ship." Save for the liaison officers and the Portuguese commander the château was apparently uninhabited. Although General da Costa spoke English very well, Captain Graham was unable to obtain any real information. Touch had been lost with practically all the Portuguese units. The general idea seemed to be that they had evacuated their trenches and were still dispersed. This was actually the case.

What was happening ? Put yourself, reader, in the position of a soldier in the front line of the 119th Brigade. Picture to yourself a mist everywhere. Imagine shells bursting all round with a deafening roar; great clouds of earth spurting up; gas everywhere; you have your respirator on, and it does not make things clearer. Remember you are under the impression that you have been sent here because it is a quiet sector, and to have a kind of " stand easy " after the fighting on the Somme. It cannot surely be a raid. Perhaps it is merely a vigorous artillery *strafe,* just to intimidate us newcomers. Then flies Rumour, trumpet tongued, down the line. " The Portuguese have retired." And then, before you can well realize what *is* happening, the mist is full of moving Germans. Thousands of rifles seem to be firing rapid all at once, and there are Huns swarming, shouting, shooting and cursing in your front line. You are asking yourself every moment, " What's up?"

Well, what was " up " was this. It has been stated earlier in this chapter that the failure of the Big Push on the Somme to achieve complete success had induced Ludendorff to make a further effort on the Lys. The German Sixth Army was to attack along the line Armentières—La Bassée Canal, with Hazebrouck as the general objective, towards which the wings of that army should fold in when the Lys was crossed. Further, should this push succeed, another German army—the Fourth— was to throw itself into the fight north of Armentières. It is the Sixth Army, however, with which we have now to do. Seventeen divisions had been placed in readiness; an immense amount of artillery had been collected; and other divisions from neighbouring armies would be available to put in. Of the divisions of the Sixth Army, nine were to be in the first line, five in the second, and three in rear. The line to be broken was manned chiefly by the 40th Division and the Portuguese; and these latter were not credited with any great power of resistance. The conditions were favourable to carrying out the operation, for a spell of dry weather held out hopes that the ditch-intersected Lys plain would prove easy going. Everything, it was realized, would depend on surprise and speed. As a preliminary the Portuguese were to be thrown out; the gap was then to be instantly widened, and then, with guns and transport following hard on the heels of the infantry, the German Sixth Army was, so to speak, to clear the Lys in its stride as a sprinter clears a hurdle. All this will explain why the Germans seemed particularly in a hurry on that misty morning of April 9th, 1918.

To a certain extent the German bombardment had come upon the 119th Brigade as a surprise. During the night, patrols from both the 18th Welch and 13th East Surreys had entered the German lines and worked down trenches known as Necklace and Nephew. All was found quiet; no enemy was met; there was no indication of an impending attack; and most of the patrols were back safely in our lines by 3 a.m. Some of the 18th Welch were, however, apparently caught in the German advance. Just one hour and a quarter later the whole brigade in length and depth was being drenched with gas shells, and, the alarm having been given, all stood-to—"such a hurricane bombardment as I never wish to experience again : many gas shells were intermixed with high explosive and common shell, entailing the wearing of our gas helmets for two hours on end." For nearly an hour and three-quarters the tornado continued, and then, shortly before six o'clock, while an extremely heavy barrage was being put down on the support line, a report was received at brigade headquarters that German troops were going over the Portuguese.

At this time the transport of the brigade was occupying lines on the northern bank of the river, near Nouveau Monde, the journey to the front being made nightly under cover of darkness. In the trip just before the German attack, *i.e.*, during the night of the 8th/9th, the enemy shelling on the roads was particularly severe, and the return journey was, in consequence, exceedingly slow. When dawn broke, with a white mist, the considerable increase in the volume of shelling warned the transport officers that it might be advisable to take precautions against surprise attack, but before any steps could be taken something dramatic had occurred. "The Portuguese were seen running along the main road from the line and past the transport, and in their anxiety had abandoned weapons and everything else likely to impede them." The brigade transport at once gave orders for the transport to inspan and await orders.

To return now to the front line of the 119th Brigade.

It was apparently exactly at 6 a.m. that the Germans forced their way into the line: "the enemy broke through and entered our front (or outpost) line between right and left battalion posts," to quote the words of the official brigade narrative. This was apparently the work of advanced units of the enemy only, for German narratives give the actual infantry assault as having taken place more than two hours later. However that may be, the immediate crumpling up of the Portuguese, coupled with the fact that speed meant everything to the Germans, now afforded them an opportunity which was to be exploited to the utmost. Through the large gap formed by the retirement of the 2nd Portuguese Division the German infantry poured, and as the 18th Welch was the unit closest to the gap the full brunt of the attack fell on them. Except for the heavy shelling, the 13th East Surreys, on the left of the brigade, were for the moment undisturbed.

At half past six the position on the right of the 40th Division was roughly as follows: The 18th Welch were being heavily attacked; so heavily that the commanding officer had to ask for reinforcements, but " he was told there was none for him, and that he must use his nearest posts if they could be moved without risk to the situation," to quote the Narrative of Events of the 119th Infantry Brigade once again. The left battalion, the 13th East Surreys, was still intact and unassailed. Curiously enough, in spite of the terrific bombardment, the telephone wire from the reserve battalion—the 21st Middlesex—to brigade headquarters remained uncut, and Lieutenant-Colonel Metcalfe was able to transmit by this means half-hour situation reports.

In still further detail, at 4.15 a.m. the shells of the Germans fell simultaneously on the front, the support line, and the battalion headquarters of the 18th Welch Regiment. The order was at once given to stand-to, and the company commanders in the front line reported many casualties but no sign of the enemy. At

4.45 a.m. a few of the enemy were observed from the front line and checked by Lewis gun fire. Artillery support was now asked for. The 57th Division guns quickly responded, " but the very heavy shelling from the enemy side quite wiped out the sound of our guns." At half-past five the officer commanding " D " Company, who held Exeter Trench—the right defensive flank—reported the enemy making a flank march across his front, " and that he had killed hundreds." " On investigation, however, it would appear that these were the Portuguese leaving their line on account of the bombardment, and the thick fog caused the mistake, the colour of the uniforms being very similar." A quarter of an hour later the enemy advanced in force on the Portuguese front and apparently found the line empty, for no rifle fire was heard by the 18th Welch. The Germans now turned quickly upon the defensive right flank of that battalion, and at the same moment struck against the extreme left, i.e., at the junction with the 13th East Surreys, while also attacking the posts in the front line with parties of two-platoon strength. The frontal attack cost the Germans dear. " Here they were mowed down by Lewis gun and rifle fire; reports from men and officers mentioning piles of dead in front of the detached posts." The right company was now quite cut off, and at 6 a.m. the commander of the left company reported that the enemy were in force on his left rear and between him and his support line. Both these companies fought on to the bitter end.

Although we are for the moment dealing with the 119th Brigade, it will help in a realization of the story of the day if we glance for a moment at other portions of the Division at this hour of 6.30 a.m. In the 121st Brigade, on the left, the situation was still " normal "— it was enduring the tornado of gas and high-explosive shells, but there were as yet no other developments. The 120th Brigade was just starting on its trek to Laventie station, a destination it was destined not to reach owing to the rapid advance of the Germans. The

artillery—of the 57th Division—was, of course, in
action, and as for the engineers, they were just " getting
down to it " with placing the twenty-one subsidiary
bridges over the Lys in position.

For the next two hours and a half the actual hand-to-
hand, or close fighting was confined to the right of
the Division. At 7.10 a.m. the commander of the
119th Brigade reported to divisional headquarters the
development of the enemy attack which had broken
through the right sub-sector in two places, notwith-
standing which, the Welshmen were still resisting
stoutly. Meanwhile, the 120th Brigade, coming up
from its position in reserve, had received orders which
were practically to the effect to form a defensive flank
on the right of the Division and to dam the German
flood which was surging through the broken barrier of
Portuguese. The rapid advance of the Germans prevented the 120th Brigade from reaching the position
assigned, and the mist, in which the Germans were
sometimes taken for the retiring Portuguese owing to
the similarity of uniforms, was a handicap for the
defenders. The Germans appear to have jumped to the
situation, and gladly used the Portuguese as a
convenient screen. The line of the 13th East Surreys
was still intact, but by eight o'clock there were indications that the real pressure by the enemy would not be
long delayed, for along the whole front of the Division
intense drum fire was now put down upon the support
line of breastworks, and a quarter of an hour later the
officer commanding the 18th Welch reported that his
two support companies were now surrounded, but that
they were fighting it out. Against the sturdy break-
water formed by this indomitable battalion the wave of
the German onrush had broken. For a while the
human mole had withstood the immense momentum,
but was at last shattered by the pressure. No survivors
reached battalion headquarters, and there fell into the
hands of the enemy merely 2 officers and 14 other ranks,
all wounded.

The actual infantry assault on a grand scale was now beginning, and, with the right of the 119th Brigade battered in, the Germans pushed on rapidly in the direction of Fleurbaix. As a result of this movement the Germans got in rear of the East Surreys, whose support trenches they suddenly attacked from the right and rear about 9 a.m. A telephone message was sent at once to brigade headquarters with the information— the last telephone message to be received from the battalion. Very soon the whole of the 13th East Surrey Regiment was surrounded.

Meanwhile, at divisional headquarters the reports which had been coming in showed that the situation was becoming grave, but, owing to the rapid advance of the Germans, communication was interrupted and delay necessarily ensued in transmitting information. At 8.35 a.m. it was known that up till then the East Surreys had not been attacked; but by 8.45 a.m., although it was known that the 18th Welch were engaged, the information was apparently limited to the knowledge that " large bodies of the enemy were in the front line posts " and that " troops had been sent forward to kill them." By this hour, however, the 18th Welch had been practically annihilated and the Germans were streaming in behind the East Surreys. The fact that intense drum fire was being put down on the whole of the support line had got through to divisional headquarters, where this demonstration was rightly construed as the preliminary to a general assault by the enemy. Word was accordingly sent to the 121st Brigade warning them that the attack would probably extend to the left sector : the instructions were acknowledged, with the information that the situation was normal, but that Fleurbaix was under hot fire. Immediately afterwards—at 9 a.m. to be exact—orders were sent out from divisional headquarters to brigades to say " that, as the troops were not thoroughly familiar with the defences of the sector, there was to be no retrograde movement, but that units were to fight it out where they stood."

Such order was, however, impossible of fulfilment. In the 119th Brigade the 18th Welch were no more. The 13th East Surreys were indeed fighting where they stood, but were facing in two directions. The brigade of artillery which was acting with the 119th was forced to withdraw some of its guns in the face of large bodies of Germans approaching from the south and south-west. The machine guns on the extreme right had brought a heavy fire upon these attackers, but were soon practically surrounded; the crews continued to fight until all the guns were destroyed except one. Even in the 121st Brigade, where for some hours the situation had been normal, the pressure was now being felt. At 9 a.m. the officer commanding the right battalion—the 20th Middlesex—was told that the front line of the 13th East Surreys had gone. Lieutenant-Colonel Richards at once ordered his right company to form a defensive flank. Also "I sent an officer to H.Q. East Surreys. Two minutes later a very excited and wounded company sergeant-major of the East Surreys rushed into my H.Q. and informed me that their support line had gone, and that the enemy were advancing on my headquarters. My adjutant and second-in-command immediately took all orderlies to man Gunners' Walk. I then went in that direction and saw a large body of Germans advancing in extended order and in a N.E. direction. My adjutant and second-in-command were surrounded by overwhelming numbers before reaching Gunners' Walk." Thus the current was now sweeping round the right of the 121st Brigade, though the left battalion—the 13th Yorkshires —was not yet engaged. The barrage, however, had done much damage. One officer and ten men of the battalion had been killed, and exactly the same number wounded.

By ten o'clock all chance of a counter-attack had gone, and it was indeed a question whether the 40th Division, which had an unfordable river at its back, might not be cut off. One of the emergency pontoon bridges at Bac St. Maur was destroyed by hostile shell fire. The Germans were still making progress on the right of the Division, so much so that the guns supporting it were in increasing difficulty. In the 286th Field Artillery Brigade all the teams of " C " Battery were destroyed by machine gun fire while limbering up; " B " Battery likewise had no time to get its guns away, but in each case the guns' crews removed the breech-blocks and sights. In the 119th Brigade the Germans were now almost up to the head-quarters of the 18th Welch Regiment. Two reserve Lewis guns of the battalion kept up a spirited combat, but the guns were put out of action and the teams destroyed. By this time the Germans were within a hundred yards, and Lieutenant-Colonel Brown, after telephoning to brigade headquarters, gave the order to withdraw. A rear-guard action was accordingly carried out at point blank range.

Of this action the commanding officer writes : " A small action was carried out until about 10 a.m., when both guns were smashed by shell fire and the crews were all dead or wounded. The enemy were now only some hundred yards on each side of battalion headquarters, and were engaged by the signallers, the remnants of Headquarters Company, the signals officer and O.C. battalion. After about fifteen minutes, the enemy approaching steadily and also firing from the rear, I decided to make for Winter's Night Post and fought a rear-guard action all the way, losing, unfortunately, Lieut. Anthony and the medical officer and adjutant wounded, and most of headquarters killed or wounded. The enemy were at times well under 25 yards away, and we had the pleasure of shooting at them and knowing that we could not miss. On arrival at Winter's Night Post, where we found the commanding officer of the 21st Middlesex and a remnant of that battalion, the 18th Welch were represented by the commanding officer and 7 other ranks, including the signals sergeant. The enemy still approached, and

we fell back to a point just in front of Sailly, being
continually shelled."

As for the 21st Middlesex, just before this the
remaining two companies, from brigade reserve, had
been ordered to move forward to the support of
the machine gun line, but were unable to get
so far. Very shortly afterwards the commanding
officer reported that Germans were in the vicinity of
Rouge de Bout, and were streaming towards Sailly,
Bac St. Maur, and Fleurbaix. It was now decided to
withdraw the headquarters of the 21st Middlesex
towards the Lys. The headquarters, from a personnel
of about 100, had been reduced, through casualties, to
4 officers and 58 other ranks. Leaving the doctor and
the padré to look after the wounded, the headquarters
started for the river; none too soon, for Germans were
seen creeping round the exposed flank. On nearing
Sailly a strong point, in which were some 200 Royal
Engineers, was entered with a view to making a stand
there. But the place was clearly untenable, and there
was nothing for it but to cross the river and line the
opposite bank.

As for the remainder of the 119th Brigade, the East
Surreys had been surrounded. Only a few succeeded
in fighting their way out, and these struggled towards
Sailly. By this time all details had been ordered up
to brigade headquarters, which had been shifted back
to a position just south of Bac St. Maur, and here, by
eleven o'clock, some of the 12th Yorkshire Regiment,
details from the trench mortar batteries and stragglers
were holding a line facing south, with the right
"connected with a Scotch battalion who threw their
flank back to the River Lys."

It will be remembered that in the 121st Brigade the
20th Middlesex was on the right, and that when the 13th
East Surreys were surrounded the pressure of the
Germans was instantly felt by the Middlesex. The
commanding officer of that battalion had endeavoured
to form a defensive flank, but the Germans had been

too quick. Two more attempts were made in rapid succession, but without avail. Accordingly, at 10 a.m., the brigade commander telephoned to his left battalion —the 13th Yorkshire Regiment—informing him of the situation and directing him without delay to form a defensive flank. This was carried into effect at once along a communication known as Shaftesbury Avenue, and the line proved to be a refuge for the 20th Middlesex Regiment, in which the casualties had been very severe. Lieutenant-Colonel Richards and his headquarters were in an extremely tight place, " but by pluck and good leading he managed to extricate himself and his men." After his several attempts to form a defensive flank, which were frustrated by rapidity of the enemy's advance in a north-easterly direction, the officer commanding the 20th Middlesex " then tried to form a flank on Greatwood Avenue, but could find no men. The enemy were advancing rapidly, and we came constantly under short range machine gun fire. I collected what men I could and fell back to the 13th Yorkshire Regiment, who were holding Shaftesbury Avenue. I saw the O.C. 13th Yorkshire Regiment, and as he had the situation well in hand, and it was his sector, I decided to place my men under his command and that I would stay with him."

This was about 11.20 a.m. on April 9th—or 12 noon according to the report of the commanding officer of the 13th Yorkshires, who wrote : " O.C. 20th Middlesex Regiment arrived at my B.H.Q. and stated enemy then near Red House Farm. His battalion practically annihilated." It was just about six minutes earlier that the 13th Yorkshire Regiment itself had begun to feel the enemy's attack, for at 11.54 a.m. the Germans were reported to be attacking the battalion's right flank post—called Peter and Paul. The S.O.S. was transmitted by pigeon, by runner, by two rockets, and through the 9th Northumberland Fusiliers, the neighbouring battalion of the division on the left. There was no response from the artillery—not to be wondered at, seeing that the Germans had got right up to the guns, as already reported. But the machine guns and trench mortars of the battalion managed to beat off the attack, and another attempt by a strong enemy patrol to enter the line was also stopped.

The 12th Suffolks, in reserve to the 121st Brigade, were still intact. Two companies had manned the Fleurbaix defences at 7 a.m. These defences had been under heavy shell fire since 4.15 a.m., " a tremendous amount of gas being used." The first actual view of the enemy was gained by a patrol of the battalion, which was sent forward towards Croix Blanche about 10 a.m. and came in contact with a party of Germans, near the cross roads, estimated at sixty strong. At half-past ten the battalion headquarters were withdrawn to the farm behind Fleurbaix where the brigade headquarters were installed, and just at this time word came from the patrol near Croix Blanche that a large party of enemy cyclists had been spotted near Croix Maréchal, moving towards Bois Grenier. The Suffolks were now holding a defensive line, and, although nominally in reserve, were hotly engaged. The whole line was under heavy machine gun fire from the Germans who had got through, or at any rate well into, the Battle Zone of the Division. In the line of the Suffolks were the battalion Lewis guns in concrete emplacements and in shell holes. Three of the Lewis guns were put out of action by the enemy fire, one gun being destroyed by a shell which killed all the team. The fighting was severe and continuous, but great loss was inflicted on the enemy, who continued to move in sections or single file across the Suffolks' front towards the west.

How far the Germans had now penetrated into the sector of the 40th Division will be understood when it is mentioned that at 11 a.m. the *artillery* supporting the 121st Brigade reported Germans to the left rear of Fleurbaix, and a few minutes later a medical officer of the artillery reported that he had been captured in that village while evacuating wounded, but had been

released. All men who could be collected at the brigade
headquarters were now hurriedly sent forward, and the
officer commanding the Fleurbaix defences was told to
hold on at all costs. Shortly afterwards, with the
approval of Division, the headquarters of the 121st
Brigade were moved back to Fort Rompu, near the
Lys. The fort was found to be evacuated, and was
under heavy shell fire. The headquarters were accordingly moved to the northern bank and temporarily
installed at a place called Essex Post.

The reserve brigade of the Division, *i.e.*, the 120th,
had originally been ordered—shortly after 6 a.m.—to
support the Portuguese left; and, when it was found
there was no Portuguese flank to support, the 120th was
soon in danger of envelopment itself. Consequently,
the right of the brigade was folded back to the bridges
at Nouveau Monde, and an effort was made to extend
the left to Charred Post—just south-east of Rouge de
Bout—so as to form a defensive flank along the right
edge of the Battle Zone and Rear Zone of the Division's
sector. The occupation of Rouge de Bout rendered
the carrying out of this plan impracticable. The left
flank of the 120th Brigade was now much exposed.
Here was the 14th Highland Light Infantry; and the
2nd Royal Scots Fusiliers, with a section of machine
guns, were sent up from brigade reserve to strengthen
it and to prolong the left on the general line north of
Laventie—Barlette Farm—Fleurbaix.

General du Cane, the corps commander, had visited
divisional headquarters about 9 a.m. and brought the
news that the Germans were attacking Givenchy, to
the south. " As the morning went on reports came
streaming in that the Bosch was penetrating everywhere." And at 10.45 a.m. from XV Corps came word
that charges were to be placed in position ready for the
destruction of the permanent bridges over the Lys. To
the commander of the 40th Division—so far as the
Division's sector was concerned—was left the responsibility of "saying when "; this responsibility had

naturally to be passed on to the C.R.E. of the Division
—since it was of the utmost importance that no delay
should arise from reference to higher authority when the
decisive moment should arrive.   In practice the devolu-
tion had to go still further, *i.e.*, to the Royal Engineers
officer at each bridge.   The general instructions by
which they were to be guided were as follows : the
bridges were not to be destroyed so long as they could
be defended, but they were to be blown up immediately
the enemy reached their vicinity in force.

For a few minutes after 12 noon there was a slight,
but perceptible, slackening of the German effort, and
in the temporary lull we may endeavour to mark the
position of the Division after eight hours of terrible
effort.   Working from right to left, the line now held
by the 40th Division was approximately as follows : The
120th Brigade was holding the main road on the south
bank of the Lys from Nouveau Monde to Sailly
inclusive, with advanced troops holding the railway at
Sailly station.   Then came what was left of the 119th
Brigade, which continued the line to Barlette Farm.
The holding of this sector was somewhat nominal, for,
as will be understood from the above narrative, the
119th Brigade was now reduced by the attrition of
battle to a mere shadow of itself.   Of its three
battalions the 18th Welch was represented by merely
the commanding officer and 7 other ranks, including
the signals sergeant.   The 21st Middlesex was likewise
reduced to the commanding officer and a remnant of
the battalion.   The 13th East Surreys had been
surrounded, and on this day alone had in killed,
wounded and missing a casualty list of 524 : it was,
therefore, also but a remnant.   And as these three
remnants had coalesced round Sailly the remainder of
the brigade line must have been more nominal than
real, although brigade headquarters had raked together
every available man and thrust them into the line.   The
situation in this particular sector had, however, been
relieved by a brigade of the 34th Division marching

from Erquinghem towards Bac St. Maur. This brigade helped to fill out the line of the 119th Brigade, and to link up with the 121st. The 121st was still holding on to the Fleurbaix defences, but with a front here somewhat disjointed; the left still held part of its original front line, with a defensive flank holding what was known as Shaftesbury Avenue.

Such, then, was the position of the 40th Division about 12.15 p.m. on this 9th April. The line ran athwart the three zones into which the sector allotted to the Division had been divided. The right of the Division was in the Rear Zone; the centre in the Battle Zone; and the left of the Division was in the Forward Zone. The Division was now facing due south. This paragraph needs throughout the qualifying phrases "approximately" and "generally speaking," but otherwise the situation now given fairly represents the position of the 40th Division at midday on this, the first day of the Battles of the Lys.

So far as was possible the units of the Division made use of the temporary lull to rectify their alignment and to get touch one with another. The lull, such as it was, lasted, however, for but a short time, and there is a pregnant entry in a brigade narrative to the effect that "things now began to move very rapidly." So rapidly, in fact, that exact chronology broke down. One incident, on which the correct narration of the remainder of the day's fighting depends, is the blowing up of the bridges over the Lys, and more particularly the main bridge at Bac St. Maur. But although the historian is working from several official and first-hand sources of evidence, it is not easy to fix this occurrence with certainty. Various times are mentioned, from noon till 2.30 p.m., and it is difficult sometimes to differentiate between the permanent structures and the temporary foot-bridges. Such discrepancies are, however, inevitable; but although they cause some difficulty in the construction of the narrative, such difficulties yield to patient comparison and investigation. And here let a tribute be paid to the work of the staff of the Division, whose records and diaries in thoroughness, detail and accuracy are nothing short of wonderful considering the circumstances in which they were first assembled.

It seems clear that somewhere about one o'clock the troops of the 120th and 119th Brigades had been forced to cross the Lys, and by that hour they were holding the northern bank actually defending the bridges—that is to say, both the permanent iron and stone structures as well as the temporary floating bridges. The first of the former class to be destroyed was almost certainly that at Bac St. Maur. This village was in the sector of the 119th Brigade, and the hard-pressed headquarters had, about one o'clock, fallen back to that portion of the village which was on the northern bank, having crossed the river by one of the temporary foot-bridges. Major Amery Parkes, of the 40th Battalion Machine Gun Corps, was put in command of details in Bac St. Maur—*i.e.*, the north side—consisting of 2 machine guns, 1 Lewis gun, and some brigade headquarter details, and ordered to hold the bridge and village at all costs. This little detachment did great execution, but the gunners were all killed or wounded, including Major Amery Parkes seriously wounded and Captain Herbert killed. A counter-attack was now actually made " with remnants," which cleared a few of the enemy from the north side of the river.

It was this sequence of events which was prefaced by Brigadier-General Crozier, in his official narrative, with the remark, " Things now began to move very rapidly." The hour is given as 1.45 p.m., and there then occurs the sentence : " Somewhere about this time a R.E. officer reported and said he wanted to blow the main bridge, as he was afraid the leads would be cut by the shelling. He was told to blow." This agrees fairly well with the official Division narrative, which says the bridge at Bac St. Maur was " abandoned and blown up about 2.30 p.m." We shall

probably not be far wrong if we assert that the
demolition of this bridge took place at 2.15 p.m. The
exact hour may seem to be a matter of small moment,
but it is of great assistance to the historian to have one
outstanding fact definitely fixed as regards time.

While this History was actually in the press a
detailed account of the blowing up of the Bac St. Maur
bridge was contributed, and this invaluable narrative
is now reproduced. It will be noticed that the hour of
the demolition is given as 2.15 p.m., the exact time
which the historian had arrived at by a process of
deduction.

" As the morning advanced and the fog cleared, it
became evident to those stationed at Bac St. Maur that
the enemy must be advancing fairly rapidly if the
volume of traffic westward over the bridge could be
taken as an index. For hours a mixed multitude, consisting of civilian refugees, Portuguese soldiers, and
transport of every description streamed steadily across
the Lys.

" The bridge, which was built on the remains of the
permanent bridge wrecked in the earlier months of the
war, consisted of heavy timber trestles, bedded on to
the old stone foundation piers, carrying a substantial
roadway capable of taking all ordinary traffic. The
demolition charges had been laid for months, successive
field companies taking and handing over the responsibility for the same as division relieved division in the
sector. In course of time various alterations had been
made in the original scheme, and the guncotton charges,
amounting to just over 900lb. in weight (as nearly as
could be calculated) were distributed in a very thorough
manner. The charges were laid with the object of
simultaneously wrecking the two centre trestles and cutting through the road bearers at the centre of the three
middle bays. Electrical detonation was arranged for,
and the firing leads were laid in duplicate to a dug-out
on the south-west bank of the Lys, where they ended in
a watertight, heavily-protected terminal box. The

224th and 229th Field Companies relieved the field companies of the 57th Division on April 3rd, and the demolition system for the Bac St. Maur bridge was taken over by one section of the 224th Field Company, commanded by Lieutenant Carr, an officer who won his M.C. in the La Vacquerie raid in 1917. The charges were carefully inspected on or about April 5th, and the resistance and conductivity of the detonators and connecting wires measured at the same time.

"Shortly after the intensive bombardment began in the early hours of April 9th, and it became clear that something more than an ordinary raid was contemplated, the sappers detailed for bridge duty took up their station under the direct command of Lieutenant Carr, M.C., who had received instructions to defer the destruction of the bridge until the last possible moment, in order to allow the maximum amount of transport to cross the river in the event of a retreat. The terminal box in the dug-out was unfastened, and the leads tested for continuity at hourly intervals.

"During the morning Bac St. Maur was heavily shelled with high explosive, shrapnel and gas shells, and there were several casualties round and near the bridge. Towards noon tests of the cables were taken almost continuously, in order to make sure that no flying pieces of shrapnel or other missiles had cut through any of the all-important wires. Shortly after noon, orders were received to remove all transport on the west side of the Lys, as far back as Croix du Bac, and by this time all the civilian refugees were across the bridge and the end had been seen of the Portuguese. Shortly after one o'clock the 57th Division Royal Field Artillery brought their last gun across the bridge, followed by two 6in. howitzers of the Royal Garrison Artillery. Unfortunately, a direct hit knocked out the horses of the leading gun just as the same cleared the bridge on the west side, and completely blocked the roadway for some minutes.

"By two o'clock the enemy machine gunners had

obtained a footing in the high houses on the east side
of the Lys, and commenced machine gun fire on the
bridge. A few minutes later, enterprising bodies of
Germans opened fire from the windows of the houses
overlooking the bridge, with trench mortars. It was
obvious that no further purpose could be served by
keeping the bridge standing, and at 2.15, just as the
first detachment of the enemy were setting foot on the
approach, Lieutenant Carr fired the exploder, and
the bridge blew up with a tremendous report. Unfortunately, during the bombardment, some of the sub-leads
suffered damage, as the demolition of one of the trestles
was not complete, but the bridge was hopelessly
wrecked, and it says much for the enterprise and fore-
thought of the enemy that they were able to fix their
temporary bridge, which they brought up from the rear
on lorries, before midnight. Lieutenant Carr and his
four sappers got away safely behind the high west bank
of the Lys, but, unfortunately, Lieutenant Carr was
killed by a shell later in the day."

At Bac St. Maur the situation was not reassuring.
Although the permanent bridge had been blown up,
three floating bridges still spanned the river. Further,
the village on the south bank, now held by the
Germans, was well adapted for fire action. From the
river, which was lined with houses, the ground rises
abruptly, and the slope, covered with still more houses,
formed, so to speak, terraces from which tiers of fire
could be directed on the northern bank, which was
much less thickly covered with houses, and on the
bridges below. Again, the defenders, in the shape of
details of 119th Brigade headquarters, were now
reduced to very small numbers indeed, and were quite
inadequate to withstand any determined efforts by the
Germans to rush the crossing.

To this critical situation arrived a welcome ally
in the shape of Lieutenant-Colonel W. E. Brown. It
has been related earlier in this chapter how Colonel
Brown, with a handful of his battalion headquarters,

fought a rear-guard action back to Winter's Night
Post, where he found the commanding officer of the
21st Middlesex with a similar remnant.   Pushed hard
by immensely superior numbers of Germans, these two
fragments had fallen back to Sailly and across the river.
Here Colonel Brown and Colonel Metcalfe disintegrated
again, each performing invaluable work, and, leaving
Colonel Metcalfe for the moment, we shall follow the
commanding officer of the 18th Welch.

At Sailly, Colonel Brown found a hundred or so of
reinforcements " who had been sent up and did not
know where they were."   Taking command of these,
and adding them to his own tiny remnant, Colonel
Brown made his way to Bac St. Maur, where he formed
a line on the northern bank.   The time given in some
narratives is 2 p.m., but this is probably too early;
from internal evidence it is clear that the main bridge
no longer existed, and as this seems from various
deductions to have been destroyed about 2.15 p.m. the
posting of Colonel Brown's detachment must be timed
after that hour.   However this may be, there were still
three floating bridges over the river, and it was imperative to deny these to the enemy.   The task was an
exceedingly difficult one.   The detachment was under
heavy fire from snipers in the houses on the other bank,
and the Germans could be seen advancing in lines of
platoons two deep, with machine guns on sledges.
Colonel Brown's party succeeded in cutting the
mooring ropes of two of the bridges and setting them
adrift down stream, but the third bridge was swept by
heavy machine gun fire and, after several casualties, the
attempt had to be dropped.   In addition to machine
guns the Germans, favoured by the haze which hung
over the valley this sultry April afternoon, had been
able to rush up some field guns, which opened fire on
the northern bank of Bac St. Maur at about 1,000 yards
range.   *Grenatenwerfer* were also installed in the upper
stories of the houses on the south bank, and did
considerable havoc among the defenders on the other

side. Enfilade and oblique machine gun fire now added
to the difficulties of the defence. It was clear that the
northern portion of Bac St. Maur could not be held
much longer, and at 4.5 p.m. the headquarters of the
119th Brigade fell back in extended order to Croix
du Bac.

It was here that the headquarters of the Division had
been installed, but the tide of battle had by this
rolled almost up to the very walls of the place. The
staff had been working at very high pressure all through
the morning. The driving in of the right flank of the
Division had presented a great problem to " G," for
the battle was soon divided into two halves, the 121st
Brigade being pushed gradually away from the
remainder of the Division; while for " Q " the Lys was
an immense difficulty. All movements to and from the
line " bottle-necked " at the bridges, and this obstacle
made ammunition supply and the evacuation of
wounded more than usually hard. Then, too, in the
course of the fighting, divisional headquarters had
acquired control of various brigades and odd units to
help on the right. " A curious fact and merciful " was
that scarcely a single shell dropped in Croix du Bac; it
was thought at the time that the Germans wished to
" nurse " the village for their own use later on, and
this view was confirmed by subsequent events.

There was, however, no such immunity from rifle
and machine gun fire once the Germans had reached
the Lys. After a hasty luncheon the divisional
commander was told that " the Bosch had crossed the
river and was advancing on our headquarters; matters
became uncommonly unpleasant as bullets began
coming in by the door and through the windows."
The first statement was, it is now clear, an exaggera-
tion; but the bullets were very real, and were those
probably fired from the upper stories of the houses at
Bac St. Maur at a range of about 1,400 yards. Evacuation was now urgent, and " was carried out in the
approved theatrical fashion as the place was full of

wounded, and maps, papers, etc., had to be hurriedly
burnt in bonfires in the gardens." The civilian inhabitants of the place were now panic stricken, and their
removal was another difficulty. General Ponsonby first
made his way to Steenwerck, where he reported the
situation and was informed that eight German divisions
had been attacking during the morning. The road to
Steenwerck was crowded with refugees, many of whom
were wounded, all flying for their lives, very old women
carrying their beds on their shoulders, and " babies
being wheeled along three in a perambulator." " It
was 1914 over again, only rather worse, for these people
had lived in comparative safety here for over three
years." Since October 15th, 1914, to be exact, on
which night the author's company, the vanguard of
the 17th Brigade, stole cautiously into Croix du Bac on
the heels of the retiring Germans, being the first unit
to enter that village in the war.

General Ponsonby's intention was to establish his
headquarters at Doulieu. Here he was met by a deputation of priests, " who asked me to tell them what
was going on." The situation was briefly described,
although, perhaps, in more hopeful colours than things
warranted at the moment. News, however, came in
that the 50th Division was coming up on the right and
that probably the 29th would arrive next day. Later
the headquarters were moved further back to Vieux
Berquin. It is worthy of mention that a staff officer of
the Division, in describing the departure from Croix du
Bac, writes as follows : " I recollect, on leaving, seeing
our infantry retiring, wave by wave, across the fields
to a line of trenches just outside the village, and the
movement was being done as if on a field day."

Having deposited divisional headquarters in their
new abode, we must now return to the Lys and put the
clock back some hours. A dozen or so paragraphs
back it was related how Lieutenant-Colonels Metcalfe
and Brown arrived, fighting a rear-guard action, at
Sailly. The subsequent movements of the latter have

been traced, and it has been told how he found a reinforcement of 100 men or so and led them to Bac St.
Maur. Colonel Metcalfe likewise found "various
detached parties of men of different units, *e.g.*, pioneers,
labour, heavy gunners, some with officers and some
without." These were all roped in by Colonel
Metcalfe who, as senior officer on the spot, assumed
command of a mixed "commando" of 400 men, of
whose grit and determination during that afternoon and
the next two days their temporary chief writes in the
highest terms of praise. It was during this afternoon
that the present Chief Constable of Somerset laid himself open to penal servitude. "A patrol reported that
a lorry with mails for the troops had broken down in
the vicinity. A party was at once despatched to bring
in the mail bags, which I opened, extracting therefrom
all parcels likely to contain food or tobacco. Quite a
haul of both was made and distributed to the commando. Eventually I closed up and resealed the bags,
sending them—much lighter—to the rear." "I have
often thought since," muses Colonel Metcalfe, "that a
policeman robbing H.M.'s mails was a bit of a
paradox." But his withers are unwrung by the recollection, for he adds, defiantly, "Anyhow, we all very
much appreciated the swag." Jesting apart, the action
of an officer who put new life into undaunted but tired
and hungry men with a sudden issue of commandeered
chocolate and cigarettes, and damned the consequences,
is worthy of record in the history of the Division.
Many were the sound decisions Lieutenant-Colonel
Metcalfe made in the war, and this was not the least
of them.

It is now, say, half-past four. For twelve hours
the battle has been raging, and we may pause in the
detailed narrative just to take a bird's-eye view of the
whole situation of the Division. The general line of
the Division was roughly as follows. The right flank
was on the north bank of the river, opposite Sailly, and
the line ran thence on the northern shore to Bac St.

Maur and thence to opposite Fort Rompu. From that post the line was carried on by the 34th Division—which now included most of the 121st Brigade—via Streaky Bacon Farm to the original left of the Division, and beyond. Working from the rear to the front, divisional headquarters are still at Doulieu, on the Lys. The 120th Brigade, which now numbered about 200 rifles with only two Lewis guns, was holding the right sector in conjunction with troops of the 150th Brigade. The Germans made repeated attempts to cross by the Sailly bridge, but were driven back every time by the 2nd Royal Scots Fusiliers. As for the 119th Brigade, it was now represented but by some remnants of head-quarters and the scratch commandos of Lieutenant-Colonels Brown and Metcalfe whose doings have been narrated. All these were on the north side of the Lys. Of the bridges over the Lys the two at Sailly were still standing. That at Bac St. Maur was destroyed about 2.15 p.m. Shortly afterwards those between Sailly and Estaires were blown up; and about 4 p.m. those between Sailly and Bac St. Maur. In several cases the destruc-tion was only partial, and in the case of the Pont Levis bridge at Estaires an entire failure, owing to the leads having been destroyed by shell fire. The 121st Brigade —to which we shall soon come—was still battling stoutly south of the river; but, before doing so, it may be stated that somewhere between 4 and 5 p.m. the 74th and 150th Brigades had been put in along the River Line Defences north of the Lys, and the units of the 40th Division in that area were ordered to withdraw and concentrate in a position of reserve about Le Petit Mortier.

The operations of the troops of the 121st Brigade were altogether different from those just related. The right of the 121st Brigade, as will be remembered, had naturally been compromised by the destruction of the 119th, and when during the morning the enemy's attack extended eastwards in considerable strength the defenders of the Forward Zone, with the exception of a

small portion on the extreme left, had been forced back
on the Fleurbaix defences. These were held by the
12th Battalion Suffolk Regiment, who continued to hold
on with great gallantry until late in the afternoon.
The fighting had been continuous and severe, and the
defences were gradually surrounded by the enemy, a
post at Canteen Farm, east of Fleurbaix and held by
one company of the 12th Suffolks, being captured by
the Germans. This company then came under orders
of a battalion of the 34th Division which was holding
posts north and east of Canteen Farm; oddly enough,
this battalion proved to be the 11th Suffolk Regiment.
Meanwhile, Brigadier-General Campbell had proceeded
to the headquarters of the 101st Brigade (of the 34th
Division) at Erquinghem, endeavouring to get touch
with his battalions from which he had been cut off,
Lieutenant Richards being despatched from here to
gain touch with the 13th Yorkshires and to ascertain
the situation there. This was about half-past two, and
not long afterwards the Germans were on the railway
in rear of the 12th Suffolks and actually attacking near
Fort Rompu, where a battalion of the 16th Royal
Scots, of the 101st Brigade, was now in position. The
12th Suffolk Regiment was now an island rising from
a sea of Germans; in more military language, its flanks
were turned; in plainer speech, its position was very
serious.

Accordingly, at 4.30 p.m., after a brief consultation,
it was decided to fall back fighting a rear-guard—and
flank-guard—action. Under covering fire of Lewis
guns the garrison moved out and fought their way
towards the river, arriving at the railway east of Fort
Rompu, where the battalion filled a gap between the
16th Royal Scots on the right and the 11th Suffolks on
the left. Here the 12th Suffolks dug in and remained
all night. The casualties were very heavy, particularly in " B " and " C " Companies. The headquarters had been cut off from the battalion in the
retirement and came under a very brisk machine gun

fire, but eventually got to Fort Rompu. Three times before half-past six the enemy formed up to attack this post, but each time the fire of the defenders frustrated the design. The 12th Suffolks were, about this time apparently, placed under the command of the 16th Royal Scots. The records are, however, not very clear, and it may be mentioned here that, according to the official narrative of the Division, the 12th Suffolks were withdrawn north of the Lys at 6 p.m. This is obviously a slip, for both the battalion and brigade narratives give the crossing of the river as not taking place till the afternoon of April 10th.

But though the records are confusing and uncertain —and, unfortunately, the fighting between 11 a.m. and 4.30 p.m. is not described in the battalion narrative— there is nothing uncertain about the gallant and protracted defence put up by the 12th Suffolk Regiment, nor of the effect it had upon the battle. So long as the Fleurbaix defences held out the Germans could not leave them safely in their rear, and delay was thus imposed upon the attackers; and delay was just what the Germans were frantically anxious to avoid at all costs. Further, and no less important, the tenacity of the 12th Suffolks was of immense value to the 34th Division upon the left, whose right flank was thereby greatly strengthened. The 34th Division did not fail to recognize the fact, and about 4 p.m. the G.S.O.2 of that division had come to Erquinghem full of "the splendid defence of Fleurbaix by the 12th Suffolks." He stated that he feared they had been overrun by the enemy. This, as we know, was luckily not the case, but the staff officer's anxiety is pretty clear testimony to the fact that the 12th Suffolks held out to the last possible moment.

Shortly after the lull which had taken place in the middle of the day it was found necessary to withdraw three posts on the front of the 13th Yorkshire Regiment and to readjust the line. Even with this readjustment, and even including the reinforcement provided by the

remnant of the 20th Middlesex, the front to be held by
the battalion exceeded 3,000 yards. This was the line
on which Major Miskin decided to stand, and he
gave orders that it was to be held at all costs. An
observation post named Peach Barr was kept manned
continuously, and gave valuable information as to the
enemy's movements. This was forwarded by pigeons
while they lasted, and through the 9th Northumberland
Fusiliers, but in the hurly-burly of the battle no answer
was ever received. At about half-past three Germans
were seen massing to the south-east of Bois Grenier, but
any attack was frustrated by the activity of the machine
guns and rifle grenades of the defence, so that by 4.30
p.m. the possibility of an attack had been removed.

Such was, generally speaking, the state of affairs at
half-past four in the afternoon; the Division being
astride of the Lys with both wings mixed up with other
troops. Somewhere about 5 p.m. divisional headquarters issued an order for a concentration of the
remnants of the 120th and 119th Brigades at Le Petit
Mortier. When the order reached the former brigade
there were no troops available to relieve the 2nd Royal
Scots Fusiliers, covering Sailly bridge; they were
accordingly left in position and the other two battalions
fell back as ordered, together with some drafts that had
arrived, and "elements of carrying parties." About
300 rifles in all thus concentrated at Le Petit Mortier,
and were formed into a composite battalion. Similarly
the remnants of the 119th Brigade—on being relieved
by some of the 25th Division—likewise fell back to
Le Petit Mortier, where a composite battalion was
formed. The enemy was now reported to have crossed
the river in large numbers at Bac St. Maur and to have
taken Croix du Bac. The 74th Brigade, with the 12th
Yorkshire Regiment co-operating on the right, was
sent to counter-attack, but not much progress was
made.

The destruction of the bridge at Sailly deserves
some notice. While the 224th Field Company carried

through the destruction of the Bac St. Maur bridge, as narrated earlier in this chapter, the 229th Field Company, who were also stationed in Bac St. Maur village, had the demolition in hand of the permanent bridge at Sailly-sur-la-Lys, higher up the river, and the closely adjacent pontoon bridge, together with three small floating footbridges between Bac St. Maur and Sailly-sur-la-Lys. The enemy did not reach Sailly until about 5.30 p.m., where similar scenes were witnessed to those at Bac St. Maur, and throughout the morning and early afternoon the permanent bridge was practically solid with refugees and transport moving westward.

Towards noon Lieutenant J. G. Voce, commanding the No. 1 Section of the 229th Field Company, destroyed the foot-bridges and the pontoon bridge, and thereafter remained with his men, who were responsible for the demolition of the permanent structure. At 6 p.m., when the enemy was practically on the foot-step of the bridge, Lieutenant Voce fired the exploder, and the demolition was very largely successful. Three trestle legs, however, were left standing, and, in the face of intensive machine gun firing and trench mortar bombardment, Lieutenant Voce, with his section sergeant and four sappers, made repeated efforts with mobile charges to effect the demolition of the remaining portions. Finally, when the supply of guncotton was exhausted, this gallant officer, who lost an eye in the early days of the war, withdrew his men, with two minor casualties only.

At 7 p.m. the situation of that portion of the 40th Division north of the river was as follows: Of the 119th Brigade, what was left of the 21st Middlesex was holding part of the Steenwerck Switch (which ran parallel to and east of the river shown on the map running from Steenwerck into the Lys); the composite battalion was acting as an outpost line round Le Petit Mortier. Of the 120th Brigade the composite battalion was in reserve to the 119th, with the

2nd Royal Scots Fusiliers still guarding the river about Sailly. The night thereafter was very disturbed, the enemy having, it is believed, reached Steenwerck and sending up Véry lights along the whole front; and as heavy rain fell the conditions were most uncomfortable. Several attacks were made on individual posts, but were all beaten off, and four prisoners were made from the enemy.

At the divisional headquarters at Vieux Berquin there was a hard night's work for all concerned. The various brigade headquarters were out of touch with their first line transport, and the three " A " and " Q " divisional staff officers practically took control of the whole of the horsed transport of the Division. " We collected the majority in the vicinity of Vieux Berquin, gave the transport officers all available information as to the locality of their units, and got them off during the night with rations and water and much-needed supplies. It says a great deal for these transport officers and their men that, in spite of great difficulties, they found their units in practically every case. The principal difficulty was in gaining touch with the units of the 121st Brigade who were now far away on our left." During the night much essential information was collected, and communication improved by the 40th Divisional Signal Company Royal Engineers, who worked very hard and well. Vieux Berquin, from being a fairly back-area, comfortable place, became a great centre of activity and was under fairly constant shell fire. The difficulties were aggravated by the necessity of evacuating a large civil population, " with mountains of possessions, cattle and live stock of all kinds."

South of the Lys, nothing in the way of any sustained attack was experienced by the 12th Suffolk Regiment during the night, the position of the battalion being on the right bank of the river, just east of Fort Rompu, with the battalion headquarters, which now consisted of 2 officers and 7 runners, amalgamated with the headquarters of the 16th Royal Scots at Erquinghem. On the extreme left of the Division the Germans attacked a post of the 13th Yorkshires at 7.30 p.m. with two parties, each about 40 strong, but after an hour's fight were driven off, the Stokes gun of the defenders doing excellent work. After this the night passed without incident. Reserve rations and hot tea put new life into the troops, and ammunition was replenished from the reserve of the 9th Northumberland Fusiliers. At the request of the commander of the 34th Division, Brigadier-General Campbell placed the 13th Yorkshires and elements of the 20th Middlesex under the orders of the 103rd Brigade, the 12th Suffolks being now attached to the 101st Brigade. The headquarters of the 121st Brigade were then transferred to Doulieu.

Such is the tale of 'April 9th, 1918.

CHAPTER XII.

APRIL, 1918. THE BATTLES OF THE LYS (*continued*).

THE 40th Division was now separated into two portions with the River Lys, and incidentally thousands of Germans, between the two wings. When dealing with the fighting of April 10th it will therefore be convenient to treat of that portion north of the Lys first, and to carry on the story so far as it affects what we may call the "right wing," leaving the 121st Brigade, which, as a matter of fact, was for the moment part of the 34th Division, until later in the chapter.

Shortly after 4 a.m. Lieutenant-Colonel Brown was ordered to hold the Steenwerck Switch, and took the composite battalion of the 119th Brigade into the line, having now on his right details of the 21st Middlesex and the 12th Yorkshires (Pioneers) on his left. The extreme right of this line was now on Sailly Bridge. The composite battalion from the 120th Brigade moved into a position of reserve north-west of Le Petit Mortier, and dug a line facing generally south-west. At about six o'clock Colonel Brown's men were shelled with 8·9's, which did much damage, " but the men stuck to their posts with really admirable fortitude."

Meanwhile the information at divisional headquarters showed that the German attack was even bigger than had at first been expected. The corps commander looked in early at Vieux Berquin and announced that "the enemy are attacking hard upon our left, and are going for the Messines Ridge." It had been discovered that his objective on the previous day had been the

Lys River, but that the reports as to the number of Germans who had crossed to the northern bank were probably exaggerated. This may or may not have been the case, but there is a note in the divisional commander's diary : " Heavy fighting is going on everywhere, and I have now ordered Crozier to hold the line of the Steenwerck Switch." This is what has been described in the previous paragraph.

About 9 a.m. an order was received from corps for the 40th Division relative to a counter-attack. If the reader will look at the map to illustrate the battles of the Lys he will see that the Lys south of Croix du Bac forms a loop concave to the defenders. The 119th and 120th Brigade elements were at the western end of the chord ; the 74th Brigade (of the 25th Division) was apparently somewhere near Croix du Bac. At any rate, the plan was that the three brigades (or what was left of them, for the 74th was also very weak) were to endeavour to push the Germans into this bight and squeeze them into the river. The hour was fixed for 3 p.m., but long before this, while the arrangements were in progress, the 74th Brigade, under pressure from the enemy, commenced to withdraw northwards. There was now the unpleasant possibility that the enemy, flushed with success, might butt against the Steenwerck Switch, which, indeed, he began to do, while the left flank of the 119th Brigade was very much in the air. In consultation with General Crozier, the commander of the 120th Brigade decided to send his composite battalion to prolong to the left, and it was in position about 12 noon.

Meanwhile considerable enemy activity was developing about La Boudrette, and the troops on both flanks of the 2nd Royal Scots Fusiliers, opposite the Sailly Bridge, withdrew. For a considerable time the Fusiliers were left entirely alone hanging on to this position, but later the troops on either flank were again brought on to a line some 200 yards in rear of the original one. 'As the situation at this point looked rather serious, one com-

R

pany of the Pioneer battalion was moved round towards
La Boudrette to be at the disposal of the commanding
officer of the 2nd Royal Scots Fusiliers.

Divisional headquarters were still at Vieux Berquin,
" which village was beginning to show signs of the
hammering it was receiving from artillery fire." " A "
and " Q " continued their control of all transport, and
there was a good deal of re-arrangement of horse lines,
etc., as well as much activity in arranging for supplies
of every nature. Information was more readily obtainable on this day at headquarters as numerous wounded
officers were " cleared " through Vieux Berquin by the
Royal Army Medical Corps, who worked hard and well.
As it was clear that a further retrograde movement
might be necessary, fresh refilling points and dumps of
all kinds were formed. Drafts kept coming in; usually
" at most inopportune moments." Much difficulty, too,
was experienced in getting rid of the civilian population,
and their effects and the roads were full of refugees.
Some of the scenes were pathetic in the extreme; dead
women and children lying about everywhere, and priests
administering the sacrament to many of the wounded
on the roadway.

Somewhere about two o'clock it was reported that the
Germans had got in behind the 120th Brigade; while
they were also pushing against the front of the
Steenwerck Switch. The situation was now very
obscure, the only thing really clear being that the attack
was very heavy. Of the 119th Brigade composite
battalion, Lieutenant-Colonel Brown writes: " We
improved our line, but the shelling was terrible
(8-inch). In front were several small copses in
which the enemy had installed machine gun nests
during the night. These harried us all the time,
and an attempt by one of my companies to surround one was repulsed with heavy loss. The ground
was perfectly flat, and we could not get to our objective
for lack of cover." The report that the enemy were in
rear of the 120th Brigade seems to have been an over-

statement, but that brigade had other trouble, for it seems that when the 74th Brigade was pushed back it took up a position facing west, and for some time fired into the 120th Brigade composite battalion. The situation about this time is succinctly described in one narrative in these words : " Continual and heavy pressure was maintained all along the line of the Steenwerck Switch, and the situation remained obscure. Gaps were known to exist at several places, but battalions were ordered to hold on at all points as information was received that the 29th Division was going to counter-attack." The worst gap was apparently between the 119th and 74th Brigades. The enemy was now west of Steenwerck, and his machine gun fire was very severe. " At this time the enemy put down a most accurate barrage of 8-inch on our new line—an aeroplane had previously been over." Thus the narrative of the 119th Brigade and the shelling is obviously that described by Colonel Brown at the beginning of this paragraph.

About four o'clock—or possibly somewhat later—Lieutenant-Colonel Brown ordered his whole line to advance with fixed bayonets. This was carried out in really fine style, with the result that some shallow depressions in front were occupied, and the whole of the attacking line was advanced about a quarter of a mile. This opportune offensive had its reward, for the line was now out of the shell zone. Four hours' respite was thus gained, and it was dark before the enemy artillery had grasped the new state of affairs.

This was not the only counter-attack, and, indeed, it would seem that the one now to be mentioned was carried out practically simultaneously with that described in the preceding paragraph. That now claiming attention is one which was carried out by the men of the 14th Highland Light Infantry, the 10th/11th Highland Light Infantry, 2nd Royal Scots Fusiliers, and the 21st Middlesex. By this offensive the Germans were driven back some 600 yards, a few prisoners were made, and an enemy machine gun was captured. The

120th Brigade composite battalion was now in touch with the 119th Brigade upon the right, but no touch could be gained with any troops on the left.

On the whole, the night of the 10th/11th was uneventful. Indeed, from 8 p.m. till midnight everything was comparatively quiet, and except for attempts by enemy scouts to penetrate the line there was nothing to report. In one narrative an optimist actually records : " 10th/11th April, midnight. Things looked better." The strain, however, had been terrific, and the reader will realize from the account of the battle so far given how little rest had been possible from 4.15 a.m. on the 9th till 8 p.m. on the 10th. The news that the 29th Division was hurrying forward and would counter-attack gave great encouragement, but unless help came soon the exhausted survivors of the 40th would reach the limit of endurance. Nevertheless, the *moral* of the remnant of the Division still stood high, as the following incident will prove :—" About dusk a rumour was passed down the line of detached shelter pits (which had not yet developed into a continuous trench) to the effect that a further retirement had been ordered. How this rumour got about I am not prepared to say "—it is Lieutenant-Colonel Metcalfe who speaks—" but I heard early next morning that a Bosch dressed in the uniform of a British staff officer had been captured in the neighbourhood from which the rumour came. The effect of it was that troops began to dribble back, amongst others my own remnant of 21st Middlesex men, who were posted in the centre of the commando. These, when called upon and told that the order to retire was erroneous, at once turned and retraced their steps, the remainder of the commando following suit. But it was touch and go, as a gap at this stage would have been disastrous, for the Bosch were pressing up hard, and were close up."

It is an intriguing problem to endeavour to plot the positions of units north of the Lys during the night of April 10th/11th, but only a conjecture can be made.

The records consulted contain many errors and incon-
sistencies. Thus the 119th Brigade narrative states that
at 5 p.m.: " As the right was very obscure brigade
headquarters moved to an estaminet at F.22.d "—a spot
miles on the enemy's side of Lille. The following,
however, seems a rough approximation. A mile or so
north-west of Steenwerck was the 88th Brigade of the
29th Division. A little south of Steenwerck or there-
abouts was the 74th Brigade of the 25th Division. Of
the 120th Brigade the composite battalion had its left
(which was not in touch with the 88th Brigade) at the
little triangle of two roads and a river west of Steenwerck, and its right a mile due south. Then from
about Le Petit Mortier the composite battalion of the
119th Brigade carried on, although from some accounts
it would appear that it was further forward, or echeloned
to the right front of the 120th Brigade composite
battalion. The 2nd Royal Scots Fusiliers (of the 120th
Brigade) had been pushed back from Sailly Bridge to
about a mile to the north-west of it, and to the left rear
of that battalion was another brigade of the 29th
Division dug in and facing south and south-east.

We can now, in accordance with the arrangement
made at the beginning of the chapter, transport ourselves across the intervening wedge of Germans and
reach the south side of the Lys about Fort Rompu.
Here were the 12th Suffolks, dovetailed into the 101st
Brigade of the 34th Division. At eight o'clock in the
morning heavy shelling, as well as machine gun fire
from front and left, followed by an enemy attack, forced
the troops back towards Erquinghem. Severe fighting
continued throughout the day, and at 4 p.m. orders
were received to cross the Lys and then to hold portion
of a line known as the Erquinghem Switch. This movement was successfully carried out in conjunction with the
16th Royal Scots, but meanwhile the Germans had been
steadily streaming across at Bac St. Maur, and some
of them were heading north-east. The 12th Suffolks
and Royal Scots were in touch with the 102nd Brigade

on the left, but the right flank was in the air until, as will be related, the 13th Yorkshires got near Nieppe.

The extent to which the 40th Division had been riven asunder will be realized when it is borne in mind that the 13th Yorkshires—still near Bois Grenier—were seven miles, and separated by a river, from their brigade headquarters, which were now at Doulieu. At half-past four in the morning three patrols were sent out from the battalion, which got into touch with the enemy, some of whom were digging in. Nothing much happened till 8.45 a.m., when the Germans made an attack upon one of the posts held by the 13th Yorkshires, but this was repulsed. An hour or so later there was some heavy shelling, and at 1 p.m. the enemy attacked, forcing their way into the position of the Yorkshires so that touch was temporarily lost between " A " Company on the right and " B " Company on the left. A counter-attack threw out the Germans, and two enemy identifications were obtained—of the 22nd and 369th Regiments. The attackers were, however, still massed outside the trench line known as the Haymarket, and arrangements were now put in hand to drive them back by a further counter-attack to be launched at 4 p.m.

Shortly before that time, however, it was found necessary to assemble a conference of the commanding officers of the 13th Yorkshires, the 20th Middlesex (the remnant of which was absorbed in the former battalion), the 9th Northumberland Fusiliers, and 1st Lincolns—the two latter of the 34th Division. The disturbing feature was that it was now known that the Germans were closing on Erquinghem. It was in these circumstances decided to endeavour to secure the river between that place and Armentières, and that the bulk of the four battalions should be withdrawn across the Lys by the railway bridge and be concentrated at Touquet Parmentier, where the road running south-west from Nieppe crosses the railway. The proposed counter-attack was therefore cancelled. At 4.15 p.m. the

Germans rushed Shaftesbury Avenue. A mist now began to form, and this facilitated the withdrawal of the 13th Yorkshires, which began at five o'clock. Machine gun fire was, however, very annoying, and on approaching the southern edge of Armentières Germans were seen advancing about 500 yards away. A force under Captain de Quetteville deployed and moved out to the attack at 6 p.m. At this time the Germans were plastering the southern suburb of Armentières—known as Rue Marle—with a heavy barrage from both light and heavy guns, and the suburb was in flames. The battalion skirted Rue Marle, and thence moved along the railway to the Armentières-Sailly road. It was now reported that the railway bridge was down, but that the one on the Nieppe road was still standing. The companies passed over by this bridge after brushing aside an enemy patrol, under an officer, in Armentières, the officer being killed. In spite of the railway bridge being down, the battalion headquarters scrambled across by it, and by 8 p.m. arrived at Touquet Parmentier. Touch was now gained with headquarters of the 103rd Brigade, and orders were received to hold a strip of the railway in front. This was carried out at midnight, " very dark and impossible to see the lie of the land."

If the reader has followed this chapter he will see that the two wings of the Division were now facing each other from the opposite sides of a triangle, of which the base was the River Lys, between Sailly and Armentières; and the apex roughly Steenwerck. And so ended April 10th, 1918.

During the morning of April 11th "things were not going too well" at Vieux Berquin, where were the divisional headquarters. The actual building where these were installed was fortunate enough, but much damage was done all around, and a waggon delivering rations at the door was destroyed by a shell. Food was now running short, and the divisional staff were beginning to regret the "open house" policy which it had maintained throughout the battle. Some anguish was caused by "a selfish C.O. who blew in and finished our last tin of bully without a murmur." Why one should murmur while eating bully beef is not stated. It is currently believed to this day that he finished the whisky as well; and in one divisional narrative it is not difficult, by reading between the lines, to note the despondency caused by the calamity.

During the morning General Ponsonby, with two of his staff, made his way to Doulieu. At this village Brigadier-General Campbell had established the headquarters of the 121st Brigade, and was busy collecting all stragglers and posting them for the defence of the village, which was being shelled rather heavily. The divisional commander then went on to a small farm north of Doulieu, "where I found Crozier and Hobkirk: they both seemed tired out. All I could tell them was that divisions were coming up behind us and that we must all hang on as long as possible and stop the Bosch." General Ponsonby also records seeing some of the 12th Yorkshires and 21st Middlesex, with whom he spoke. "They were all right, but pretty nearly all out with fatigue."

The shelling now seemed to be increasing as the divisional commander was returning to Vieux Berquin. Soon after his return the corps commander came in, who reported that "26 German divisions are now in front of us, and he thinks their objective is Hazebrouck and the railway." The corps commander was loud in his praise "for the way the Division had fought and stuck it out." Then came the welcome tidings that the 40th were to be relieved and to be withdrawn right behind.

So far as the 119th and 120th Brigades are concerned the day's work was simply to hang on and to hold off the Germans until the promised relief should be effected. At dawn the enemy started a heavy bombardment of the southern portion of the line, and, massing about La Boudrelle and to the south of that village, made some heavy attacks.   La Boudrelle is not marked upon the map accompanying this chapter, but is about half a mile due north of La Boudrette.   About ten o'clock the troops on the right of the 2nd Royal Scots Fusiliers began to withdraw rapidly and the enemy worked round the right flank of this battalion, causing it rather heavy casualties and eventually forcing it back on to the line of the 29th Division, which was slowly falling back on Doulieu.   The enforced retirement of the Royal Scots Fusiliers caused General Crozier to ask the 29th Division for a battalion to stiffen up the front held by the composite battalion of the 119th Brigade, and accordingly a battalion of the South Wales Borderers was sent up.   Here the situation was critical.   The line was very thin.   The men were at twenty paces interval.   There was practically no reserve.   At 10.45 a.m., after heavy drum fire, the Germans made an attack upon the centre, which fell back but reformed again with hardly any loss of ground.   Oddly enough, the enemy made no attempt here to follow up his temporary advantage.   It was about this time that the brigade major, who had been sent out to ascertain the situation, returned and reported "the enemy pressing very heavily on our sides and centre."   The head-quarters of the 119th Brigade now moved to Vieux Berquin, and here orders were received relative to the relief by the 31st Division.

By 12 noon the situation of the 119th and 120th Brigades was roughly as follows : The right flank was about a mile north-west of La Boudrette; the left flank, which was sharply refused and "in the air," was from a mile to a mile and a half due west of Steenwerck. Although the line was composed nominally of two brigades, the total bayonets was less than two full battalions.   During the afternoon the right was steadily driven back towards Doulieu, and the situation in the centre became very serious, as the line was very thin and strong attacks were being made.   It will be remembered that the 2nd Royal Scots Fusiliers were on the

extreme right, but by the end of the afternoon only
3 officers and 20 other ranks were together, and these
were withdrawn behind the 29th Division at Doulieu.
Owing to the serious position on the left flank the
commanding officer of the 2nd Royal Scots Fusiliers
was ordered to move the remnants of his battalion, with
stragglers of other battalions, to support the left.

Somewhere about 5 p.m. the withdrawal of the troops
in the forward area was placed under the orders of
Lieutenant-Colonel Brown. The operation was rendered possible by a successful attack by a brigade of
the 31st Division, by which La Becque was regained.
With some difficulty Lieutenant-Colonel Brown
managed to get in touch with the relieving brigade,
and by 11 p.m. had withdrawn his men to a position
in rear of the line, ready to march off. The troops
were ordered to retire to the Forêt de Nieppe, but this
destination was altered to Strazeele. The movement
was delayed by a difficulty over the " relief chit," with
the result that the withdrawal had perforce to be
postponed till dawn. Divisional headquarters were
transferred to the château at La Motte, where some
confusion ensued owing to the fact that three other
divisions had already installed their headquarters there.

To pass now across to the other wing of the Division,
at 2 a.m. on this day, the 11th, the remnants of the
12th Suffolk Regiment had coalesced with the 13th
Yorkshires and what was left of the 20th Middlesex, the
whole coming under the command of Lieutenant-
Colonel Richards, of the last-named battalion. The
composite battalion thus formed was, about 8 a.m.,
withdrawn into support at Pont d'Achelles, where it
dug in. Nothing of any outstanding importance
appears to have taken place during the forenoon, but
at 2 p.m. reports were received that the enemy had
broken the front line and had got round almost as far
as Romarin. The 12th Suffolks, supported by the
13th Yorkshires, were ordered to counter-attack and
restore the situation. The operation was successful,

the enemy retiring in a northerly direction, having abandoned several machine guns. At five o'clock the Suffolks received orders not to press the attack further, as an advance in a northerly direction might prejudice the withdrawal which was to take place during the night. In this withdrawal the 13th Yorkshires were to act as a rear-guard to enable the 12th Suffolks to pass through. The operation began at 8.30 p.m., and the destination of the composite battalion which now represented the 121st Brigade was Strazeele, where it would join up with the main body of the 40th Division. Keeping to the north of the Armentières—Bailleul railway, the composite battalion reached Strazeele about 5 a.m. on the 12th, and came again under the orders of Brigadier-General J. Campbell.

The Division was now united once more, for the 120th Brigade—or what was left of it—concentrated about Strazeele during the morning, as did also the 119th Brigade. The latter had a rather rough passage, for owing to the difficulty over the relief chit already referred to the withdrawal had to be carried out in broad daylight in full view of the enemy, so that the retiring troops were badly harassed by low-flying aeroplanes. " If here and there there was a little moving at the double instead of in quick time it was checked at once; the 21st Middlesex remnant setting a splendid example and firing all the time under a perfect hail of machine gun bullets. In his ' History of the Peninsular War ' Napier wrote stirring lines concerning the ' Die-Hards ' at Albuhera, and right worthily their scions of the 21st Middlesex played *their* part in this retreat, and in that of the Somme, before overwhelming numbers." The words are those of Lieutenant-Colonel Metcalfe, the commander of the battalion, who was seriously wounded in the retirement, and to whose inspiriting example the steadiness of his battalion is largely due. It is breaking no confidence to state that the divisional commander's private diary talks of " old Metcalfe, who commanded his battalion splendidly for the last three days," and that, in the Somme affair, a similar document by his brigadier states that "old Metcalfe was wonderful." After the latter little episode, when every one else was pretty " done to the world," Lieutenant-Colonel Metcalfe calmly went out trout fishing. He was fortunate in the unit he commanded, taking it over in December, 1917, when, as he himself writes, " it did not take me long to discover that I had got hold of a real live unit which had ' found itself ' at Bourlon Wood and had got its tail up."

The forenoon of April 12th thus found the Division reunited again, and the XV Corps to which it belonged was transferred to the Second Army this day. The divisional headquarters had been moved back to a school at Au Souverain, just south of Hazebrouck, and orders were received to take up defensive positions round that town and Strazeele. During the night the chaplain of the 119th Brigade—Watson by name—had died of wounds. "An extraordinarily brave padre; he was killed trying to help the wounded along."

When April 12th dawned the great German thrust was by no means over, but so far as the 40th Division was concerned it had fought itself to a standstill, and it took, and indeed was incapable of taking, any further real share in the battle. In that sector of the fighting represented by the map accompanying this chapter it may be mentioned that by now the German X Reserve Corps had overrun Ploegsteert Wood (the " Plug- street " of all time) and had its left wing about Romarin. The town of Armentières, with more than 3,000 men, 45 guns and ample stores, had fallen into the hands of the enemy. The II Bavarian Corps had pushed through Nieppe (not to be confused with the Forêt de Nieppe at the other side of the map) to Steenwerck station. The XIX Corps had succeeded in reaching Neuf Berquin Church, while the IV Corps had taken Lestrem and Merville. On the British side it was all important to prevent any increase in the hole made by the Germans, and to the 40th Division fell the defence of Strazeele and Hazebrouck. For the security of the former place the remnants of the 119th, 120th and 121st Brigades were placed under Brigadier-General Crozier, and at 3 p.m. the 119th and 121st were ordered to dig a defensive line, the 120th Brigade engineers and pioneers forming the reserve. Brigadier-General Campbell, with such units as could be got together, was entrusted with the safety of Hazebrouck. It was, however, not found necessary actually to utilize the troops thus detailed, and on the 13th, on the 1st Australian Division coming up, the 40th was withdrawn to an area west of St. Omer.

For three days the 40th Division had been continuously in action. More leaves had been added to the laurels won at Bourlon and the Somme. But the price paid had been a high one. The killed, definitely known as such, amounted to 221; the wounded numbered 1,251; and the figure of missing was 3,020, a number which obviously includes many who perished. These figures are exclusive of the losses of the 57th Division artillery, attached to the 40th, which amounted to 38 killed, 165 wounded, and 83 missing, so that the total casualties of the Division in action amounted to nearly 4,800. Coming as it did practically on top of the losses on the Somme, this fresh depletion necessitated the complete reorganization of the 40th Division.

" Although it may be invidious "—so runs the official narrative of the Division—" to select for special mention any particular battalion when all were doing their utmost to stop the advance of German troops who outnumbered them so greatly, the following battalions may be mentioned for having done particularly good work: The 18th Battalion Welch Regiment, who at the end of the first day's fighting were still holding on, though numbering only 5 officers and 120 men. [This number evidently includes reinforcements picked up at Sailly on the 9th.] The 12th Battalion Suffolk Regiment, for their gallant defence of Fleurbaix and Canteen Farm. The 2nd Battalion Royal Scots Fusiliers, for their defence of the bridge-heads at Nouveau Monde and Sailly. The 40th Battalion Machine Gun Corps, for consistent good work in heavy and continuous fighting, especially about the bridges over the Lys. Other battalions which distinguished themselves were the 21st Battalion Middlesex Regiment and the 14th Highland Light Infantry." It would be an impertinence for the historian to venture to add anything to an official recommendation, but a close study of all records of the battle has left him with a certain wistfulness at the omission of the 13th Yorkshire Regiment. He has, however, the pleasure of quoting a memorandum concerning the 20th Middlesex Regiment, which will speak for itself :—

" CONFIDENTIAL.

" *The Officer Commanding,*
    " *20th Middlesex Regiment.*

"On the evening of the 10th April 2nd/Lieut. E. C. P. Williams, 2nd/Lieut. A. H. Glover, and 2nd/Lieut. Bowden, with about 120 men, came under my command in action. I wish to place on record my high appreciation of the services of this detachment of your unit. The way in which the officers and men co-operated with the unit under my command was most praiseworthy. The conduct of 2nd/Lieut. A. H. Glover was more especially gallant, and I attach a copy of a recommendation which I am forwarding through the usual channels. Unfortunately 2nd/Lieut. Bowden was killed by enemy shell fire on the 11th. I am despatching the detachment under 2nd/Lieut. E. C. P. Williams by march route to Hazebrouck.

" H. C. WESTMORELAND,

" *Lt.-Colonel,*
    " *Comdg. 2nd Hampshire Regiment.*

" 15/4/17 " [*sic*].

Now that the battle has been described at some length it is of interest to summarize the views held by those in high places in the Division and recorded within a few days of the event. In spite of the absence of any indications of an attack upon a large scale prior to April 9th, it seemed to be the general impression that the Germans would follow up their success in the south by an attempt in the north; also that the choice of place might be one where the Allies felt secure. The Armentières sector was about the "cushiest" in the whole line, and for this very reason there should have been more divisions in reserve than there actually were. So far as the 40th Division was concerned the danger was of course the right flank. The Portuguese had never come in for a very strong bombardment or a strong attack, and a long sojourn in a "cushy" sector had rendered them perhaps over-confident. The 40th Division was handicapped slightly by the change in the reserve brigade—the 120th. It was reorganizing when the battle started, for the 14th Argyll and Sutherland Highlanders had just been broken up, and the new battalion—the 2nd Royal Scots Fusiliers—had only just arrived, after a very severe gruelling with the Fifth Army on the Somme; it was therefore imperative to allow it twenty-four hours' rest. It is worth recording the opinion that if more concrete emplacements for machine guns had been made the Division might have held out longer. There were, indeed, concrete "pill-boxes," but only half of them had been completed with loopholes. As it was, the defences at Fleurbaix and at Canteen Farm held out for some eight hours, although surrounded.

The question of the River Lys is a difficult one, and has already been discussed in part, but the view has received support that it might have been better to take up a position north of the river, using it as an obstacle. A difficulty, of course, was that so many villages and towns like Bac St. Maur, Estaires and others were really for the most part on the south side of the river, and would have to have been evacuated. In the position actually occupied wire was in abundance—perhaps too much so, and in one account there is a complaint about the limitations to manœuvre thus caused. The worst part of the whole battle was the evacuation of the French civil population. "This was left in the hands of the French Mission, who were apparently helpless and did nothing. The people refused to leave their houses, as they could not realize, after three years of comparative safety, that the Bosch would ever attack in these parts. The result was that the casualties among the poor women and children must have been very terrible. I think the French ought never to have allowed the civil population to be so close up to the front line."

As regards the tactics of the Germans, they undoubtedly knew how to exploit a success. They pushed their light machine guns well forward, taking advantage of any fold in the ground, and invariably tried to push their guns up on any exposed flank, with a view to enfilade fire. Communications worked well throughout the whole affair, but it was a "soldier's battle," and one almost impossible to direct from divisional headquarters. The value of leadership on the part of regimental officers was well brought out, and it was shown time and again that the best way to stop an enemy rush was to counter-attack. "This, of course, takes some organizing, but whenever it was carried out it was immediately successful." Gaps were, of course, of frequent occurrence, and perpetual messages came through to say "we are not in touch with the brigades on our right and left"; "the brigade on our right has fallen back"; "the enemy are now moving in large numbers round our right rear," and so on. The divisions which came up in support were used chiefly to fill the gaps, or what was called at the time "to plug the holes." They became involved in the fighting before they knew where they were. It would possibly have been better for these new divisions to have established themselves on some definite line of defence in rear, instead of being pushed up. The difficulty in this case was that the troops in front were not only dead beat, but were completely out-numbered, and in order to check a bad break through it was necessary at all costs to support those in front, who were doing their utmost.

In concluding this account of the share of the 40th Division in the Battle of the Lys, the historian feels that he must allude to a special difficulty with which he was confronted in writing it. Enclosed—or " intercalated," to use the scientific jargon—in a sector held by British troops was a division of another nation, and a nation which was not amongst the leading Powers in military organization or experience. For political reasons it was obviously inexpedient to wound the feelings of an ally who had made great sacrifices to enter the war on the side of right and justice, and accordingly the despatches subsequently transmitted by the British commander-in-chief were written under a certain difficulty. It is clear, however, and it is now common knowledge, that the Portuguese were driven out of their position; that they were unable to re-form; and that this hurried withdrawal reacted at once upon their neighbours—the 40th Division. That division had its right suddenly un-covered, and, in a sector where it was expected that it might in part recuperate from the severe fighting on the Somme, it was forced to battle for its very existence. The losses incurred were very severe; so severe, indeed, that the 40th Division, in the shape in which it had originally arrived in France, henceforth ceased to exist. In its great effort the Division performed a duty than which there is no nobler in war. It sacrificed itself to retrieve the effect of mishap elsewhere. A considerate tact for the misfortune of an old ally is undoubtedly a good thing; but it is not so good as justice to the Division which had to pour out its blood like water in its splendid endeavour to make things good.

This is not to mean that the Portuguese have altogether deserved the derision which clung to them

s

from that fateful day in April, 1918, right up to the end of the war. The test by which they were tried was a terrible one. It is clear, and is now indeed admitted by the Germans, that the strip held by the Portuguese had been marked down as the point of thrust. It is as certain as anything can be that the bombardment to which they were subjected was not less severe than that which fell upon the 40th Division; and it is highly probable that it was even more intensive. Again, unlike all the other divisions on the Western Front, the Portuguese had had practically no chance of being really "blooded" or tried out. They had been put into a "cushy" sector, and had quite obviously been "nursed" by the Germans. Designedly, the enemy allowed the Portuguese to get into the state of taking things easy, with the result that a fatal over-confidence was engendered. The records and narratives supplied by members of the 40th Division leave no doubt whatever on this point, and there is before the historian an account of a visit to a Portuguese post just before the battle, which tells its tale. The inferno which was opened on these nervy troops on April 9th was all the more terrible on account of the unexpected nature of the storm. And then things happened, and happened quickly, which was just what the Germans had played for.

CHAPTER XIII.

The Division Reconstituted.

DURING April 13th divisional headquarters remained at Au Souverain, and it was amusing to see the staff in the large schoolroom trying to make themselves comfortable at the desks so recently occupied by little children of this thickly populated area. What were left of the sorely tried troops were collected in the Strazeele and Hazebrouck areas, and the time was occupied in seeing "how we stood" and in arriving at the losses in men and material. The latter item was a large one, and the Division was found to be in such a depleted condition that obviously it was of no further immediate use.

On the following day headquarters were transferred to Renescure, where orders were received that they were to be again shifted to Longuenesse, just west of St. Omer. Passing through the latter town the staff noticed many signs of alarm on the part of the civil population. Most of the shops were shut, and a good many people were packing up and leaving the place. This was probably due to a severe bombing which the town had suffered the previous night. The news from the front was now decidedly better, and it looked as if the Germans had been definitely brought to a standstill. In order to secure better accommodation the headquarters were shifted to Wizernes on the 16th. Bailleul was reported on the 17th to have fallen into the enemy's hands, " but as the Huns were all round it this was only to be expected. But on other sides the news is quite good." On the same day the Division was transferred from the XV to the VIII Corps,

" coming under the command of Hunter-Weston, generally known as Hunter-Bunter." Orders were now received that a composite brigade, to be ready for any emergency, was to be formed out of the Division. Drafts were being despatched freely, and some 1,250 proceeded about this time to sister battalions of other divisions, so that the formation even of a composite brigade was not too simple. However, it was duly made up of three battalions as follows : " A " Battalion, three companies 20th Middlesex Regiment and one company 21st Middlesex Regiment; " B " Battalion, one company 21st Middlesex Regiment, one company 13th East Surrey Regiment, and two companies 13th Yorkshire Regiment; " C " Battalion, three companies 12th Suffolk Regiment and one company 13th East Surrey Regiment; the whole under the command of Brigadier-General John Campbell.

The actual work now carried out by the Division consisted of a mild form of training coupled with a transfusion of blood—in the shape of huge drafts to other formations—on a very generous scale. Consequently the period for the moment was one of enforced inactivity, and advantage may be taken of it to give here a *résumé* of an aspect of the Division which has so far been touched upon here and there— the work of the medical units.

The third week of November, 1915, saw the birth of the medical units which were to be eventually part of the 40th Division, at the Royal Army Medical Corps Training Centre, Crookham, Hants. The men arrived in a variety of uniforms of different first aid societies, those of the Red Cross and St. John of Jesusalem predominating, and were soon allotted for training purposes to three units—135th Field Ambulance, under command of Lieutenant R. V. Graham, Royal Army Medical Corps; 136th Field Ambulance, under Lieutenant H. Graham; and 137th Field Ambulance, under Lieutenant J. O'S. Beveridge, Royal Army Medical Corps. Under the direction of Major (later

Colonel) A. H. Safford, C.M.G., Royal Army Medical
Corps, the units carried out the preliminary training
until February, 1916, when commands of the units were
assumed by Major R. N. Hunt (135th), Major F. E.
Rowan Robinson (136th), and Major N. E. Dunkerton
(137th), all Royal Army Medical Corps, and subsequently lieutenant-colonels. The general and field
training was carried out at Crookham, whilst the
specialist training, i.e., nursing duties, was carried out
at various London hospitals (Guy's, Bart.'s, London,
St. Thomas's, etc.). Eventually, in the middle of April,
1916, the field ambulances were officially allotted to the
newly-formed 40th Division.

About May 15th they were inspected by the
A.D.M.S., Colonel A. J. Luther, A.M.S., who considered them sufficiently trained to join the Division in
training. On May 16th they moved to Bullswater
Camp (near Woking), where they finished their field
training. On June 3rd they embarked at Southampton
and arrived the following day at Le Havre. Here they
remained one day, and then undertook the monotonous
railway journey to Lillers. Many of the discomforts
of travelling could have been alleviated if any of the
personnel had had previous experience in the Expeditionary Force. On arrival at Lillers the medical units
were allotted to their respective brigades to take in such
sick and casualties as occurred. The Division was
billeted in villages surrounding Lillers. Up to this
time the units had horse transport only, and while
stationed outside Lillers the motor transport arrived—
seven motor ambulances, six Siddley Deaseys, and one
Ford ambulance for each field ambulance. Of these
cars scarcely one remained to the end.

Training in active warfare was now undertaken, personnel from each ambulance (2 officers and 40 other
ranks) being attached to a corresponding unit of the
16th (Irish) Division and the 1st Division, which were
then stationed at Noeux-les-Mines and Braquemont
respectively. These divisions were then holding the

line from south of Hulluch to Double Crassier, including the village of Loos. This training was completed in a fortnight. On July 4th the 40th Division took over a sector of the line from the 1st Division. The ambulances were situated at Braquemont; the main advanced dressing station was in the theatre of Les Brebis, in the same road as brigade headquarters. A more advanced dressing station was situated at Maroc and one at Calonne. About the middle of August, Captain Allingham, Royal Army Medical Corps, attached 21st Middlesex Regiment, was severely wounded in the chest by a rifle grenade. His place with the regiment was filled by Captain C. O'Malley, Royal Army Medical Corps, who remained with the regiment till April, 1918, when he was taken prisoner. About the middle of November the Division was relieved and moved to Pont Remi district (Abbeville) for a period of rest and refitting, and in the middle of December made its way slowly to the Somme area, coming to rest at Suzanne and surrounding district. The dreadful weather of the months of December and January caused a great deal of sickness in the Division. Some extracts from diaries show that the percentage of sick amongst battalions at rest ran as high as twenty per cent. (normal, three per cent.). A large number of these were frostbite in its different forms. Trench foot was also very prevalent, in spite of every known precaution for its prevention being tried.

In February, 1917, the Division moved out and the medical units were situated in Bray and district. They moved back to the north bank of the Somme about the first week in March. The advance of March 17th came, and with it the work of the medical units was supplemented by the formation of camps for the evacuation of refugees. One of these was formed at Bray by the 137th Field Ambulance, under Captain J. Linnell, Royal Army Medical Corps, in a camp close to the railway station. It was a difficult work, as there was a number of suspected spies amongst the 1,700 refugees dealt with at this camp. The camp was eventually closed on April 1st.

The Division now moved up to Péronne, and eventually came to rest at Mannencourt and district, prior to taking over the line Gonnelieu—Gouzeaucourt—Villers-Plouich. While stationed at Mannencourt, Major Carl Reilly, Royal Army Medical Corps, D.A.D.M.S. of the Division, died suddenly, falling from his horse when visiting the 137th Field Ambulance. He was a great loss to the Division, and the vacancy was filled by Captain Thatcher, Royal Army Medical Corps, About the middle of April the line referred to was taken over, the advanced dressing station being situated in Gouzeaucourt and Villers-Plouich, while the divisional main dressing station was situated at Fins, formed by the 136th Field Ambulance. The Division remained here till the second week in October, when it moved out to Gouy-en-Artois and surrounding district. When stationed in the above line the medical units of the Division attained a very high standard of efficiency. Two examples are given. A private of the 21st Middlesex received a very severe abdominal wound about 12.15 p.m., and was brought to the regimental aid post. He was evacuated through the advanced dressing station straight to the casualty clearing station, and was operated upon immediately on arrival. His operation was completed two and a half hours after he received his wound. A raid on a large scale was carried out by the 12th Suffolks on September 25th, 1916, involving 72 casualties, of which over 50 were stretcher cases. The raid commenced at 7.30 p.m., and all casualties were clear of the advanced dressing station at 1.30 a.m. —a very fine record, considering that the transport of only one field ambulance was used. For this the medical units of the Division were congratulated by the consulting surgeon of the army, who was present at the advanced station during the period.

While the units were stationed at Fins the first American doctor to the Division joined No. 137 Field

Ambulance, Lieutenant Buckley, U.S.M.C. He was the predecessor of many excellent Americans who served with the Division. The Division spent the end of October and beginning of November in training for the Battle of Cambrai, and on November 17th it moved forward and concentrated south of Bapaume (Rocquigny and district). On November 21st it moved forward and took up a position in reserve, where it remained till 3 p.m. on the 22nd. It then moved forward, the 119th and 121st Brigades in the line and the 120th in reserve—the 137th Field Ambulance forming an advanced dressing station at Graincourt.

On the march to take up positions the 121st Brigade was badly shelled, and the 12th Suffolks received many casualties, especially amongst the stretcher-bearers. One shell was responsible for 15 casualties, amongst whom was Captain J. O'S. Beveridge, Royal Army Medical Corps, who was so severely wounded that he died that night at the main dressing station at Beugny. He was a very great loss to the Division, having served with his unit from the time of its formation. The battle is described elsewhere in detail. The casualties were very heavy on the 23rd, and evacuation conditions very difficult. On that day most of the casualties were carried a distance of about four miles to the nearest point to which ambulances could be brought. The route lay through very muddy ground, so increasing the difficulty of carrying. The following day casualties were evacuated to Flesquières, where the Guards Division had a field ambulance. Here the casualties were collected in barns, from whence they were eventually cleared by a motor ambulance convoy procured by Colonel Meek, A.M.S., D.D.M.S., III Corps. On the 27th the Division was relieved by the 59th Division and taken out to rest and refit. Captain P. Gaffikin, Royal Army Medical Corps, and 50 other ranks Royal Army Medical Corps, were left behind to clear the remaining wounded when the Division moved out of the line. The A.D.M.S. (Colonel A. J. Luther) was promoted to

D.D.M.S. XV Army Corps, and Colonel A. Humphry, late officer commanding 11th Casualty Clearing Station, became A.D.M.S. The Division now moved back to the line on December 10th, having its headquarters at Hamelincourt. The ambulances took it in turn to clear the line, while a corps hospital for the treatment of skin diseases was situated at Ervillers. They remained here till February 10th, 1918, when the Division moved out to rest, and on March 16th moved back to their old area, Hamelincourt, in reserve.

On March 21st the attack began at dawn. For five days the ambulances put in what was probably some of their hardest work during the war. The clearing of the casualties was under the direction of Lieutenant-Colonel W. McK. McCullagh, D.S.O., M.C., who did magnificent work, as, indeed, did all ranks under him. Unfortunately the ambulances lost about 25 men taken prisoners in this "show." The Division was relieved on March 25th, and, after two days' rest, made its way north where it took over the Fleurbaix section of the line on the Lys, south of Armentières, divisional headquarters being at Croix du Bac. The attack was launched by the Germans on April 9th, when the Division was in the line. A large number of men were lost as prisoners, including about 4 officers and 40 other ranks, Royal Army Medical Corps. The remnants of the Division remained in action for five days, when it was withdrawn and remained at rest during the following two months, refitting. In June, Captain Thatcher was killed, and the vacancy as D.A.D.M.S. was filled by Captain A. Jebb, Royal Army Medical Corps. During a bombing raid on St. Omer on May 30th, 1918, Captain Thatcher ran out into the street to see if any wounded required help, and was himself wounded. He was taken to the Duchess of Sutherland's hospital at Longuenesse, where he died a couple of days later. He was an excellent staff officer while with the Division, most conscientious and hardworking.

Of the professional side the work of the medical units

was of a very high standard, and it is invidious to mention any particular officers—they were all excellent, some eminently fitted for the bearer sections, and some of more mature years for the tent sub-divisions, though all took their turn at all duties. Of the non-commissioned officers and men, who represented for the most part Leeds and Bradford, with a sprinkling from Manchester, Wales, Scotland and Ireland, one cannot speak too highly. They were of an excellent type, and worked hard at their special duties. The commands of the units engaged at different periods, and at the Armistice, were : 135th, Lieutenant-Colonel H. Harding; 136th, Lieutenant-Colonel I. R. Hudleston, D.S.O.; and 137th, Lieutenant-Colonel W. McK. McCullagh, D.S.O., M.C. Mention must not be forgotten of the regimental medical officers, whose excellent work richly earned them the splendid reputation they bore. The 40th Division Sanitary Section was undoubtedly responsible for the prevention of infectious diseases which have been the bugbear of previous campaigns.

On April 17th General Ruggles-Brise, who was now military secretary at General Headquarters, came to see the headquarters of his old Division. Two days later a conference was held " concerning lessons to be learnt for the future." The weather was now cold and dreary, but a cheerful note was introduced by the receipt of congratulatory messages from army and corps. In the former the First Army commander wrote : " I wish to express my great appreciation of the bravery and endurance with which all ranks have fought and held out against overwhelming numbers. It has been necessary to call for great exertions, and more must still be asked for, but I am confident that, at this critical moment when the existence of the British Empire is at stake, all ranks of the First Army will do their very best." From the commander of the XV Corps came an appreciation of the services of the Division " during the operations of the 9th/13th April."

The commander of the First Army had not minced his words. He had declared that the existence of the British Empire was at stake. The Germans were straining every nerve to force the issue before the troops which were pouring across the Atlantic from America should make their weight felt and turn the scale. Apart from this, and so far as the northern sector of the Western Front was concerned, there could be no question of the Germans breaking off the offensive. They were practically committed to a continuance of it. The attack by the German Sixth Army which had begun on April 9th had to a great extent taken the Allies by surprise. The whole stretch of the Lys at Sailly was rapidly taken, but the battles of the next few days, though successful, were very costly, and it appeared doubtful whether a real break through would result. The German left wing had not succeeded in taking Festubert and Givenchy, or in reaching the canal. It was, however, impossible for the Germans merely to consolidate their gains, for the inner wings of the Sixth Army and of the Fourth Army north of it were in difficult tactical positions, although some relief was gained by the capture of the Bailleul and Neuve Eglise heights. Still, the German Higher Command could not overlook the fact that the advantages of initial surprise had passed, and that the Allies were getting their second wind. The French had been hurrying up reinforcements, and by skilful manœuvring the Allies were eluding a carefully built up attack by the German Fourth Army on the Belgian front. General Ludendorff clearly recognized that it was only by a remorseless continuance of the offensive that he could hope to achieve real success. Accordingly, on April 20th, another great German attack began. Mount Kemmel was carried, but the piecemeal capture of Festubert and Givenchy did not succeed. The end of April saw a cessation of these strenuous efforts, but although the Germans passed temporarily to the defensive they had achieved much. The Portuguese

were destroyed as a fighting entity, and another heavy
blow had been directed on the British, so heavy that
General Foch had been forced to send about eighteen
French divisions and six cavalry divisions to reinforce
the Flanders front.   Nevertheless, looking back now at
1918, it is obvious that the German Higher Command
must have been wracked by anxiety. A decisive
victory was as far off as ever.   German man-power was
ebbing fast.   But streams of American troops were
swelling from a trickle to a torrent which threatened to
submerge the weakened German line.

The 40th Division, however, knew of this further
offensive merely at second hand.   Its dissolution was
continuing, and no news of its re-formation had been
received.   On April 20th there was a further transfusion of blood : 400 men of the 13th Yorkshires and
200 from the Highland Light Infantry were ordered
to join other divisions.   As for the active work of the
Division, the staff of it was ordered to reconnoitre a
line east of Cassel to be occupied in an emergency, and
this was duly done.   In such a period of the life of the
Division both war diaries and private records naturally
lack the wealth of reminiscence which characterize
more stirring times.   There is the record, however, of
a curious benediction when the Deputy Chaplain-
General (the Bishop of Khartoum), preaching at a
Nonconformist service, added to his blessing the
unorthodox but noble prayer "that we might all be
given strength to stick it out to the end."

The period of uncertainty was, however, sharply
interrupted on April 22nd.   On that day General
Ponsonby was lunching with the corps commander at
Cassel, and was informed that probably the 40th
Division would be broken up and the personnel
distributed to other divisions.   The staff and headquarters would, however, remain, as it was hoped to
re-form the Division within three months.   Naturally
the news of the breaking up "caused much consterna-
tion and grief throughout the whole Division," and it

was felt that in view of its fine *esprit de corps* and its
fine record in the last two great battles the 40th
Division might have been spared.

It was now definitely decided that the Division was
to be broken up, but all headquarters, that is to say
divisional, brigade and battalion, were to remain, with
their staffs and small training cadres, and in the meantime it was thought more than probable that the cadres
would be employed in training Americans. The new
line east of Cassel was being dug; the trenches were
carefully concealed behind hedges, and arrangements
were made for camouflaging them with branches and
green turf. It was not clear what part the Division
would ever take in manning them, for on the 25th
another depletion took place when the 2nd Royal Scots
Fusiliers left to join the 9th Division. Two days later
Brigadier-General John Campbell, of the 121st Brigade,
who had been promoted major-general, left to take over
command of the 31st Division. An order was now
received that two composite brigades were to be formed
instead of one, and a rumour was started about a move
to Poperinghe, but this was quickly postponed, and
was followed by another rumour that the Division would
move farther back. In this atmosphere of doubt closed
April, 1918, a month of mist and wet with hardly a
gleam of sunshine. For the 40th Division it had been
a momentous four weeks, including as it did the Battle
of the Lys and the dissolution of the Division itself.

May opened with " conflicting orders arriving every
hour." The corps commander was anxious to hold
on to the Division to the very last moment, and was
always telephoning to say " we may be thrown into
the fight any moment." The view taken at divisional
headquarters was that, if it were intended to use the
Division actively, opportunity should be given to
organize it properly. To do this it was hoped that
such reinforcements as were about should be sent to
the 40th, and that opportunity should be given to reconnoitre the position properly and to organize things for

the attack. There was a marked and natural objection to being "messed about," *i.e.*, to be taken up to the line and marched back again. "Make up your mind one way or the other; either break up the Division or leave it and reorganize it. As it is at present we get nothing but contradictory orders every hour, which upsets everybody." This is how one diary reflects the situation.

Another transfer took place on May 2nd, this time from the VIII to VII Corps. This perpetual shifting from one corps to another may have been necessary, but it had its drawbacks, for no sooner did headquarters begin to know the new corps staff than "off one goes to another corps." During the six months which were now ending, the Division had formed part of the following corps : the III Corps, under General Pulteney; the V, under General Fanshawe; the IV, under General Woollcombe; the VI, under General Haldane; the XV, under General Du Cane; the VIII, under General Hunter-Weston; and now the VII, under General Whigham. These changes may have been unavoidable, but as Nebuchadnezzar exclaimed when he took to a grass diet, "It may be wholesome, but it is not good."

A further ebbing of the life blood of the Division took place upon the 4th, when half the personnel of the 40th Battalion Machine Gun Corps left for the base, followed by the remainder on the next day. On the same day the 12th Yorkshire Regiment left, and practically all that was left of the 119th Brigade, while on the 6th there were further heavy drafts from the 120th and 121st Brigades. Only the skeletons of battalions were now left, that is to say commanding officers, adjutants, sergeant-majors, some training specialists, and the brigade staffs as well. As to what was to be the next phase everything seemed undecided. There was a rumour that the Division was to superintend Chinese Labour Companies, which induced the divisional commander to put in at once for three weeks' leave, but the application had to remain in abeyance, as the army commander, Sir Herbert Plumer, was averse from granting any leave at the time.

Meanwhile the Division, or rather the skeleton of it, was in a shadowy way involved in what was known as the Winnezeele line, Winnezeele being a village some three miles north-east of Cassel. It is curious to note that even as late as May, 1918, opinions were still divided as to how far the various lines—observation, resistance, and reserve—ought to be apart; and there were still the old arguments for and against the siting of defensive lines on the reverse slope of a hill. This question had thrust itself into prominence in 1914, but was apparently still undecided. The reverse slope was favoured provided that a field of fire of at least 500 yards could be obtained; without this, no sooner is the observation line driven in than the enemy is " on top of you." As for the forward slope, it meant that the trenches were under direct artillery observation, and " you are shelled out of it in no time." The historian experiences a certain fascination in discovering in diaries of 1918 the same arguments and doubts which confronted him personally four years earlier in 1914.

A little mild supervision of the work in the Winnezeele line, and a good many air raids—which were anything but mild—over St. Omer were now the chief diversions of the 40th Division. In one air raid No. 10 Stationary Hospital was hit, 2 doctors and 18 wounded soldiers being killed. St. Omer was becoming more deserted than ever, and at nights the majority of the inhabitants used to leave the town and sleep in the fields a mile away. On May 25th a corps order was received to the effect that, on the completion of the Winnezeele line, the 40th Division should proceed with the organization of an intermediate one between that place and St. Omer. General Foch was at this time anxious to have four defensive lines between St. Omer and Ypres. All these were to have an outpost line, and a main line of defence with a support trench and also a reserve line. This meant that about 500 miles of trenches had to be dug, the actual manual work being carried out by British and Chinese Labour Companies.

The month closed with news of some import. The Germans had once more passed to the offensive, though this time in another sector of the Western Front. By May 27th the Germans had accumulated sufficient fresh reserves, and it was still imperative that they should lose no time. If the Allies were now allowed time, and were able at a self-chosen moment to use their fighting force, with its ever-growing superiority in personnel and material, Germany might give up the war as lost at once. The choice of the sector of attack had been carefully considered by the German Higher Command. There seemed to be two alternatives; either to attack on the Arras—Amiens front, with Paris as the ultimate objective, or in Flanders, with the idea of pushing the Allies into the sea and gaining the Channel ports. Ludendorff had decided on the latter; but as there were considerable French reserves in this sector it was proposed to open with a diversion in another place, with the idea of drawing off these reserves and so weakening the Flanders front. Such diversion was fixed to take place upon the Aisne. It began on May 27th and succeeded beyond all hopes, at the end of the first day the Germans claiming 25,000 prisoners, British and French, and 150 guns.

The D.A.D.M.S.—Thatcher, by name—had been badly wounded in an air raid, and died on the morning of June 1st in the Duchess of Sutherland's Hospital. So bad had the air raids now become that Sir Herbert Plumer strongly advised the divisional commander to shift his headquarters from St. Omer, and on the 3rd this was carried out, the new headquarters being Lenderzeele, a small but peaceful village six miles away; and on the same day the training cadres of the following units left on transfer to the 34th Division, to assist in training American troops: 21st Middlesex, 13th East Surreys, 10th/11th Highland Light Infantry,

14th Highland Light Infantry, and 13th Yorkshires. In some cases, if not all, this fell through, and although it is impossible to follow the further fortunes of all the fine battalions which were scattered on the dissolution of the Division, the experience of two is somewhat similar to that of the others.

The training staff of the 13th East Surrey Regiment proceeded by rail to Rinxent, near Boulogne, whence it marched to Hardinghem, on transfer to the 102nd Brigade of the 34th Division. On the 11th it was transferred to the 101st Brigade at Bayenghem, where it was joined by two battalions of the 310th United States Infantry, which it was to instruct. The training, however, lasted but a fortnight, for on June 27th the training staff of 9 officers and 47 other ranks received orders to proceed to England, arriving at Frimley on the 30th. On July 16th the training staff proceeded to Lowestoft, and by the end of the month about 400 men had been drafted in. A month later the strength was 825, of which, however, only 393 were passed fit for service overseas. Then on September 7th an order came for disbandment; the men were rapidly drafted to other units, and just before the Armistice the battalion officially ceased to exist.

To take another case, that of the 18th Welch Regiment; the cadre of 10 officers and 50 other ranks returned to England and proceeded to Folkestone for Aldershot, whence it was despatched on June 21st to North Walsham, to " fill up." The new officers were of good material, chiefly Northern Cyclist Battalion, with a sprinkling of Army Service Corps and 3rd Welch. The men, however, were of a poor class physically, including many discharged from hospital for wounds, debility, mental breakdown, and rheumatism; "so crippled and unfit were the larger proportion of the men that it was with the greatest difficulty that they managed the march from Aldershot station to Bourley Camp." As a result of constant application, permission was given to cast 800 of the

T

most hopeless cases—advanced heart disease, consump-
tion, lameness, blindness, deafness, and so on—and by
an influx of better drafts the battalion was eventually
able to embark for France with 39 officers and 739 other,
ranks, nominally "garrison" troops, but actually
intended to carry out the rôle of a normal battalion in
the line, which it did, arriving in France for the second
time in its career at the end of July, 1918. These two
examples of the subsequent history of these two
battalions are given to show the difficulties of man-
power at this time, difficulties which the 40th Division
was to experience to the full.

It was on June 9th that the Division learned definitely
what was to happen to it. Orders came that sixteen of
what were called "garrison guard" battalions had been
collected from various labour companies—all B1 men,
that is to say of low physique—and that these would be
incorporated into the 40th Division. Five of them
were at once allotted and turned over to the 120th
Brigade, and a few days later it was officially notified
that the 40th was to be reorganized as a "garrison," or
"semi-mobile," division of ten garrison battalions, four
being transferred from the First Army. The light and
medium trench-mortar batteries were to be formed under
Second Army arrangements, and the small arms ammunition section of the divisional ammunition column by
General Headquarters. It was stated that the Division
would be required to hold a "quiet" sector, and that
"all efforts were to be concentrated on training with
this object." Mere eyewash, of course, and immediately recognized as such by the survivors of the
Division, who remembered how far from "quiet" the
Armentières sector had proved, and that it was just
these "quiet" sectors that the Germans loved to attack.
However, there it was. The man-power question was a
burning one, and this will be recognized on examining
the orders for the Division in case of attack. In the
event of an enemy attack on the Second Army front,
the 40th Division and attached troops were to man part

of the reserve line, known as the West Hazebrouck line. It was divided into three sectors. The southern sector was to be held by the 120th Brigade, a company of Royal Engineers and two labour companies; the centre by the 121st Brigade, two companies of Royal Engineers and five labour companies; while the 119th Brigade, a company of Royal Engineers and seven labour companies, were responsible for the north. This was, so far as personnel was concerned, the "last ditch" with a vengeance.

The three brigades of the Division were, of course, but a scratch lot and but a shadow of their predecessors of Bourlon Wood, the Somme, and of the Lys. Many of the men had done no military training for a very long time; numbers had never fired a rifle; and about twenty per cent. in each battalion were useless. Representations were made to XV Corps, of which the Division was now a part, but it all came to this: an attack was considered imminent (as it often was in a "quiet" sector at this time); and "men with rifles in their hands, trained or untrained, are absolutely required to hold, if possible, the reserve line." That was the man-power situation, and an interesting sidelight on the condition of the Division is thrown by a remark of the corps commander to the effect that, as it was unfit to march any distance, it should be moved forward to a position nearer the line it would have to occupy on emergency.

This lugubrious "close up" of the Division has been designedly thrown on the screen so that its growth once more into a fighting unit may be the more thoroughly appreciated. The first phase of the phœnix process may be said to have started on June 21st. On that date a conference was held, at which were present the three brigadiers and all the commanding officers of the new battalions. It was then decided that the designation "Garrison" should be eliminated from the names of battalions; that opportunity should be given to Irishmen and Scotsmen to join units of their respective

T 2

nationalities, and that a Welsh battalion should be formed should the numbers of Welshmen in the Division warrant it. Commanding officers were to pay particular attention to the smartening up of their men, to the cleanliness of billets, and to the matter of saluting. There was also a general discussion on training, musketry, and route marching, which were to be carried out without delay. The Division as now reconstituted dates officially from June 14th, 1918, and was as follows, though the epithet "Garrison" was not formally dropped till about a month later.

119th Brigade.

13th Royal Inniskilling Fusiliers.

13th East Lancashire Regiment (commanded by Lieutenant-Colonel Plunkett, formerly of the 19th Royal Welch Fusiliers).

12th North Staffordshire Regiment.

120th Brigade.

10th King's Own Scottish Borderers.

15th King's Own Yorkshire Light Infantry.

11th Queen's Own Cameron Highlanders.

121st Brigade.

8th Royal Irish Regiment.

23rd Lancashire Fusiliers.

23rd Cheshire Regiment.

On June 24th the commander-in-chief came over to see the Division, and inspected one battalion from each brigade. He spoke to many of the officers and men, and told them that their duty was to hold one of the back lines in case of a break through by the enemy; that everybody who could handle a rifle might be required, and that, until the Americans were ready, everything must be done to stop the Germans reaching the Channel ports. Sir Douglas Haig drove off about 1.30 p.m., saying that on the whole the B1 men looked a better lot than he had expected. It should be remembered that an immense number of labour troops were to come under the divisional commander in case of emergency. They numbered about 14,000, and consisted of " all sorts and conditions of men." About half of them had never handled a rifle, but arrangements were now made that they should receive an hour's musketry instruction every day.

On the last day of the month General Ponsonby was unofficially informed that he had been selected to command the 5th Division. The news was not welcome, for General Ponsonby was extremely loth to leave the Division, which under him had achieved such success. The army commander, however, represented to him very strongly that to refuse would be tantamount to declining promotion. The 5th was a Regular division, reputed to be one of the best in the Army, and round its bayonets still played the glory of Mons, of Le Cateau, of the Marne, the Aisne, and Ypres, 1914. In the circumstances, General Ponsonby accepted, and, following a parting dinner on July 1st, he bade farewell two days later to the 40th Division. " I felt very sick at leaving the 40th, where I have had a most happy time " is the entry in his diary. He was succeeded by Major-General Sir William Peyton.

The dominant feature of July was training, and again training. It was becoming clear to all in the Division that it was being organized for something more strenuous and active than merely defensive purposes in an emergency. Each battalion received a quota of A1 category officers; there was a further pruning out of the men; fresh drafts arrived. For a time conditions were exceedingly pleasant, for the brigades were called upon to do nothing more severe than drill, musketry, and a few route marches, relieved by a few days' tour in portions of the Hazebrouck reserve line, which was used as an imaginary front. The troops moved up at night, sentries were posted, and were on duty throughout the night in the fire bays. Patrols were sent out, but although the work was seriously undertaken it had

no terrors for the men, inasmuch as 500 yards in front
of the line was an excellent canteen, belonging to one
of the " resting " battalions of the 31st Division.
Patrolling, in these circumstances, was robbed of many
of its drawbacks.

About the middle of July things began to move.
An important conference was summoned. All
commanding officers, seconds-in-command, company
commanders and their second captains, from every
battalion in the Division, were bidden to attend to meet
the divisional commander. Sir William Peyton
explained that the time had now come when the recon-
structed 40th Division was going to justify its existence
by taking its place in the line. It was pointed out that
only a " quiet sector " was contemplated, and that the
Division would be worked as lightly as possible. Only
one brigade would be in the front line at a time. A
difficulty was foreseen. The troops in the Division were
what was known as "category" men who had regarded
themselves as immune from further fighting. In fact, it
appears that an official letter was received from High
Authority to say that B1 men were not to be used for
offensive action, and that it was ordered that the letter
should be read out to such men. A valuable correspondent to this History describes this tersely as " a political
dodge." Events proved, however, that these men
scorned to exploit their " rights " and gave of their very
best. Amongst them was some extraordinarily good
fighting material, and in the end it so happened that
many who most distinguished themselves in the final
advance were those who had earlier become casualties
from wounds or sickness.

At this time the Division was daily expecting a
further enemy attack upon its front, July 18th being
freely mentioned by those in the know as the date on
which the Germans were coming over. This rumour
lent a certain piquancy to the order which detailed the
Division to do its bit in the line on that date—the real
line, that is, with Huns, and not a wet conteen, in front.

The honour fell to the 119th Brigade, which, accompanied by one company of the 17th (Pioneer) Battalion of the Worcestershire Regiment, relieved the 87th Brigade and came under the 1st Australian Division. On the last night of the month the 121st relieved the 119th Brigade. It was a strange form of warfare to many, especially to those brought up on the full diet of orthodox trench warfare. The line was but lightly held by isolated posts, and there was a considerable distance between the front line and the supports, as well as between supports and reserves. To take the case of an individual battalion, the front line of the 23rd Lancashire Fusiliers was on the edge of a little stream called La Becque, the enemy being in the village of Vieux Berquin, some 600 yards away. This village, and most of the places mentioned in the remainder of this chapter, can be located on the map which illustrates the Battles of the Lys. The Germans kept most of their troops in the cellars of the old ruined houses in the main street. During the day they held the ground in front lightly with machine gun posts, which at night were considerably reinforced. These posts were dotted about in shell holes or behind natural cover in the long grass of which No Man's Land was composed

Information was received during this tour that the Germans were retiring, and the battalion was ordered to send out patrols to explore. This gave the brigade, as reconstituted, its first chance to distinguish itself, and the 23rd Lancashire Fusiliers did especially good work. Two particularly daring daylight patrols had exactly dissimilar results; in the one case Lieutenant Henderson, accompanied by a non-commissioned officer and three men, engaged an enemy machine gun team at close quarters, with disastrous results to themselves, two of the patrol being killed, and Lieutenant Henderson, after a prolonged struggle, being captured. In the other case Lieutenant Anderson, M.C., accompanied by a sergeant and five men, succeeded in surprising an enemy machine gun post and taking all the team prisoners and capturing their gun, without any casualties to ourselves. One German was wounded. For this exploit Lieutenant Anderson was awarded a bar to his Military Cross. Later on, another daring patrol was undertaken by two officers, Captain Brown and Lieutenant Farrell, M.C., who that evening led a strong raiding party, which succeeded in capturing prisoners and obtaining much valuable information. The casualties were light, but, unfortunately, Lieutenant Farrell was wounded and taken prisoner. Captain Brown was awarded the Military Cross for his share in this exploit.

On August 2nd the divisional commander proceeded on sixteen days' leave, his place being temporarily taken by Brigadier-General F. P. Crozier. The first half of the month was quiet, and no item more exciting than routine reliefs and the divisional horse show is to be chronicled. On the 21st orders were received for the 40th to take over the whole of the front occupied by the 31st Division, the line, generally speaking, being Vier Houck—Kew Cross Roads—Bracken Farm—Bleu—West of Cutlet Corner, and this line is quite sufficiently indicated if the reader will look at the map illustrating the Lys battles, and imagine a pencil line from just east of Merris to just north-west of Neuf Berquin. There was a good deal of talk about a general retirement of the enemy—the reason for which we shall soon see—but, as a matter of fact, patrols pushed out from the Division did not find much to bank on. The war diaries consulted now show all the old features: there are the same old references to shelling; the same old daily intelligence reports; and the same old tale of work done in and on the trenches. During the night of the 23rd there took place the first real " scrap." The 120th Brigade attempted to alter a line of posts; to this the Huns objected; the 120th Brigade pushed forward; the enemy counter-attacked, but this attempt was beaten off. Three days later the 119th Brigade captured a wounded prisoner of the

140th Regiment, 4th Saxon Division. Someone was the richer for this exploit, for the brigadier had promised £5 for the first captive brought in, and £1 a head for subsequent bags.

It was on August 27th that the first real piece of fighting by the reconstituted Division occurred. The 13th Royal Inniskilling Fusiliers, from the 119th Brigade, with a company of the 12th North Staffordshire Regiment, and with the 15th King's Own Yorkshire Light Infantry, of the 120th Brigade, co-operating, attacked with the object of effecting a slight rectification of terrain. It was a real battle in miniature, as is proved by the respective casualties. Fifty German dead were counted, and there were 32 German prisoners, 26 of them unwounded. In material, 2 heavy machine guns, 7 light machine guns, and 3 Lewis guns were taken. The attackers also lost heavily. In the Inniskillings 2 officers were killed and 9 wounded, while in other ranks the figures were 15 and 60 respectively; the King's Own Yorkshire Light Infantry got off more lightly with a total of 15 casualties, all in other ranks, and 3 being killed. This had been a smart engagement, and with it the new 40th Division had been well and truly blooded.

On the 29th the 11th Cameron Highlanders carried out a daylight attack. It began at 1.30 p.m. and was directed against Rue Provost, a small hamlet about half a mile due north of Neuf Berquin, and some annoying cottages in the vicinity. The attempt was completely successful. All of the objective was taken, and the enemy was "seen to run." The Highlanders had 29 casualties, all wounded. The following day there was a slight general advance, and on the last day of the month patrols worked their way forward to the line Aileron Farm—Pont Wemeau—Corin. Lack of space prevents these names being shown upon the map, but the line indicated ran from north to south, passing just west of Doulieu.

A reference to the map and a perusal of this chapter

will show that in about six weeks the 40th Division had made an advance of nearly four miles, a phenomenal rate of progress in the static warfare which had lasted now more than three and a half years. And we shall see, in the remainder of this chapter, the 40th Division maintaining and increasing its pace, and engaged not so much in attacking positions as in pursuing a retreating enemy. To confine the narrative of the History, at this juncture, entirely to the 40th Division, would be to evince a complete absence of any sense of proportion or value; and the situation now existing on the Lys can be understood only by a brief survey of the whole of the Western Front.

It has already been mentioned that Ludendorff was determined to repeat the blow in Flanders which the Allies had managed to parry on the Lys in April. His first object was to entice away the French divisions which General Foch had hurried north, and for this purpose he staged a diversion on the Aisne. This began on May 27th, and had succeeded beyond all hopes. The effect of the attack was felt in Flanders, where the Allied fighting activity diminished and whence a portion of the French reserves destined to support the British vanished from the scene. All the same, this effect produced upon the Allies did not seem to the German Supreme Command to warrant for the present the carrying out of the planned and prepared attack on the Flanders front. The Germans proposed first to carry out another diversion, by which the remaining French divisions in the north might be lured away, and even the British might be forced to detach units southward. Then, when the Lys and Flanders had sunk sufficiently to the level of a " quiet " sector, a hurricane attack might be launched there; the British line broken; the Channel ports reached; and, incidentally, the 40th Division would be chewed up into little bits.

Such was the general plan, and the diversion which Ludendorff now envisaged was a Marne-Champagne offensive, to begin in the middle of July. In many ways the project was sound, but Ludendorff deceived himself in two vital particulars. He exaggerated the loss of *moral* from which the French Army had been suffering, and he belittled not only the numbers of the Americans, but their fighting skill. As a matter of fact, these latter had arrived in numbers of staggering magnitude when compared with our initial effort of 1914; they were inspired with almost fanatical enthusiasm for the Allied cause; they had submitted themselves to rigorous and thorough training; and burned to show their fighting worth and "to put it across the Hun."

Consequently, the great German diversion failed The French Army showed itself anything but a beaten force. Three days later, on July 18th, the supposedly non-existent Americans established alike their presence and fighting ability by marching through the German lines south of Soissons in a fashion which compelled the evacuation of the whole Marne salient. The scales now dropped from the eyes of the German soldiers, and there was a very general feeling prevalent that it was now time to go home.

Ludendorff still clung to his idea of a new Lys offensive, but even his stubbornness had to admit the necessity of postponing it indefinitely. He was, however, spared any further worry on the subject by the fact that the initiative had passed out of his hands. After the brilliant, and, indeed, unexpected success of the counter-attack of July 18th, the Allied commanders had met to discuss the best means of exploiting the new situation. A policy of continuous offensive action was favoured. On August 8th, General Rawlinson delivered a terrific punch at the German salient facing Amiens. It was a staggering blow to German pride, and a deadly one to the declining *moral* of the German soldier. Ludendorff called August 8th the "Black Day" of the German Army. Five days later German military commanders and ministers met

at Spa. It was there agreed that the game was up,
and that peace would have to be negotiated at the first
favourable opportunity.

Such opportunity never came. The Allies saw to
that. Foch threw in the Americans—there were one
and a quarter millions of them in France—to reduce
the St. Mihiel salient, near Verdun. On August 20th
a French attack near Oise and Aisne forced back the
German line. Still more serious for the Germans, on
the following day, was the attack by the British Third
Army, north of the Somme, on the line Bapaume—
Péronne, which brought about another crisis. By the
end of August the military situation had become
sufficiently defined to enable the Allied leaders to look
beyond merely driving back the Germans to a fortified
position in rear. It was now a question of ultimate
victory following a knock-out blow.

Of the Allies, the British Army had been made up
approximately to its nominal fighting strength—a process rendered easier by the enormous contingent
retained in the United Kingdom after the dubious
Battle of Jutland and by utilizing " low category "
men. The French Army had suffered the greatest
losses, and France was almost bled white. The
Americans were numerous and spoiling for a fight.
The Belgians were relatively insignificant in numbers.
Marshal Foch—he had been elevated to that rank on
August 6th—therefore determined on two main offensives, to be carried out chiefly by the British and
Americans. The British, supported on their right by
the French, were to break the Hindenburg Line in the
direction of Cambrai—St. Quentin. The Americans,
after completing the reduction of the St. Mihiel salient,
were to break through the German lines north of
Verdun and to advance in the direction of Mézières.
In other words, the German line, where it bulged
forward in an immense salient, was to be pinched on
each flank. In these circumstances Ludendorff's
grandiose scheme of capturing the Channel ports defi-

nitely collapsed, and by the end of August the German High Command ordered the evacuation of the Lys salient.

This brief summary of what was going on not only on the stage but behind the scenes, will show the enormous difference in the situation, as it affected the 40th Division, between April and September, 1918. Put very briefly, the tide had definitely turned within this period. There had been ebb and flow, high water and low, in regular recurrence since 1914, but the tide which flowed this time for the Allies was to have no succeeding ebb. If the flood could be kept up long enough the waters would never come back, and there would be no more ebb because there would be no more sea.

At the same time it would be absurd to imagine that the 40th Division was to have a walk-over for the remainder of the war. The German Army still preserved the bearing of a splendid force, and was still imbued with magnificent traditions of victories in the past. Although the enemy were undoubtedly making plans for a general retirement they succeeded in holding their lines to the last minute, and made very advantageous use of machine guns in fighting their rear-guard actions. The reported " general retire-ment " was not an accomplished fact, as most battalions found to their cost, but as day succeeded day new ground was captured, and the Division ultimately found itself taking part in the general advance of the British line.

" I remember particularly well," writes an officer of the 120th Brigade, " one morning towards the end of August ; we had occupied a line at Grand-Sec-Bois and Petit-Sec-Bois for one night, and were to move forward that evening, through Vieux Berquin, to relieve parts of the 119th Brigade, who by this time had gained con-siderable ground ; news was received that the enemy was retiring rapidly and the troops in front were pursuing him. General Garnett—who had succeeded

General Hobkirk—walked into our mess and said that
there would be no formal relief of the battalion in the
line; the 23rd Lancashire Fusiliers were now part of an
advanced guard and must push on until they reached a
particular spot, automatically relieving and sending
back any of our troops that were met or overtaken in
the process.

" Things didn't work out quite according to plan, and
we encountered considerable opposition and severe
shelling in the neighbourhood of Tiger Farm, near Le
Verrier, but two days later the enemy had made a
further retirement, and we had walked across the open of
something like 3,000 yards without encountering serious
opposition, eventually reaching the river Steenbecque.
Here, however, the enemy was found in considerable
numbers, and further progress was delayed for some
days.   Meanwhile, a sharp engagement was fought at
Croix du Bac, on September 2nd, which resulted in a
considerable number of casualties to the brigade.   The
Lancashire Fusiliers lost two good officers, as well as a
large number of N.C.Os. and men, but much good
work was accomplished by the battalion, Corporal
(afterwards Sergeant) Williams, M.M., especially distinguishing himself by capturing a German officer,
sergeant-major and two men with their machine gun.
For this Corporal Williams was awarded the D.C.M.
After the fighting at Croix du Bac a further small
advance was made, the right of the brigade then resting
on the river Lys and the left extending to Nieppe.

" The 8th Royal Irish, who were on our left,
encountered considerable trouble here, and had the
misfortune to lose a whole company, taken prisoners.
That time we were continually receiving orders to push
on through open country, and it became exceedingly
difficult at times to retain communication.   These
unfortunate people were believed to have walked into
the village of Nieppe, thinking it was their own line,
only to be surprised.

" The country through which we had recently passed,

and in which we were now fighting, was in fairly good condition. After leaving our own line in the beginning of August, and going through Vieux Berquin, we had passed through all kinds of country, through shell-ridden areas, with main roads that had been pounded to bits by our own guns—roads which were littered with limbers, dead horses, water carts, etc.—eventually pushing out into better country with quite peaceful-looking fields, many farm-houses, and cottages remaining intact.

" At the side of the Steenwerck road I well remember coming across one of our own guns which had been abandoned in the big German advance in the previous April. One of our troops promptly stuck a label on the gun, on which was printed in large letters, ' Absent without leave since April !' The Germans had left behind a number of booby-traps, which required careful handling, and there was also a certain amount of propaganda; I still retain a souvenir of this, which I think is worth recalling. I refer to a pamphlet which was to be found in every farm-house, cottage, and even in the fields over which our men were advancing. On this was printed, in bold letters, the following :—

' DEAR TOMMY,
    ' You are quite welcome to what we are leaving. When we stop, we shall stop, and stop you in a manner you won't appreciate.
                                                ' FRITZ.'

" This did not have quite the moral effect intended by the enemy, but it certainly caused a number of our troops to pause and think, especially when they came up against a particularly nasty burst of machine gun or shell fire."

To turn from this graphic little pen-picture to the aridity of the war diaries, it may be said that early on the morning of September 1st the 121st Brigade captured Doulieu and Le Verrier, and by the forenoon of the 2nd had reached the line of the Steenbecque. At this time the 29th Division was on the left, holding Steenwerck, and the 61st Division was echeloned about 1,500 yards in rear of the right flank. The great thing now was to keep the enemy on the move, and by the morning of September 5th the 40th Division, still north of the Lys, was facing Armentières, with its right on Jesus Farm. If the reader will look at the map illustrating the Battles of the Lys he will see that the Lys makes a slight bulge northwards, just west of Erquinghem. Jesus Farm is at the apex of that bulge, on the northern bank of the river. To the right, and echeloned in rear, was the 61st Division, with its left on Bac St. Maur and its line extending thence to the south.

It was on the 5th that the company of the 8th Royal Irish disappeared into the unknown as already related. Apparently it had been sent out on some mission from L'Epinette, a small hamlet between Jesus Farm and the railway. On September 7th there took place an advance on rather an extended scale. Arrangements were made between the 119th Brigade and the 92nd Brigade (of the 31st Division) to attack Pont de Nieppe (which is not a bridge, but a long village running up from the river in the direction of Nieppe) and the line of the river Lys to the top of the loop due north of Armentières. Beyond this, that is to say to the north, the advance would be carried on by the 31st Division. The advance started at 10 a.m., and was supported by four brigades of artillery, which put down a creeping barrage. One company from the 119th Brigade succeeded in working its way through Pont de Nieppe and establishing a bit of line, beyond it, along the Lys. The co-operating brigade, however, was able to make no headway, and a smart counter-attack by the Germans caused a withdrawal into what was called the Nieppe system.

For the next three weeks or so there was a good deal of shelling, of patrolling, and smart, if minor, scrapping; with a good deal of rather annoying " aerial

activity" which is diarese for "being bombed." It
was clear that the Germans were by no means on the
run, and those who had counted upon it began to
wonder how many more years the war would last. On
the 10th what is called in the war diary a "bridge-
head" was established at dusk at the river end of the
village of Pont de Nieppe. The map consulted shows
this post as being on the northern bank, which would
indicate that the term "bridgehead" is not rightly
used. Similar posts were also established near
Erquinghem. Three days later fighting patrols from
the 119th Brigade attempted to cross the Lys in three
places, under cover of darkness, but one party was
detected, and in the case of the other two the bridges
were found to be demolished, so that the effort was
unsuccessful. On the 16th a large enemy aeroplane
from Lille was brought down near the Division. Before
the month was over a further advance resulted in the
driving in of the enemy covering screen and the establishment of a line which ran as follows : The right was
at Pont de Nieppe, and thence the line followed the
northern bank of the river Lys to the apex of the bulge
north of Armentières, from which point it ran to a
point some 2,000 yards farther north, but in a zig-zag
course. The divisional headquarters, which had been
at La Motte, were now moved forward to the vicinity
of Steenwerck.

Up to almost the end of the month the continued
advance of the Division was merely part of a natural
policy of keeping the Germans on the move, and did
not form a piece of any definite plan of action. This
was now to be changed. The general withdrawal and
the accumulating evidences of increasing demoralization
of the German Army made it evident to the Allied
commanders that offensive operations on a still larger
scale could be safely indicated. And Marshal Foch, in
a conference with the British and Belgian commanders-
in-chief at Cassel on September 9th, had arranged for
a fourth offensive, on the extreme northern sector of

U

the Western Front in order to force the Germans back towards Ghent. On September 28th, therefore, the Belgians, under King Albert, supported by a French army and the British Second Army under Sir Herbert Plumer, attacked the line from the coast southward to beyond Ypres. This was to prove one of the most rapid and thorough offensives of the war. We shall follow the doings of the 40th Division in a chapter headed " The Advance to Victory."

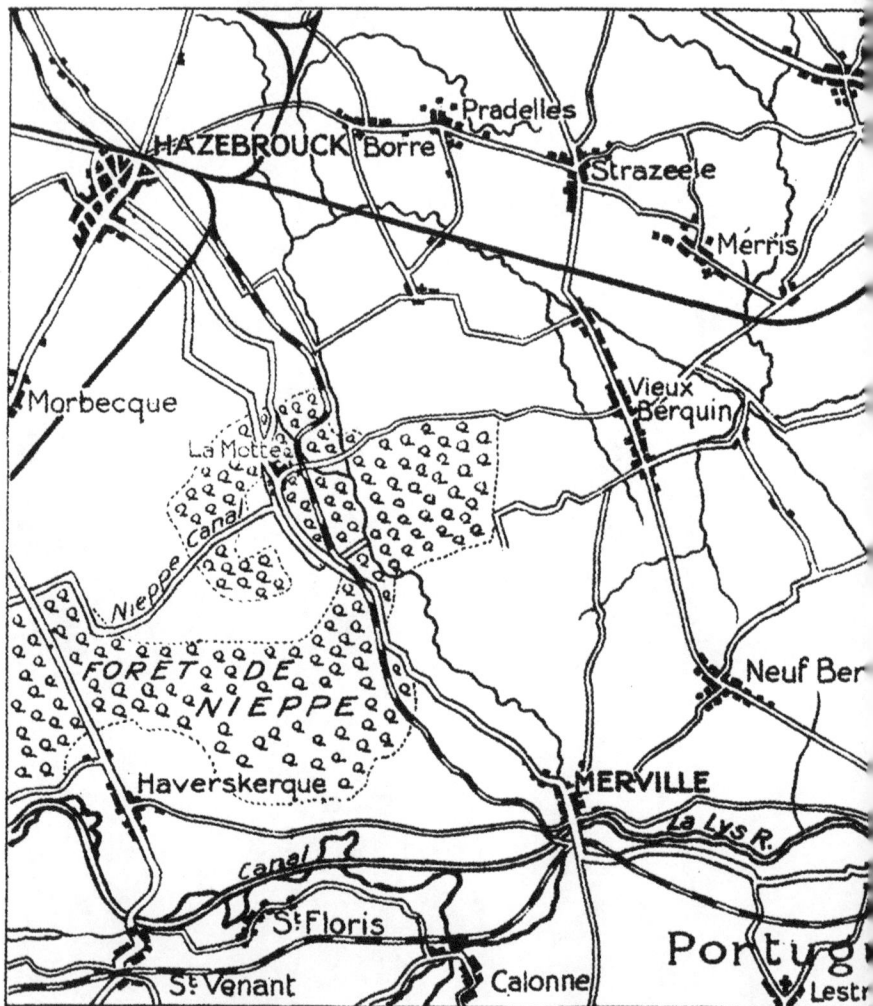

Pradelles

HAZEBROUCK Borre

Strazeele

Mérris

Morbecque

Vieux Berquin

La Motte

Nieppe Canal

Neuf Ber

FORÊT DE NIEPPE

MERVILLE

Haverskerque

La Lys R.

Canal

St Floris

Portu

St Venant

Calonne

Lestr

REFERENCE

Railways (Double).

" (Single)

Mi

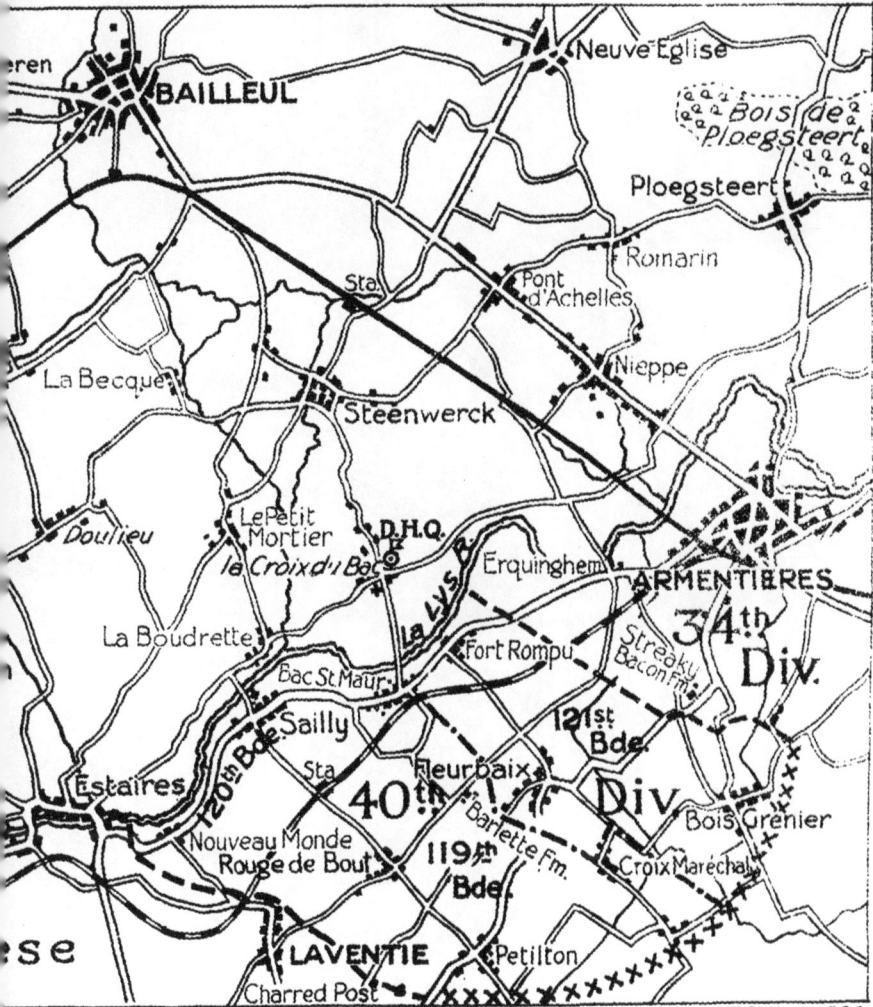

eren

Neuve Eglise

BAILLEUL

Bois de
Ploegsteert

Ploegsteert

Romarin

Sta.

Pont
d'Achelles

Nieppe

La Becque

Steenwerck

Doulieu

Le Petit
Mortier

D.H.Q.

le Croix d'1 Bac

Erquinghem

ARMENTIÈRES

La Lys

34th

La Boudrette

Fort Rompu

Streaky
Bacon Fm.

Div.

Bac St Maur

121st
Bde.

120th Bde.

Sailly

Sta.

Fleurbaix

40th

Div.

Bois Grenier

Estaires

Nouveau Monde
Rouge de Bout

Barlette Fm.

Croix Maréchal

119th
Bde.

se

LAVENTIE

Petilton

Charred Post

Scale

To face page 290

½   0   1   2   3   4   5 Miles

CHAPTER XIV.

THE ADVANCE TO VICTORY.

OCTOBER began with more nibbling along the loop of the Lys, north of Armentières. Just at the north-east of it is the little village of Le Bizet, to which the Germans were still clinging and from which it was necessary to dislodge them. This was carried out during the night of October 1st/2nd, the village being surrounded and then captured. Two prisoners were taken, who proved to be of the 3rd Company, 186th Regiment, 56th Division, and a useful identification was thus secured, although as a matter of fact identification had now lost some of its importance, for the Germans were being hammered all along the Western Front, and a surprise movement of enemy divisions from one sector to another was, therefore, unlikely. New posts were established after the capture of Le Bizet, and on the following day the left brigade reached the northern outskirts of Armentières—*i.e.*, the suburbs north of the Lys—without opposition. The right brigade, meanwhile, crossed the river at Erquinghem and pushed forward south of Armentières, with its right in touch with the 61st Division. Armentières, therefore, was being gradually surrounded.

During the night of October 3rd/4th a foot bridge was thrown across the Lys about a mile north-east of Armentières, and troops crossing by it pushed forward and occupied portions of the "original British front line," an expression which probably means the line

U 2

held just prior to the fighting of April, 1918—for the expression " original " would properly refer to the far-off days of October, 1914. In sympathy with this movement the right brigade also moved forward. The Germans, however, were not disposed to give up the Lys without a struggle, and the troops which had crossed by the foot bridge, as above, and pushed forward, were heavily shelled at 5 a.m. on the 6th, and one post was raided. A non-commissioned officer and 7 men were missing after the affair, and the Germans left one of their number dead behind them—this time from the 118th Regiment of the 56th Division. Then ensued a couple of days quiet, occupied with the inevitable establishment of new posts. On the 9th a thrilling aerial combat was observed. Two British scouts engaged a German two-seater aeroplane, with the result that one scout was sent down. The enemy 'plane however, was compelled to make a forced landing behind Steenwerck, the occupants—a pilot and officer observer—being captured.

On the 12th the 40th Division was holding a line east of Armentières, with its left practically on the Lys and the right upon the Armentières—Lille railway. The city had by this time been evacuated, and occupied by units of the Division, some of them going into billets in the lunatic asylum at the south-east edge of the city. This building had proved a regular paradise in 1914, provided as it was with excellent hot baths, drying-rooms, etc. Curiously enough, although it was then a most conspicuous target, it was shelled to a surprisingly small extent. Possibly the Germans had marked it down for their own subsequent occupation.

The Germans this time gave Armentières a really good shelling one night. It was, however, obviously a Parthian shot : " the 8th Royal Irish, who were holding the front line, reported that the enemy had got right away." Certain it is that in divisional orders issued on the 15th it was stated that the enemy would probably carry out an early withdrawal, and that the

40th was to be ready to push forward at once in an easterly direction, having the 31st Division on the left and the 59th upon the right flank. An advanced guard was detailed in these orders to consist of the 121st Brigade, the 331st Brigade Royal Field Artillery and " B " Company, 39th Battalion Machine Gun Corps, the whole under the command of Brigadier-General E. C. Stubbs, who had succeeded to the command of the 121st Brigade on September 17th.

In a forward march on the heels of a retreating enemy it is naturally the advanced guard which sees most of the game, and the personal impressions of one who formed part of it cannot fail to be of more interest than the jejune extract obtained from an official war diary. " Orders were issued "—says the narrator, a company commander of the 23rd Lancashire Fusiliers— "that the 121st Brigade would leave the trenches they were then occupying, and form up on the road and march in fours towards the enemy's lines—no one knew exactly where or for how long. It was a great adventure. When we looked at our maps and were given some idea of the route which was to be taken, we saw what appeared to be passable roads, tracks, etc., but before we got into anything like a reasonably good road we had to pass through the old original German front, support and reserve lines—a maze of shell holes, barbed wire, and débris of every description.

" That night march will never be forgotten by all those who took part in it. There was one occasion when the whole brigade had to descend a huge crater and mount the other side, officers meanwhile holding torches to show the men the way—it took an hour or more for the files to close up. There was uncanny stillness in the air, and no sound of firing anywhere, though one imagined that any moment a fury of shelling might descend upon us. We had to cut whole depths of barbed wire, and negotiate all sorts of objects, but eventually at dawn, very tired, but still very interested, we got into better country and the leading battalion had reached Quesnoy, where a halt was made. During the whole of this time we had been marching with bayonets fixed and rifles loaded. There was more than one narrow escape as men fell into disused trenches or shell holes or tripped over barbed wire, and in my company a couple of rifles went off accidentally, fortunately without causing any damage. Arriving at Quesnoy, we halted and awaited further orders. Information was received that the 31st Division, on our left, had got so far ahead that they were believed to be across our immediate front.

" For two days there had been no sign of the enemy, and for our part we had no idea when we should catch up to him again. After spending a whole day at Quesnoy, company commanders received instructions from headquarters to go ahead, and see what accommodation there was for the billeting of the troops in the little town of Wambrechies. My company (" C ") was at this time working in conjunction with " B " Company, commanded by Captain Rae, the other half of the battalion being some considerable distance away on the right. Captain Rae and I, leaving our seconds-in-command in charge, and accompanied by two runners, went forward at dawn to Wambrechies.

" When we had gone half the distance we saw with a thrill French civilians ! It must be remembered that we had now come many miles, and the last civilians we had seen were miles behind Hazebrouck. It turned out that at this particular place we were the first English troops these people had seen for four years, and naturally we got a great reception. In the little town of Wambrechies we found flags flying ; everywhere people came out and made us welcome, old ladies and young women doing their best to offer what little hospitality they could. The last of the Germans, we were told, had left the previous night. We explored an old château which had been used as a dressing station, and there were grim signs of very recent occupation, bloodstained field dressings, bandages, etc., lying about the floor, and there were parts of uniforms, caps, etc., of both British and German soldiers. This hospital had evidently been abandoned in a great hurry. Later we returned to Quesnoy, and the same morning the battalion marched over into Wambrechies. We understood we were to remain there for a day, occupying the billets which the advanced party had selected, but after two hours we got orders to push on again.

" The journey through Wambrechies was extremely interesting, as we had to cross the canal, which at this point had a particularly high embankment, the bridge over which, of course, had been blown up. We had to descend by step ladders and cross on rafts, and then had a big climb on the other side. It took a very long time for the whole battalion to get across, but the utmost good feeling prevailed. The banks of the canal were lined with crowds of shouting and cheering children, and one of our aeroplanes caused great excitement by flying very low, the observer standing up in his seat and waving to the crowds below, who acclaimed him with great enthusiasm.

" We made a further halt some two miles out of Wambrechies, and were then told that we were to make for the manufacturing town of Croix, which is really a southern offshoot from Roubaix. The troops, who had had no proper food and had marched a very considerable distance on the preceding days, were tired and hungry, but so novel was the experience and so exciting the situation generally, that personal discomforts were forgotten, and everybody thoroughly enjoyed the march and the progress we were making.

" Our great triumph was our arrival at Croix, which was accomplished about six o'clock in the evening. We had been marching light-heartedly along the roads, frequently being cheered by civilians in isolated farmhouses. Of course, we had cyclists and infantry patrols ahead of us, and we were marching at company intervals of about two hundred yards, still with bayonets fixed and rifles loaded, but nobody seemed to imagine in the least that it was at all likely that he would be called upon to use his rifle, though actually the Germans were not very far away, and of course, had they chosen, they could very easily have shelled us, and caused a great deal of trouble.

" Before entering Croix we had another very difficult canal to negotiate. Everywhere bridges had been blown up, and our progress in the advance was considerably hampered. We were able to get into Croix, however, through a particularly efficient piece of work by some of our leading troops, who were ably assisted by a number of French civilians, in building a plank bridge, across which the whole battalion passed in single file. The battalion cyclists' orderlies had rather a trying time in crossing with their bicycles on their shoulders, but eventually everybody negotiated the canal safely.

" It was at this stage, on entering the outskirts of the town, that our progress developed into a triumphal march. Crowds of people surged around us—they were mostly women and children, as nearly all their men-folk had been sent back by the Germans before they evacuated the place, but there was any amount of enthusiasm, and, what astonished us most, a most lavish display of bunting. It was said that the Germans had had a stock of British flags for a very long time, which they sold to the civilians before departing ! Be that as it may, the fact remains that flags were flying everywhere, which was an astonishing thing when it is remembered that the last of the Germans had left only a few hours earlier.

" There was one amusing incident in which ' B ' Company were concerned. The officer of the leading platoon was informed that in one of the houses which we were passing there was a German spy. He immediately detailed a sergeant and half a dozen men to surround the place, and himself went in to investigate. It turned out, however, to be nothing more serious than a violent quarrel between two French women, one of whom was accusing the other of being too friendly

with the Germans during their four years' occupation.
The accuser had a large number of sympathizers, who
crowded round and were in a state of great excitement.
The Lancashire Fusiliers subaltern officer, Lieutenant
Brittlebank, of course left them to their quarrel, but not
before he had received nearly the whole contents of a
bucket of water, which somebody was attempting to
throw over the accused woman!

" This little incident caused a temporary halt, which,
of course, held up all the companies behind. I was
about two hundred yards in the rear of 'B' Company,
leading 'C,' and immediately we halted we were surrounded by an excited crowd of women and children,
who came out with coffee and biscuits, and very
indifferent beer. One girl dashed up to me and threw
her arms vigorously round my neck and kissed me,
and then promptly turned to my sergeant-major and
treated him in a like manner!

" Eventually we pushed on through the town, to the
accompaniment of wild demonstrations of enthusiasm,
until we sought the safety of a quiet street, across which
at either end we had to draw a cordon of troops to keep
the crowd away—we were in danger of being killed by
kindness! This street was flanked on either side by
high walls, which enclosed the wool-combing works
of Houlden et Fils—in peace-time a very important
concern, closely associated with the wool industry of
Bradford; the firm itself, we understood, being connected with the Illingworths of that town. A
temporary resting place was found for us in this
factory, which for a long time had been used by the
Germans as a munition store.

" By this time we were beginning to feel the effects
of our long march, and the fact that we had had no
proper food for forty-eight hours. We understood that
we were to push on again early next morning, and
there was a conference about midnight, in which the
details of the advance were explained to company
commanders, who were alarmed to hear that it was

expected of them to occupy whole villages with one company—only about eighty strong ! However, these plans were not carried out. At seven o'clock the next morning we were still there, and our rations came up ; our limbers had succeeded in crossing the canal on the hastily constructed, and now enlarged, plank bridge.

" Then, during the morning, came the news that we were not to go any farther, it being understood that the divisions on our right and left had got so far ahead that they had met and cut us off. An order was issued to the effect that the category troops of the 40th Division had nobly taken their part, and were now to have a well-earned rest, but the divisional commander promised us that if he could have his way we should be in at the finish, which by now seemed well within sight. Singularly enough, the announcement that we were to remain behind caused disappointment amongst a large majority of the troops, whose enthusiasm had been so aroused by the events of the last few days that they were prepared to go on, and wanted to have a share in the advance.

" During this day, which was a Saturday, all preparations were made for our comfort, and we proceeded to have an exceedingly comfortable time. We found to our surprise that there was a little English colony in this place—subsequently explained by the aforementioned wool-combing industry. These people naturally were overjoyed to have us among them, after four years of German rule, during which time they had suffered untold hardships and privations. All the officers were found exceedingly comfortable billets, and it was a unique experience to end a tour of the line, as it were, by finding a wonderful billet after advancing twenty miles in battle order. The battalion headquarters mess was in a fine old house which had so recently been occupied by the German town commandant, and it was curious to reflect that only a few hours ago German officers had been sleeping and feeding in these quarters. On the Sunday we had a service in the English church, which was conducted by our padre, the Rev. A. E. Morris, which was most impressive, as it was attended by all the English civilians in Croix.

"I had an amusing experience the previous night; it was whilst waiting in the road outside the mills in which we were to be billeted, before orders had come or we knew what was going to happen next; the troops were standing at ease in columns of four. The road was deserted except for one little man who, in appearance, resembled a typical Frenchman. Imagine my surprise when he walked up to me, and in broad Yorkshire said, "If tha catches oop wi' yon Germans, give 'em 'ell!" It turned out afterwards that he was one of the foremen of Houlden's mill. He was from Bradford, but had lived in France for years.

"The next day I had a long chat with him; our mail came up, and somebody gave him an English Sunday paper, at the sight of which he positively wept! He told us that they hadn't seen an English paper for four years—they had forgotten the taste of meat and butter, and anything they were able to buy was only procurable at an extremely high price. On the whole, they had been fairly well treated, so long as they carried out all the orders of the area commandant without question; but here and there people had rebelled, and had been fined or imprisoned on the least provocation.

"We remained in Croix for six days, being occupied mostly in clearing away the débris caused by the terrific explosions where cross-roads, bridges, etc., had been blown up. Training was not neglected, and we did a certain amount of musketry and drill, but any idea that we were to remain there for the rest of the war was speedily dispelled. On the 25th October we got orders to go forward again, and were informed that after one night in Leers-Nord, which was actually in Belgium, just over the border, we were to go into the line again at Pecq, relieving the 15th West Yorkshires, of the 31st Division."

We may briefly annotate this vivid personal impression by some *obiter dicta* from the war diary of the Division. It was on the 16th that patrols entered Croix au Bois—which must not be confused with the Croix (part of Roubaix) just mentioned, nor with another village called La Croix which, to the searcher using a detailed map, may cause the same confusion as it produced in the present historian. It may be said that when the French are hard up for a place name they use Bailleul (of which there are hundreds in France), and when that gets overdone they utilize Croix, either with some qualification or by itself. On the 18th "Roubaix was occupied by our troops," which is probably synonymous with the entry of the 121st Brigade into Croix, as described in the previous paragraphs. The billeting in these large towns, full of inhabitants, presented some little difficulty, and the troops were requested to remember that the people had been for more than four years under German rule, and should therefore be treated with every courtesy and respect. Strict regulations were also issued as to the necessity of a smart appearance and turn-out, and troops were forbidden to wander from their respective billeting areas. The same day that Roubaix was entered the divisional headquarters moved into Armentières, and on this day, too, an important event happened. The artillery of the division, which had been detached since March, now rejoined, relieving the 66th Divisional Artillery, which was acting with the 40th. During their absence the gunners of the 40th had lived up to their reputation of being almost the best divisional artillery in France, and as the 40th Division is now resting for the moment it is a good opportunity to describe what the divisional artillery had been doing in the last seven months.

The artillery had been left in action in March, after the remainder of the Division had been relieved, as mentioned in Chapter X, and had been detached ever since. On March 25th, Brigadier-General Rotton, commanding VI Corps artillery, had written to say " how much I appreciate the excellent work done by the 40th Divisional Artillery, and tell them how proud I am to have had them in the VI Corps R.A.   Please congratulate and thank the officers, N.C.Os. and men under your command for all the gallant work they have accomplished."   Again,   on   April   8th,   General Ponsonby, commanding 40th Division, wrote from the Lys : " You seem to have had more than your share and been up to the neck in it for the last three weeks, and I really believe it is owing to the 40th Division R.A. that the Bosch has been stopped down your way. Your gunners were quite splendid, and I shall never forget how you blazed away at the Hun to the very last moment and then got every gun away."

In April the artillery covered the Guards and later the 2nd Division, with headquarters at Bretencourt Château, usually with three or four other field artillery brigades attached and a group of medium artillery.   On May 14th/15th it was relieved and went to rest at Hauteville—Fosseux—Saulty, in corps reserve, to join the 2nd Division in reserve.   Remounts were obtained, and the gunners rested and " brightened up generally." On July 4th, when General Ponsonby left the 40th Division to assume command of the 5th Division, he wrote on that date : " I want to thank you and your staff, especially Pile, for the splendid work you carried out when under my command.   I am sure the 40th gunners are the best in France, and I still hear that they are considered so by other divisional commanders they have served under."

On July 10th the VI Corps horse show was held, when the 40th Divisional Artillery and attached company of the divisional train, under Major Peters, won all the three events open to them, with one second prize in addition. The best section of a battery was won by C/178 against sixty-eight batteries competing.   Nos. 1 and 2 Sections of the divisional ammunition column, under Captains Bennett and Renwick, made a splendid show with their magnificent horses—a triumph of horse-management. On July 26th headquarters and brigades moved into line, covering the 59th Division, with headquarters at Basseux. From August 18th to 20th divisions on the right attacked successfully. Two days later headquarters moved to Bretencourt Château, and with the 40th Brigade and two army brigades—5th and 232nd—prepared to support the 52nd (Lowland) Division, attacking through the 59th on August 23rd, thus joining the XVII Corps, which had taken over part of the VI Corps front.

On August 24th, General Haldane, commanding VI Corps, wrote, in bidding farewell : " I desire to thank you for the excellent work of the 40th Divisional Artillery during the now longish time they have been under the VI Corps. I regard them as an exceptionally fine force, and by their good work and admirable administration arrangements they will always stand out in my mind as one of the very best that I have had under me during this war, and that is a very large number of artillery brigades."

Steady progress was made on August 23rd and 24th, when waiting for the Canadians on the left to complete a turning movement. On the 25th, at 4.55 a.m., the 40th Divisional Artillery fired for ten minutes on the Hindenburg Line wire with 102 18-pr. guns and thirty-six 4'5 Howitzers on a 1,200 yards front. Not a vestige of wire was left, and two battalions passed through the gap and mopped up the main trench, including Henin Hill and down to the Sensée River, by 12 noon, both 52nd and Canadians working with great dash. Fontaine Croisilles held out beyond the right flank, full of machine gun posts, and a concentration of heavy and medium artillery was required to render it untenable; it was finally taken on the 28th. On August 31st the headquarters of the artillery were commanding the 40th and 56th Divisional Artillery, and 232nd Army Brigade in support of the 52nd Division.

By September 1st the convergence of troops on Quéant caused elaborate and difficult barrages, and the forward supply of ammunition required great energy from the divisional ammunition column, a strain to which they answered admirably. Similarly the supply services worked through great difficulties with unfailing efficiency, under Major Peters. About September 5th the 40th Divisional Artillery got out to rest for a few days, and on the 10th started collecting German 77 mm. guns and their yellow and blue cross gas ammunition to fire at the enemy on the next suitable occasion. This was fired at Bourlon Wood on the 27th; thus the 40th Division got a little of its own back, and avenged those of the 119th, 120th and 121st Brigades who had perished in that great adventure of November, 1917.

Between September 19th and 26th preparations for an advance on the Cambrai area were made. On the latter date headquarters moved to Moeuvres area, covering part of the 63rd Division. On the 27th, as the attack advanced successfully, headquarters moved to the factory near Graincourt, and on the 30th to near the church in Fontaine, with brigades just in front firing on Proville and the Faubourg de Paris of Cambrai. Lieutenant-Colonel McGowan was severely wounded on the 27th. By October 2nd all the infantry of the 63rd, 57th and 52nd Divisions were too tired and short-handed to move, and the Canadians on the left were getting slower. On October 8th the forward movement recommenced, and during the advance to Niergnes three German tanks counter-attacked, "two of which were knocked out by Blundell and Bushman, of B/178." Next day the advance continued, with the 181st Brigade as advanced guard artillery, where they did very good work and were thanked by the general officer commanding 24th Division. On October 13th, having reached the Selle River, the 40th Artillery was relieved by that of the 61st Division and withdrew to the Proville area, where all hands had a welcome rest and the horses good grazing and plenty of water. A ride round Cambrai and inspection of some of the best houses there gave one an idea of the brutal work of the Hun. Beautiful panelling was hacked to pieces, fine furniture smashed to matchwood, all leather work cut away, and every house like a pigsty. "We had a dinner party in the fine dining-room at Proville Château, with a big fire, and drank the health of Major Noakes and his newly-gotten D.S.O."

On October 16th the divisional artillery complete entrained at Bapaume and Fremicourt and went north to join the 40th Division in the Armentières area. On that date General Sir Charles Fergusson, commanding XVII Corps, wrote to General Peyton, commanding 40th Division : " I want to bring to your notice the really excellent work done by Palmer and the 40th Divisional Artillery since they have been with his corps since the end of August. On each occasion of a major operation these two brigades were specially selected as the close supporting artillery, and have done splendidly. We owe a great deal to Palmer. The trench mortar personnel also did excellent work in manning the 77 mm. battery at Moeuvres and dosing Bourlon Wood with yellow cross gas, with the result that the German batteries were captured there *in situ*. Later they manned German light trench mortars at Proville. The horses, which were in excellent condition at the start, lasted well in spite of having a hard time through want of water and abominable communications."

Next day General Wardrop, commanding the artillery of the Third Army, wrote to Colonel Palmer : " You and your artillery have been a tower of strength to us." And to Sir William Peyton he wrote : " It is hard to speak too highly of them and their work." And thus the artillery rejoined its old division, covered with fresh laurels, and in time to share in the final glory of the 40th.

The phenomenal speed with which the 40th Division was now advancing, and the fact that the enemy could not be got to make any real stand, points to an obvious series of thrusts in other sectors of the Western Front. This was the case. On September 12th the Americans had attacked and captured the St. Mihiel salient. The one real hope for the Germans lay in their frankly accepting the situation and in making a timely withdrawal to the Meuse, or even to the frontier, but Ludendorff still clung to the idea of holding every foot of French territory till the last possible moment. The attempt was, however, hopeless, in view of the policy of a remorseless offensive at all points of the line directed by the Allied generalissimo. The end of the war was now plainly in sight. The Austrians suffered a *débâcle* on the Piave at the end of October. The same day Ludendorff was compelled to resign. Next day, October 28th, when the German High Seas Fleet was ordered out, the crews mutinied. Bulgaria dropped out of the struggle. Her surrender was followed by that of Turkey, whose military power had been shattered in Palestine. For Germany the sands were running out. But she now stood alone. Any defence of her frontier was rendered almost impossible by the position of her crumbling armies on the Western Front. The German Army was rapidly being demoralized; the German Navy was in a state of mutiny; the German people were in a state of open revolt. Peace—even peace at any price— was now the German aim.

It is, of course, no derogation to the newly-constituted 40th Division to say that its rapid and victorious advance was rendered possible by the imminent collapse of Germany. At the same time a sense of perspective is necessary if the doings of the new 40th are to be contrasted—as inevitably they will be—with those of the old. There is all the difference in the world between the advance of the 40th Division against Bourlon in November, 1917, and the onrush just eleven months later into Belgium; the former measured in furlongs, the latter computed in leagues; the former a wading through rivers of blood, the latter implying merely the casualties incidental to advanced guard and patrols.

x

The only operation of the old 40th with which the advance of the new Division can be justly compared is the move forward in the spring of 1917, but even here the comparison falls away. In 1917 the Germans deliberately, and in their own time, fell back to a carefully prepared position of immense strength. There is little resemblance between this orderly withdrawal in a portion of the front and the universal *sauve qui peut* which had now set in, although it is only fair to state that in that portion of the theatre of war where the 40th Division now found itself the Germans had presented as much stability as they had in any part of their line.

To take up the thread of the story of the advance to victory, on October 19th patrols advanced early in the day and reached L'Annoy, Toufflers, Leers and Leers Nord. On the same day the 40th Division was withdrawn, and for the next three days was either resting, or training, or working on the repairing of roads and railway. Divisional headquarters were brought forward to Mouveau, and on the 27th to Lannoy, by which time the 40th was again on the move. The following day, at 9 a.m., a patrol crossed the Escaut east of Pecq, but, owing to considerable enemy activity with trench mortars, machine guns and rifle fire, the patrol was compelled to withdraw. The divisional artillery was then turned on, with useful results, especially as no enemy guns apparently replied.

The final move forward to Pecq is described in the narrative of the officer of the 23rd Lancashire Fusiliers, which is now resumed from where it broke off a few pages earlier.

" The comparatively short distance to the line, which was only five or six miles away, surprised us considerably, as we had imagined that the troops in front of us were very much further ahead. Moreover, we speedily realized that though the end might be in sight, the Germans were still putting up a stout resistance, and this time they were aided by the position they had taken

up, which along our whole front was on the banks of
the River Escaut. Our line extended from Warcoing
on the left to Pecq on the right, whilst the Germans
were in the little town of Herines, where they had a
particularly good observation post from the church
tower.

" These little townships had hitherto been quite
immune from shelling or bombing, and of course the
country round about was entirely free from shell holes,
barbed wire, etc., but within a few days the enemy
commenced to shell Pecq and Warcoing, and the region
behind, heavily, and very considerable damage was
done. Despite this, however, a number of civilians
remained in their cellars, thinking that the further
enemy retirement would only be delayed a day or two,
but after a week most of them were evacuated, the
ambulance doing some particularly daring work, and
going right up to Pecq to take out of their houses
nervous old ladies whilst shelling was actually in progress. Battalion headquarters, during this tour of the
line, was in a magnificent old château surrounded by a
moat and several acres of beautiful park land. Some
heavy 8in. shells fell in the grounds, and very close to
the château, but no direct hit was recorded.

" The village of Estaimbourg, just behind, however,
came in for a heavy bombardment, and most of the
houses were very badly hit. It was here that, only two
days before our last tour of the line, we had a whole
platoon of ' A ' Company knocked out by a direct hit on
the houses in which they were all billeted. The most
noteworthy incident of this final tour of the line was a
magnificent piece of work by Captain T. Cowcher, of
' A ' Company, who from his line observed that one of
our own 'planes, which had been hit in aerial combat,
had descended on the opposite side of the river. The
'plane had come down in flames, and the pilot was
badly wounded. The observer, who was also hit,
crawled out, and was proceeding to carry his pilot to
safety, when Captain Cowcher observed that he was.

x *

walking straight towards the houses where the enemy was concealed, whereupon he shouted to them to come back, and then proceeded to swim across the river to their assistance. Then the Germans, who had hitherto remained quiet, opened fire with a machine gun, and Captain Cowcher had to swim back with the observer and the wounded pilot under a hail of bullets. He was recommended for the Victoria Cross, but only got a Military Cross, much to the disappointment of all ranks of the Division."

There was a final flicker of resistance on the Escaut. On October 29th the engineers attempted to throw a foot bridge over the river, but were prevented by the enemy's machine guns and artillery. On the following day, however, a foot bridge was placed in position at Warcoing, and a patrol, advancing in daylight, surprised an enemy post, bringing back four prisoners, including the sentry, who had been wounded. Other patrols was also operating, but, although some met with success, others encountered considerable opposition. On the last day of the month patrols attempted to push along the roads east of Pecq and Warcoing and to rush an enemy post. But, although the divisional artillery co-operated with effect, the Germans put up such a stubborn resistance that the patrols were compelled to retire.

The opening of November, 1918, found the advanced guard brigade (121st) holding an outpost line along the west bank of the Escaut from just south of Pecq to the Espines Canal on the north. On this day, after artillery preparation, patrols of the Division pushed forward and seized an enemy post which had been evacuated as a result of the bombardment. One dead German, two wounded, and a machine gun were taken. The enemy counter-attacked, but were repulsed. Nevertheless, other patrols met with strong resistance from enemy machine gun fire. The attempt to establish patrols east of the river was still persisted in on the 2nd, but some had to be given up owing to the fire from the enemy's guns and trench mortars. On the 7th preparations were made for a full-dress forcing of the Escaut, and, two days later, Clipet and Henhart were reached, patrols finally entering Velaines at 3 p.m. This was the high water mark of the final advance of the 40th Division, and on the 10th, owing to the converging of the line generally, the 40th was withdrawn in rear.

Meanwhile, Germany had been feverishly pressing for an armistice, and her envoys had been admitted through the French lines to listen to the terms imposed. So stringent were the terms laid down, and to such humiliation would Germany have to submit should she accept them, that it was thought that, even in her extremity, she must refuse. To such a state of collapse, however, had the foremost military Power in Europe been reduced that the terms were accepted, and on the morning of November 11th, 1918, this telegram was received at the headquarters of the 40th Division :—

> " Following message from G.H.Q. begins AAA Hostilities will cease 11.00 November 11th AAA Troops will stand fast on the line reached at that hour AAA Defensive precautions will be maintained 'AAA There will be no intercourse of any description with the enemy until receipt of instructions from G.H.Q. Further instructions follow AAA Ends."

The war was over. Europe was safe. The cause for which the Allies had poured forth their blood like water was attained. True to her promise, England, having drawn her sword, had not sheathed it until the military domination of Prussia had been beaten to the dust. The guns, which had not ceased to fire for more than four years in France, were now silent, and although a state of war was to exist for well on into the following year, of active hostilities there were no more. The Allies sent portions of their forces to the Rhine, but it was decided that the category troops of the 40th Division should not be called upon to stand the strain of the hard winter march into Germany. The Division remained, therefore, in and round the Roubaix district. It were but anti-climax, however, to carry on the story through the minutiæ of demobilization, and to relate how the Division melted away into civil life. Its history properly ends on the Escaut. It came into being to fight. It fought well. And, the fighting over, the tale is done. To the 40th Division England, Scotland, Ireland and Wales contributed units and personnel. Each country may well be proud of those of its sons who made the Fighting Fortieth what it was.

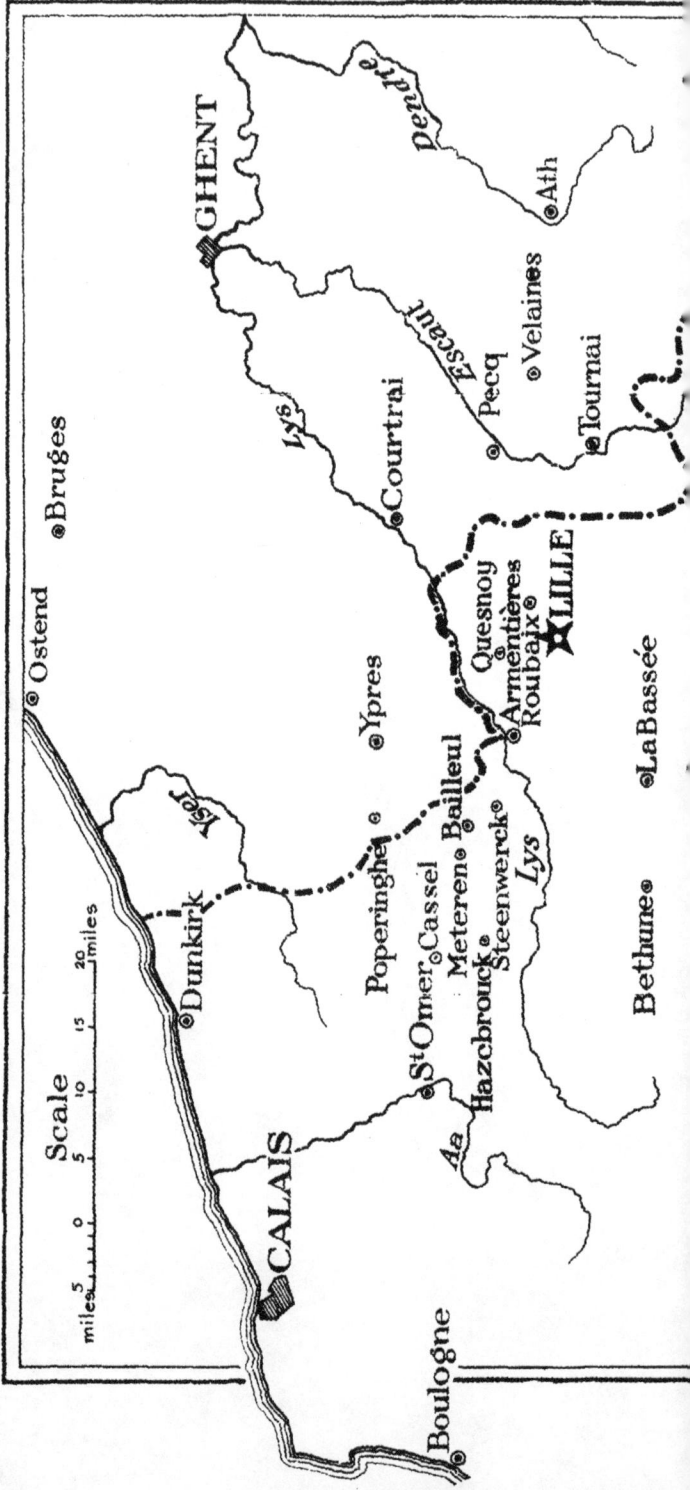

Sketch Map Illustrating British Sector on Western Front

Scale

miles 5 0 5 10 15 20 miles

Boulogne

CALAIS

Dunkirk

Ostend

Bruges

GHENT

 Aa

StOmer Cassel
Hazebrouck Meteren Bailleul
Steenwerck

Poperinghe

Ypres

Yser

Lys

Escaut

Courtrai

Pecq

Velaines

Tournai

Ath

Dendre

Quesnoy
Armentières
Roubaix
LILLE

Bethune

LaBassée

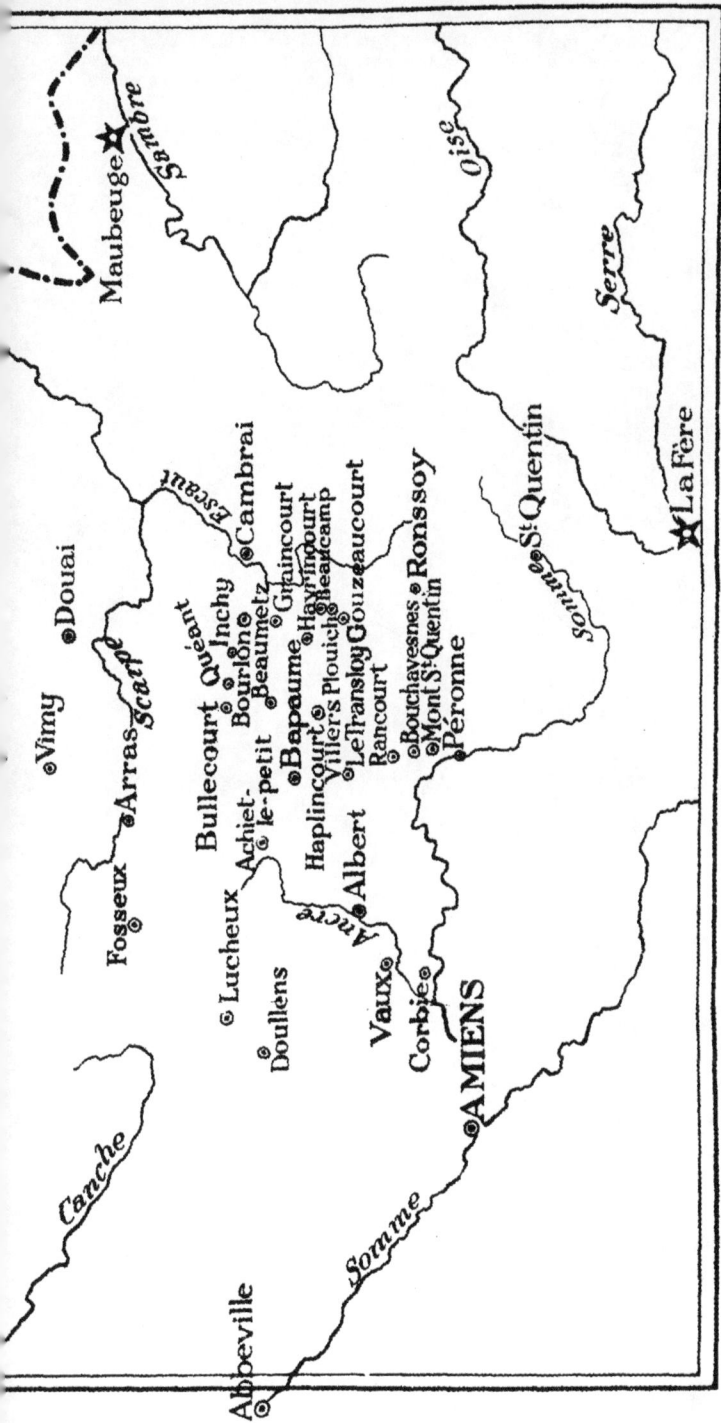

INDEX

311

www.ingramcontent.com/pod-product-compliance
Lightning Source LLC
Chambersburg PA
CBHW020807100426
42814CB00014B/362/J